Travels in a Dervish Cloak

ISAMBARD WILKINSON

Photographs by Chev Wilkinson

ELAND
London

First published in Great Britain by Eland Publishing Limited
61 Exmouth Market, London EC1R 4QL in 2017

Copyright © Isambard Wilkinson 2017
Photographs © Chev Wilkinson

ISBN 978–1–78060–078–9

Text set in Great Britain by James Morris, in Minion and Galliard
Printed in Great Britain by Clays Ltd, St Ives plc

For Granny and the Begum.
You made this possible and gave life its *masala*.

Contents

Glossary

Azan	the call to prayer
Betel nut	seed of the Areca palm, chewed as a stimulant
Bhang	marijuana
Bhangra	an upbeat pop music of Punjabi origin
Bindi	a red dot worn on the centre of the forehead
Biryani	a rice dish, often with meat
Bohreen (Ir.)	a narrow lane
Burqah	an all-enveloping outer garment worn by women
Chaat	a savoury snack, of which there are many variations
Chador	a large piece of cloth wrapped by women around their head and body, leaving the face visible
Charpoy	a bed upholstered with string
Chummcha	a follower to the point of sycophancy
Dervish	a Muslim Sufi ascetic, whose search for God follows a path of poverty, love and service
Desi	an adjective meaning local to South Asia
Dhobi	washerman/woman
Duenna (Sp.)	an older female chaperone
Durbar	a public reception, originally held by a ruler or prince
Fakir	a wandering holy man
Farang(hi)	a foreigner (foreign)
Feudal	a landowner
Gora	white, European, slightly derogatory
Gurdwara	a Sikh place of worship
Haal	a formalised greeting and sharing of news
Haveli	a traditional townhouse or mansion
Hijra	transgender individuals, born male
Hookah	a water pipe
Hujra	space where men gather and are entertained

Hur	members of the Sufi community following Pir Pagara
Iftar	sunset meal which breaks the fast in Ramazan
Jalebi	deep-fried sweets soaked in sugar syrup
Jihad(i)	the fight(er) against the enemies of Islam
Kurta	long shirt/jacket over trousers, worn by both sexes
Lassi	a yoghurt-based drink
Lungi	cloth worn by men wrapped around the lower body
Madrassa	an Islamic religious school
Masala	spice
Mehtar	title given to the rulers of Chitral
Memon	an ethnic group, originally from Gujarat, united in their use of the Memoni language
Mughal	empire, started by Babur in 1526, which continued to rule the Indian subcontinent into the 19th century
Mujra	an erotic dance, originally performed by courtesans
Mullah	a Muslim trained in Islamic law and doctrine
Nullah	a watercourse, dry riverbed or ravine
Pakora	deep-fried vegetable snack
Paratha	a flat bread
Pathan	an ethnic group in the North West Frontier Province, Pashto-speaking
Pir	a saint
Punkah	large cloth fan suspended from ceiling
Qawwali	Sufi devotional music and its performances
Ramazan	the month of fasting performed by devout Muslims
Sardar	a tribal leader
Shalwar Kameez	a combination of long shirt (kameez) and baggy trousers (shalwar)
Sharia	Islamic religious code of law
Sherwani	a long coat with a high collar
Shia	branch of Islam which believes that Muhammad designated Ali as his successor
Sufi	person who follows the mystical tradition in Islam
Sunni	branch of Islam which believes Abu Bakr, appointed by the consensus of the community, to have been the successor to Muhammad
Tabla	musical instrument consisting of a pair of drums
Takht	a low, four-legged wooden platform for sitting on

Tamasha	a fuss or commotion
Wahabism	a fundamentalist Sunni religious movement hailing from Saudi Arabia which is vehemently opposed to more moderate, mystical forms of Islam
Wallah	a person concerned with a specific thing/profession

You don't travel in order to deck yourself with exoticism and anecdotes like a Christmas tree, but so that the route plucks you, rinses you, wrings you out, makes you like one of those towels threadbare with washing that are handed out with slivers of soap in brothels.
NICOLAS BOUVIER, *The Scorpion-Fish*

This is the reason that in the insane asylum, all the lunatics whose minds were not completely gone were trapped in the dilemma of whether they were in Pakistan or Hindustan. If they were in Hindustan, then where was Pakistan? If they were in Pakistan, then how could this be, since a while ago, while staying right here, they had been in Hindustan?
SAADAT HASAN MANTO, *Toba Tek Singh*
(Trans. from Urdu by Frances W. Pritchett)

Countries, like people, are loved for their failings.
F. YEATS BROWN, *Bengal Lancer*

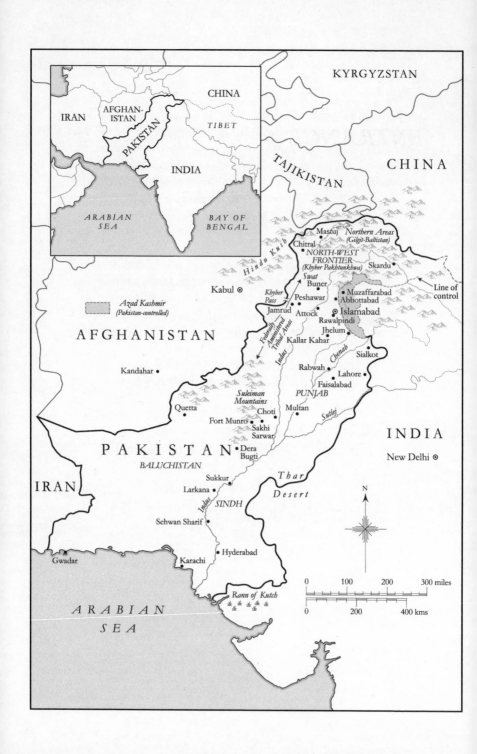

KYRGYZSTAN

IRAN

AFGHAN-
ISTAN

CHINA

TIBET

PAKISTAN

INDIA

ARABIAN
SEA

BAY OF
BENGAL

TAJIKISTAN

CHINA

Hindu Kush

Mastuj • *Northern Areas*
(Gilgit-Baltistan)

Chitral •

NORTH-WEST
FRONTIER
(Khyber Pakhtunkhwa)

Skardu •

Kabul ⊙

Swat

Buner

*Khyber
Pass*

Peshawar •

• Muzaffarabad

Line of
control

Jamrud •

Attock •

⊙ Islamabad

Rawalpindi •

Azad Kashmir
(Pakistan-controlled)

AFGHANISTAN

Federally
Administered
Tribal Areas

Indus

Jhelum •

Kallar Kahar •

Chenab

Sialkot •

Kandahar •

Suleiman
Mountains

Rabwah •

Lahore •

• Faisalabad

Quetta •

Choti •

Multan •

PUNJAB

Fort Munro •
• Sakhi
Sarwar

Sutlej

INDIA

PAKISTAN
BALUCHISTAN

• Dera
Bugti

New Delhi ⊙

Sukkur •

Thar

IRAN

Larkana •

Indus

SINDH

Desert

N

Sehwan Sharif •

• Hyderabad

Gwadar •

• Karachi

0   100   200   300 miles

ARABIAN

Rann of Kutch

0   200   400 kms

SEA

ENTRANCE

Preamble

A GALE WAS BLOWING from the north. Gusts of rain drummed down the chimney on to the smoking peat fire. From a window in my grandmother's house, deep in hilly Irish countryside, I watched thickly fleeced sheep rampage across the wintry garden, searching for refuge among clumps of rhododendron. 'Poor sods,' I thought.

Soon I'd be out in the foul evening too, trudging down the *bohreen* with my bag to wait on the road for a lift that would take me from the hearth's cosiness to Pakistan. God. All week my mood had trapezed between zeal and cowardice. Why on earth was I going back?

I was struggling with a quandary: on the one hand I wanted to become a 'proper' journalist, advance my career and lead an exciting, heroic life; on the other, the thought of returning to that part of the world summoned fearful images of falling fatally ill or of foul-breathed assassins kidnapping and beheading me. The paltry side of my nature wanted to reach old age, but my past – and a wavering professional ambition – had caught up with me. Over the past few years I'd asked my boss, the foreign editor of the *Daily Telegraph*, to move me from my comfortable billet in Madrid to somewhere more challenging. Now that he had offered me the job of correspondent in Islamabad, I could scarcely refuse.

It was January 2006, Washington's so-called War on Terror was in full swing and Pakistan was its 'frontline'. The millionaire Saudi fugitive, Osama bin Laden, who had masterminded cataclysmic attacks on America in 2001, was generally believed to be hiding in a cave in the Afghan–Pakistan borderlands, a sanctuary for Islamic militants waging global *jihad* and an insurgency that was beginning to overshadow the country.

'Pakistan' was on Western lips. Lavishly funded think-tanks recruited specialists who could locate it on a map; the American president slept with a book on the subject beside his bed; and London cabbies deemed it fit for nuclear destruction.

Pakistan was News. Anyone who had a connection to the place might be useful to a newspaper. And I did.

*

My travels there began before I stepped on to its soil, in my childhood, in my grandmother's camphor-perfumed, cramped old tower in Ireland, where every summer her Pakistani friend the Begum, Sajida Ali Khan, visited with her family. They didn't adapt themselves to the house, it succumbed to them. Servants slept on floors outside bedroom doors, fridges overflowed with sticky sweets and pungent dishes. Gifts of embroidered cloth soon covered sofas, walls and even my grandmother. In the evenings, coiled in shawls to ward off the bone-devilling damp, they told stories about their travels together in Pakistan, conjuring a hot and turbaned land where carpet-flight and slippered sprites did not seem improbable to my young imagination.

My grandmother's connection to that part of the world pre-dated her friendship with the Begum. Her family arrived in India from Europe, perhaps France or Belgium, in the 19th century, working as smalltime traders and marrying into Indian, Eurasian, British and Irish families in Mysore, Madras and Hyderabad, where, generations later, her father worked as a railway engineer. Jaunts up the line to hill stations and a verandah-ed playworld of ayahs, mongooses and cobras came to an end at the age of eighteen when she married a young British cavalry officer, my grandfather, whom she met as he made his way to fight in Burma during the Second World War. A few years later, India won its independence and, having tied her fate to my grandfather's, she left her native land in the rush of imperial withdrawal. On the night before her departure on one of the last trains out, villages in the hills above her house were set alight as Muslims, Hindus and Sikhs turned on each other in the chaos that accompanied the division of India and the creation of Pakistan. Embarking for England in a refugee ship, she sailed with her two babies – my mother and aunt – and an unfailing memory crammed with the chutneyed and chillied minutiae of Anglo-Indian life.

Her ties with the Subcontinent had not ended there for her friendship with the Begum had extended and deepened the Indianness of her life.

They had met at the last gasp of empire in 1950s Malaya and nearly every year since then my grandmother had visited Pakistan –

a place she found more similar to the India she had known than its contemporary incarnation – until she reached her nineties.

The scion of an old Lahori family, which had gradually sold off most of its lands and lived in a state of threadbare nobility, the Begum was in the traditional sense a 'Begum', a title meaning 'Lady' or 'Princess', but which increasingly now – much to her chagrin – also meant 'Mrs'.

My grandmother's diary of their journey in a Datsun Corolla from London to Pakistan in the 1970s left no doubt as to who was the dominant partner. Planting her teenage son in the driving seat, the Begum had commandeered every border official from Calais to Kandahar, fobbing off an Iranian policeman who had caught my infidel grandmother in a forbidden shrine with the tale that she was a Bosnian Muslim, and paying an angry Afghan petrol pump attendant with tea leaves when they'd run out of money.

My grandmother's Indian roots and her friendship with the Begum had suffused my own boyhood with a heady, dusty fragrance. I grew up under the spell of nursery rhymes she sang in Hindi, her improvised curries, and stories about a pet monkey with a penchant for schoolgirls and picnics on tiger-infested lakes. A contrast to the tight England of my boarding-schooled youth, the idea of the Indian subcontinent created by my grandmother exerted a fascination upon me: in a curious way I found myself experiencing nostalgia for a place I'd never known.

But I'd no idea what a large role Pakistan would play in my life until I was 18 years old and my grandmother suggested that I go with her for the marriage of the Begum's youngest son.

*

Pakistan in 1990 lived up to my imaginings. On landing at Lahore airport, my grandmother covered her hair with a scarf, and with our luggage bobbing on the heads of khaki-overalled porters we disappeared into a crowd of beards, turbans, frying samosas and inquisitive eyes. On the road to the Begum's mansion, my grandmother pointed out *fakirs* – wandering mendicant Muslim holy men, a small nomad encampment and the house of a friend, a tribal chief, who, on her last visit, had been in a foul mood because his enemies had ambushed some of his men.

The Begum put me up in a room on the roof of her house. From there, surrounded by a constellation of minarets and domes and listening to the cries of street hawkers, I saw young boys tugging the strings of kites battling above television antennae, rickshaws puttering along tiny alleys and first heard the call to prayer. We had entered a place of enchantment.

The week of the wedding neared and I was entranced by its preparations: a jeweller sitting crosslegged on the floor of an upper gallery in a golden beam of light, threading pearls with the nonchalance of a widow darning a sock; a tailor stitching a crimson, bedizened and spangled garment, his needle flashing like whitebait under the tangles of his moustache; and dress rehearsals for dancing, turban-tying and cooking.

A new well had been dug in the garden for the occasion, huge brass pots of food cooked over fires and suits of clothes and jewels exchanged. Then came the surging momentum of the ceremonies that joined the two parties. The bride and her entourage of maidens, thickly tressed, bodies caparisoned in gem-encrusted robes and noses studded with gold, danced off against stamping and twirling men. Alcohol was served discreetly in corners, rationed out by plump jolly 'uncles', the groom's entourage slipped me a few cookies loaded with hashish, and Qawwali, the meditative and ecstatic music of the Sufi mystics, was performed. The rituals of the marriage – joyous, tactile, intricate and layered – removed the last trace of any expectations, digested from Western newspapers, about a dour, depressed world of troubled Muslims.

After the wedding, at a Lahori tea party society 'Aunties' had offered prayers and then sipped tea and nibbled *pakoras*, welcoming me into their world of disputes, blessings, curses and polo matches, of feudal landlords, political skulduggery and black magic; and their openness and vivaciousness struck a chord with me, reminding me of my mother's and grandmother's own un-English emotional warmth.

And then I had struck out on my own. In the murk of polluted lanes outside the Begum's house, as I weaved among mules, starvelings, men gobbing *betel*-nut juice against walls and clerks bent over battered typewriters, grubby hands motioned me into secluded, smoky temples where gods glittered and cloth-bound scriptures were carefully unwrapped. All these were strange and yet familiar, reminiscent of things picked up in stories and replayed outlandishly in dreams, and they summoned my foolish young blood.

One night, when I was travelling in a third-class, windowless railway carriage across a freezing desert from Karachi back to Lahore, my impoverished fellow passengers offered me food and bedded me down under a blanket with one of their children. Wherever I went people gave me shelter, refusing to take money and sending me on my way with transport and introductions to friends with whom they said I must stay at the next stage along the route. How long will you remain in Pakistan, they asked. As long as my money lasts, I replied. Then you will never leave Pakistan, they said.

*

After leaving university, my curiosity about Pakistan did not dwindle and for several years I made months-long trips until finally I decided to live there and started a journey across the country to discover it more fully.

Travelling with my elder brother, we flirted and puffed on joints with urbane young women who viewed our growing interest in the country's Hindus, Sikhs, tribes, languages, folklore and mysticism as outré; plummy, cravated buffers greeted us in panelled clubs with gin and tonics and hemmed and hawed with watery eyes about the last days of the Raj; and an austere elderly aristocrat gave us lessons on Islam, during which once he observed: 'When you *junglees* were living in caves, climbing trees and eating raw meat, my ancestors lived in palaces, reciting poetry'. He told us about the Arab dhows that had brought slaves and Islam and about Mughal civilisation, and my brother and I, covertly pulling faces at one another to show we hadn't been taken in, lapped it all up.

But the plan to travel the length and breadth of the country was cut short when I suddenly fell ill and had to return home.

For a few years, I was immured in my grandmother's tower, laid low by kidney failure. Surrounded by boxes of dialysis bags and all the attendant paraphernalia of iodine, dressings and sterilising fluid, I met the disease at every turn: I was tethered, my freedom circumscribed.

Mooning about the house during this confinement, a Mughal miniature, hanging in a dimly lit passage, pricked my sense of loss. Its battered leather frame enshrined a beady-eyed, black-bearded Sufi, or Muslim mystic, painted in profile with sullen lips and a lightning streak of eyebrow. Majestic under a bulbous white turban, with a light brown Kashmiri shawl, embroidered with flowers, draped over an ankle-length white robe, and carmine slippers curling up at his toes, he held in both hands what appeared at first to be a flaming Christmas pudding, but which in fact was the world. He reminded me of all that I didn't have and all that I'd left behind in Pakistan: its *fakirs*, saints, mysticism, occult sources of power and my freedom, which the country had come to represent, prompting maudlin thoughts that I would probably never return.

After a year or so, I received a transplant of a kidney that had belonged to someone of about my age, whose family had donated it anonymously after he or she had died, most likely in a car crash.

My conscientious Dublin consultant counselled against a journey back to Pakistan. 'You are a very sick man,' he said, trying to drum into my unreceptive head the significance of my plight. 'Patients like you who take immuno-suppressive medication are more vulnerable to disease,' he cautioned, 'and have died in such places.' I shrouded my ambitions in caution and buried them at the back of my mind where I hoped they would quietly fade.

*

Another salvo of wind burst down the chimney on to the gasping fire. I chuckled as I saw my grandmother pursuing the sheep, who were beating a horn-nodding retreat to the mountains.

So what *was* I doing now, eight years later, answering my editor's call to go to Pakistan? The Begum was partly to blame: visiting Ireland the previous summer, she had reissued a longstanding invitation with an unusual caveat. 'You *must* come now before it's too late,' she had said after listening to a news bulletin about a bomb attack in Pakistan. 'The country is changing fast. Soon it will be unrecognisable from the one you knew.'

Her words had taken me by surprise and before I knew it the memories and excitement of my youthful travels came barrelling back with almost physical force and suddenly the idea hadn't seemed so mad. My mother had died two years before at the age of 59 from heart failure. 'I've lived my life to the full,' she said with mischievous defiance not long before she passed. I wanted to do the same.

So when my editor made his offer of the Islamabad post, it had seemed like a divine gift, a second chance for a life of adventure, and I accepted. But there was still that apprehension. Was it a gift or was it a temptation of providence? Would my kidney transplant hold out in such an environment? How would I survive war-torn Afghanistan, which was also to be on my beat? Was I even professionally prepared for such an assignment?

My first job as a journalist was with *Country Life*, an English magazine popular with aspirational rural dwellers, for which, most notably, I had penned articles on King Charles spaniels and military officers' relationships with their pet parrots, ostriches, and Labradors. My career since then had been untouched by danger. The *Daily Telegraph* had asked if I wanted to be posted in Africa, but I'd declined, citing kidney problems. So they had sent me to Spain, where a bomb attack on trains, a Hispano-Moroccan spat over a goat-inhabited rock in the Strait of Gibraltar and memories of the Spanish Civil War were the nearest I'd come to conflict. Recently, the newspaper had sent me on a couple of 'embeds' with American and British troops in Afghanistan and Iraq, but the only peril I'd experienced there was constipation from dry rations.

I felt ill-prepared for war.

The last of the day's coppery light had all but drained from the window and Granny and the sheep melted into the reflection of the fire. Time to grab my bag. I sighed, trying to steel myself with the thought that such fears would not have troubled my grandmother and the Begum, who both had said I should go. A friend, concerned that I was wallowing in Madrid's fleshpots – and grief over my mother's death – had also urged me to go. 'It'll be the making of you.' I repeated his phrase to myself now, without conviction.

I found Granny outside in the dusk, among wind-whipped branches, dabbling in a barren flowerbed. Maintaining her poise in spite of her shabby gardening clothes and holding on to her floppy hat, she waved me off with a raised trowel. 'I do worry about your health. Do take care, darling.' We would meet before long in Lahore, she said, adding that the Begum would be a wonderful 'guardian angel'.

Chapter 1
A Visit to the Begum

'THESE CROOKS,' THE BEGUM MUTTERED, without looking up from a newspaper. 'They should all be lined up and shot. The country has no gas, no electricity, no education, and they are siphoning off millions of rupees.'

I'd just come down to breakfast on my first morning back in Pakistan, muzzy from the flight, my thoughts scrambling to catch up with my hostess's.

She finished handing down sentence on the country's politicians, and said good morning, reclining on her usual perch, a *takht*, a low four-legged platform, propped up by bolsters in a bright, tall-ceilinged sitting-room at the back of her crumbling mansion abutting the Old City of Lahore.

Particles of dust winked in shafts of sunlight slanting in through open French windows and querulous crows disputed on the lawn outside; 1930s portraits of coolly beautiful, loosely veiled ladies and turbaned, decadently eyed princes gazed superbly from the walls. I remembered that the more risqué paintings of nudes, upstairs, were veiled with sheets when *mullahs* called.

She peered at me over the rims of her spectacles and rang a small brass bell. In her seventies, her large eyes were always brilliant with mirth, or indignity caused by some affront. She had high cheekbones and a proud nose that retained the memory of her youth's luscious beauty.

For years I'd been awed by the Begum, that is to say, terrified of her. But I'd survived her early, mettle-probing onslaughts when she would greet me with bald remarks about how I was going about a task or the character of a girlfriend. And so it was without fear but battle-ready that I now approached her *takht* – her sofa, office and seat of power, which housed her documents, bills, packages sewn in calico and an assortment of telephones and servant bells.

A few moments later a servant, Mehmud, greyer and more careworn than when I'd seen him last a decade before, bustled through a swing door, a hastily donned prayer cap askew on his head, holding a breakfast tray laden with chillied omelette, *paratha* and thick milky sweet tea, which he set down on a table in front of me. We smiled discreetly at each other. The Begum directed a short burst of Punjabi at him and he disappeared.

'Your old friend Mehmud is not to be trusted,' she said. 'He is a scoundrel. He takes advantage of your kindness. Don't leave your things lying about.'

Even during her husband's lifetime, the Begum had ruled the roost. She did so with a firm hand. Housing at times up to twenty servants and as many relations, the old mansion was a hive of continuous chatter, cooking, comings, goings and intrigues.

Servants were always absconding, getting married, coming back and in a perpetual state of war with their employer. Similarly, family members were always visiting, getting arrested, shot, promoted, transferred or being cold-shouldered for not greeting an 'auntie' with due protocol.

Life was a constant *tamasha*, a word of Persian origin meaning bustle and excitement and employed for any situation ranging from a domestic squabble to a *coup d'état*.

Events, domestic and national, were guided by conspiracy. That morning I asked the Begum what lay behind a border skirmish with Pakistan's neighbour and arch foe, India.

'These people want chaos and conflict. They are against peace,' she replied. 'Whoever they are, they'll already be cooking up their next *evil* drama.' Drama was also part of the lingua franca.

Even at night when she clamped on headphones and listened to Indian television dramas at full volume, she intercepted – through some magical facility that didn't rely on lip reading because her eyes were glued to the screen – all that was taking place around her. Occasionally, she silenced whispered conversations with a pithy remark. Once I'd witnessed her verbally demolish an attorney general in the middle of a carpet shop. It was unwise to cross her.

'You are still not married,' she observed, continuing what was to become our morning ritual on my regular visits to Lahore. 'Don't worry. We will get you married off. What about one of the girls from Heera Mundi ['the diamond market', Lahore's red-light district]?'

'How much are they going for these days?'

'But you have no money,' she said, beginning to chuckle. 'You are as poor as a church mouse. No! No! No! That would never do. They would probably charge you double as you are a *gora*.'

Gora, meaning 'white', a mildly derogatory term used for Europeans, was dished out by the Begum with relish.

Her muslin headscarf was draped like a sash over a simple cotton *shalwar kameez*, but now she unfurled it and let it float over the back of her bangled arms to amplify her lightness of mood. Here, in her domain and among her family, it was less an article of modesty than an instrument of communication.

'And then you would have to convert to Islam,' she continued. 'I'll teach you the *qalma* [the Muslim declaration of faith].'

'I don't think I'd make a very good Muslim.'

'We would make you a good Muslim. And anyway, once you convert, there's no turning back – or it's ffffattaaak,' she said slashing an imaginary sword across her throat, laughing. After wiping away a tear with a handkerchief, she sighed *'Tauba! Tauba!'* (Repentance! Repentance!) and touched the lobes of her ears with each index finger, her hands passing across her face, an old gesture of piety.

'*And* I don't think your grandmother would approve.'

She laughed again at the thought of needling her old friend. At such moments I could imagine the hockey-sticks-and-pigtails mischief of her childhood.

She resumed her riff, chuckling between phrases: 'We must find you a nice girl, a rich one. What about those sisters you met last night? They are Westernised, fat, yes, but they would make good wives. So do these Chitralis, Gilgitis. They are fair-skinned and hard-working...'

Mehmud entered waving a sheaf of bills. An exchange of rapid-fire Punjabi ensued. Mehmud retreated. The Begum turned to me again, now more serious.

'Anyway, what is your programme? You should stay here. This is your home. You are part of the family. You must live here as long as you like.'

I had to live in Islamabad, the capital, I explained. The foreign editor had said that should 'they' catch the most wanted terrorist, Osama bin Laden, or if Pakistan's military ruler, General Musharraf, were to be assassinated and I was not in the capital where all the action would be, my usefulness, and therefore my career, would be limited.

The Begum was unimpressed with my arrangements. 'You cannot organise your life around possible assassinations, on who may or may not be killed,' she mused, opening the palms of her hands and tilting her head, shaping the South Asian 'what-to-do' gesture. 'People round here drop like flies.'

She put aside her bantering tone and fixed me with a severe look.

'You must be careful doing your work here,' she cautioned, wagging a finger and arching a belligerent eyebrow. 'Military rulers don't like to read bad things about themselves. They could throw you out. And I should avoid bin Laden. Look what happened to Daniel Pearl [an American reporter who had been kidnapped and beheaded a few years before while following Osama bin Laden's trail]'.

'I have smaller fish to fry', I replied, before shovelling in the last mouthful of omelette and greasy bread. I explained that to my mind bin Laden and his ilk were distractions from the real quarry: the essence, the quiddity of Pakistan, which I hoped to find by encountering its mystics, tribal chiefs and feudal lords.

The Begum's eyebrows expressed all sorts of moods but none so articulately as scepticism; but then I saw the flicker of a ruse in her eyes.

When I was last here, Islamic militants hadn't posed an obvious threat to the country. The 'elite' had spoken with casual disparagement of Islamic zealots as 'fundos', fundamentalists. Bin Laden had been a minor celebrity, holed up with his hosts, the Taliban regime, across the border in Afghanistan. My attempts to meet him as a nascent journalist were limited to going to a point man's office in Islamabad, where I'd always fallen asleep – one of many early unnoticed signs of kidney failure – before the contact said: 'The Sheikh regrets that he cannot receive you as he is busy at this time.'

But circumstances had changed since the September 11 attacks on America. Daniel Pearl had been snagged in a web of *jihadis* clandestinely supported by military intelligence, which didn't brook revelations about its covert affairs.

Pakistan, a richly remunerated ally in America's 'war on terror', was supposed to be helping Washington hunt bin Laden and suppress a Taliban insurgency against the newly installed US-backed Afghan government; but Musharraf had other ideas, instead playing both sides. With one hand Pakistan fought *jihadis* within its borders to appease Washington, while the other nurtured them to fight on its behalf in India and Afghanistan.

The result was that conservative Islam was on the march in Pakistan, threatening the old tropes of the country, its mysticism and folkloric traditions, things that fascinated me; and from the glimmer in the Begum's eyes, I could see it was an interest that met with her approval.

'Yes, I think your plan to understand the culture is a very good idea,' she concluded, adding *sotto voce*, 'And it may keep you out of trouble.' Her policy for my safety settled, she picked up the financial pages and returned to the business of her empire, leaving me to find my bearings.

*

I went to my old spot up on the roof and idling there I felt a ghost of the excitement that my 18-year-old self had experienced sitting on the same balustrade all those years before. The city's honking traffic and minarets and domes lay beyond the house's walled lawns and trees. Already there was the first inkling of spring warmth. Wood smoke curled up from an alley below where cloaked men sat on their haunches, working frying pans and teapots over fires, celebrants reverently preparing for a ritual.

Behind the house, the humble dwellings of the servants' quarters squatted around a well. Their tin-roofed huts were obscured by washing lines hanging heavy with women's bright coloured garments and men's dour *shalwar kameez*, whose trousers, bereft of their restraining strings, stretched to six foot in width and appeared to belong to giants. Tree branches were stacked on the courtyard's bricked floor for lighting cooking fires.

This was the lot of most of the country's 190 million people (had it really only been 110 million when I first visited?): to live through heat, cold, and rain in shacks, mud huts, tents and tenements. 'The masses', as they were known. The powerless, impoverished majority.

Barefoot children burst out from under the laundry, running across the courtyard, their shrieks followed by women screeching after them in coarse Punjabi.

How unconnected this all was to the newspaper's London headquarters where a few days before the foreign editor had dispatched me with a finger drum-roll on his desk and an 'it's time to get some dust on your boots', and the desk manager had handed me my kit: a flak jacket, helmet and a thick wad of cash. 'If you get stuck in Donga Bonga or wherever,' he had said, standing up, tucking his shirt into his trousers, 'you know who to call.'

I'd been in Pakistan for less than twenty-four hours but already it seemed as if I'd wandered back into a pleasant old dream. I was almost expecting to bump into my younger self – fresh-faced, out of place and innocent as to what lay ahead in adulthood – wandering in a corridor of the Begum's house.

Now, walking back across the Begum's rooftop, I ducked to evade a kite – this time with feathers – swooping to probe my hair with its talons, made out a word or two of the ongoing hail of Punjabi from the mothers below and felt content. The country's reflexes and rhythms, phrases of a language once partially learned but now forgotten, were slowly coming back to me.

*

More gold sovereigns returned to me that afternoon when, lying on my stomach with my head at the foot of the bed, I scoured my old guidebook and map of Pakistan.

The map showed a country shaped like a scrap of paper, torn from the frontier where India, Iran, Central Asia and China meet. I placed a finger on the glacial northern border, what Lord Curzon, a former British Viceroy, called the 'southern eave of the Roof of the World'. A watershed in the Pamir Mountain Range, from here the rills of the Oxus trickle westward into Afghanistan, and streams, forded by fur-coated yak-riding Mongols, race in icy streaks to join the Indus. The river there is milky turquoise, and my finger, following its course south, traced a path through Himalayan kingdoms and ancient animist valleys far below to plains littered with the coins and statues of Indo-Greek satraps, and on farther still to its silt-clogged many-mouthed delta on the Arabian Sea. The Indus and the Punjabi rivers form a network of life-giving water shaped like the veins in the back of a hand.

Here, invaders such as Tamerlane and Alexander the Great had marched vast armies; one could stumble over shards of pottery from a civilisation with an undeciphered set of symbols as old as Mesopotamia; ancient oyster-rich coastal ports had for millennia traded in lapis; Sikhism was born and Buddha first regained human shape in the form of a statue; and manacled and chained mystics continued to wander in search of God.

Pakistan, a country of 340,000 square miles, is divided into six provinces or areas – Baluchistan, Punjab, Sindh, the Federally Administered Tribal Areas, North-West Frontier Province (Khyber Pakhtunkhwa) and Gilgit-Baltistan – and the Pakistani-controlled territory of Kashmir. Its official language is Urdu and official religion Sunni Islam; but on further examination language and faith fragment into dozens of tongues, peoples, sects and heresies.

Pakistan, Pakistan, Pakistan. I only ever heard the English translation of Pakistan, 'Land of the Pure', used with irony by its own people. According to the consensual version, it was invented a decade or so before the country's creation, by an Indian Muslim Cambridge student in the 1930s. Composed of letters taken from the names Punjab, Afghania (North-West Frontier Province), Kashmir, Iran, Sindh, Tukharistan (Bactria in northern Afghanistan) and Baluchistan, which provided the 'stan', both geographically and spiritually, it was an ambitious name, its religious purity and much of its borders being of some debate.

As I folded up the map, a small dark cloud crossed my mind. It all seemed dauntingly large, rich and dangerous, and I wondered if I'd bitten off more than I could chew.

*

The next morning, standing in the doorway to see me off on my way to the north of Punjab, to the capital, Islamabad, the Begum strained with both hands to raise a heavy old leather-bound Koran under which I ducked to receive divine protection. She resembled a classical figure holding up a torch so that I might see the good in her country. But she ushered me over the threshold with a note of caution.

'Be careful. We are a devious people. We *have* to be,' she said, leaning her head to one side in explanation. 'This is a tough country.'

Chapter 2
A Capital Place

O<small>N THE SURFACE</small>, Islamabad didn't offer much of the 'tough country' of which the Begum spoke.

A suburb-unto-itself, a capital purpose-built in the 1960s on a grid system designed unimaginatively by a Greek, it was where superannuated men and women lived and died in peace in the shadow of the Margalla Hills. Parrots and crows squawked across orderly gardens of tufted palms, potted chrysanthemums and thickets of hydrangea. Foreigners sipped metallic burgundy at the French Club over passable steak-frites, working off the fare later at gyms or on trails in the hills. The expatriate cliché was that the city was 'twelve miles from Pakistan', the distance to the nearest 'real' city, Rawalpindi.

Its few places of interest – brothels, drinking dens and militant mosques – stood out, as a British military attaché was soon to tell me, 'like a racing dog's bollocks'. At the top of the town, behind a complex of government buildings, like the puppeteers behind the show, stood the well-fenced Diplomatic Enclave, where the most influential embassies tried to pull, with greater or lesser success, Pakistan's strings.

Islamabad was without soul or conscience. It had a relatively cool climate; no rickshaws, no throngs; few trucks, buses, garbage and flies; and supplies of gas and electricity more regular than the rest of the country. The rattle of servants running errands on rickety sit-up-and-beg bicycles occasionally disturbed quiet leafy lanes; portly wives, wearing white sneakers and loose garments, worked off surfeits of *biryani* striding around the boundary of an immaculately cropped cricket pitch. The hill stations and villas of the Himalayan foothills were an hour's drive away.

In due course, the capital would become a place to enjoy clean sheets, rest and a gossip with confreres after returning from a foray into the surrounding wilds; but now I was desperate to establish a base there quickly in order to escape it. I was eager to pick up the trail of my old adventures.

At the guesthouse where I stayed for the first few weeks, my neighbour, a young American, was causing quite a stir with his noisy lovemaking to a 'Westernised' local woman.

The manager wrung his hands apologetically. 'We are having problems with the unmarried staff as they are having ears pressed up against his door the whole day.'

'Who is he?' I asked.

'He is come for earthquake duty. Working for Catholic Relief.'

In the mornings the manager briefed me on his efforts to pour water on the American's ardour, which seemed confined to asking him to 'please turn off music at midnight'. One night I found the woman sobbing on the floor outside his closed door.

I doubled my efforts to look for a place to rent.

*

House-hunting and several days off work allowed me to explore the city, which, against my expectations, harboured a gem.

Mistakenly, I'd thought Islamabad a sterile zone ('half the size of Arlington cemetery but twice as dead' was another expatriate witticism), but late one afternoon, I came across a wild olive tree, incongruous in the grid of streets, which had become entwined with a municipal lamp and white-and-pink-flowered bougainvillea. The ground around it had been tiled, oil candles and joss sticks lit at its base and bits of cloth tied to its branches. At a makeshift camp nearby, Pathans, rolling out *bhang* (cannabis) to drink in goblets, said that it was a sacred tree on an ancient pilgrimage route they had taken from their hometown, Peshawar, the capital of the North-West Frontier Province, to the shrine of Bari Imam, on the outskirts of Islamabad.

I accompanied them in the back of a small open truck to the green-roofed shrine where the air was perfumed with the woody smell of the burning *khera* plant, dervishes robed in red gowns tooted on buffalo horns and young women sat crosslegged under rosewood trees, singing a *qawwali*. These worshippers, like the majority of Pakistanis, both Shia and Sunni, follow a moderate, mystical folkloric form of Islam, Sufism – a fusion of beliefs whose formal central tenets are the universality of God, compassion, devotion and the unity of love. They revered the entombed Bari Imam, a 17th-century pacifist holy man, as a saint, or *pir*.

The place had been deemed holy for centuries – even millennia. As I picked my way about knots of people praying I saw that fire was still worshipped here – an 'eternal flame' was lit on a stand and people dipped hands into its embers, slapping their ashy palms against the shrine's walls. Some walked around the fire, an old Zoroastrian rite. Enraptured by these small discoveries, the singing, smoke and prayer, I breathed it all in, mentally holding on to a spirit formed by traditions flowing together and melding into a whole, which like the enamelled, jewelled interior of the saint's mausoleum, was as delicate as a Fabergé egg.

There was another ancient root leading back to the past. The mausoleum rested on the remains of a Buddhist stupa. Above it, in a cliff face, was a cave used by Buddhists centuries ago, and pilgrims still, as a retreat. Islam, adapted and moulded to older beliefs, was just another layer.

Then, I wandered into an official-looking building attached to the saint's mausoleum. I found it full of unshaven and overfed thugs, and the tenor changed abruptly. They answered my questions about the shrine with impatience. 'Yes, it's what you see. A holy place. Superstitions of the masses. They come here for help,' said a paunchy, red-eyed man, leaning back in a chair, tapping cigarette ash on the back of a man crouched massaging this lout's legs. They were the 'keepers of the shrine', said a minion deputed to usher me out. He confided there had been some dispute among them, members of a landowning family, over who should pocket the alms. They were minor 'feudals', as landowners are called, who lived off the peasantry.

The minion, an elderly apostle of the saint, shook his head at the turn of events. The wrangling over money was not the only difficulty. The shrine was to be modernised and built up into a 'religious attraction', the ancient fire removed and other 'non-Muslim' practices banned. He said the previous year a man had charged into a tent of Shia pilgrims at the shrine and detonated explosives strapped to his chest, killing twenty people.

Places of communal worship like Bari Imam, he said, were under threat from militant and conservative Islam, which wished to wipe out all that had gone before.

Walking away from the shrine, its fragrance and singing growing fainter, the bitter-sweet visit jangling my mind, I passed a gaunt *fakir* dressed in rags, recumbent next to a hashish pipe. Oblivious to all about him, his head resting on a knotted bundle, he was looking up at the early evening stars with the blank eyes of remote contemplation.

*

At times, the capital, like my own view of Pakistan then, seemed stuck in a time warp, appearing not to have moved on since my last visit. At a drinks party I saw the usual politicians, bureaucrats, diplomats and aid workers, a community held together by jolly local hosts, social desperation and pilates, and heard conversations repeated verbatim from a decade before: 'You see that was why they called the *mullah* "Maulana Sandwich", because he was caught *in flagrante delicto,* pressed between a woman and a *boy...*'

A few days later, on a trip to Rawalpindi, home to the headquarters of the Pakistan army, I met again the name of Maulana Sandwich – at the home of a disgruntled retired general.

General Hamid Gul had been doing the rounds for years. A former head of the ISI, the country's infamous military intelligence agency, he had crazy bulging blue eyes and grey hair, mostly dyed jet black. His vulture nose and bristly moustache gave him a look of the villainous Hedley Lamarr in *Blazing Saddles,* and he typified the establishment's support for Islamic militants.

I met him in his drab, darkened ex-officer's house in a middling suburb. He spoke pedantically and slowly in a lulling, gulling singsong voice about the scholarly acumen of the compromised *mullah,* Sami ul-Haq, a friend of the military who ran a prominent *madrassa,* a religious school, one from which the Taliban recruited in great numbers.

Dismissing the old claims about the cleric's sexual proclivities as 'disgusting propaganda cooked up' by politicians opposed to the *mullah*'s parliamentary push to impose *sharia* law on the country, he said that Israeli intelligence was behind all Pakistan's problems. He lived for conspiracy.

As a serving officer, Gul had worked alongside American officials covertly supporting *jihadis,* including Osama bin Laden, in the Soviet–Afghan war in the 1980s. He was angry about America's indifference to the region following the Soviet withdrawal from Afghanistan.

I asked him what he thought was being fought over now in Afghanistan. He said the Taliban were successors to the Afghan *mujahideen,* fighting against outsiders.

'You have let loose RAW (Indian military intelligence) in Afghanistan. We are encircled. India has never accepted Pakistan's existence. Afghanistan is turning towards India. We are in a nutcracker.

'The West, aided by Israel, wants our resources, access to Central Asian gas, you want geopolitical power, but you will only get your soft nose rubbed in the harsh soil.'

He focused his crazy bulging blue eyes on my nose.

'You have such delicate small noses. We have such big ugly noses, but with *character*. You do not want to get yours crushed in the harsh Afghan soil. You British should know better, you had your noses broken in the Afghan soil. They are natural fighters, and their Muslim brethren flock to join them in casting out the infidel.'

'You do have a very fine nose,' I replied, irritated by his caricatures. 'Much grander than my own, I was only thinking the other day how the noses here are so much more...'

'Let India come into Afghanistan and have their noses crrrushed,' he cut in, anger whitening his face.

Gul was a senior general during the military dictatorship of General Zia-ul-Haq, a conservative Muslim who Islamised Pakistan in a bid to save it (and his regime), introducing *sharia* courts and giving state backing to *madrassas*, 'letting the Islamic genie out of the bottle' in newspaper parlance, believing the more Islam, the better.

The country had needed saving, for it hadn't got off to a good start. Its first prime minister was assassinated in 1951, four years after Partition; the first military coup took place in 1958; India defeated it in wars in 1965 and again in 1971 with the humiliating loss of East Pakistan (now Bangladesh); and then, following civil unrest, in 1978 Zia staged a coup, toppling the prime minister, Zulfiqar Ali Bhutto, whom he executed the following year. Islam, Zia said, would unite the country.

Since then, things hadn't improved. Pakistan's use of Islamic militiamen in Indian-controlled Kashmir in the 1990s had further strengthened the hand of the military and those in favour of an austere Islamic state. The performance of corrupt civilian governments dominated by the feudal class had played into the hands of the military and Islamists. Village and tribal councils offered the only swift form of justice available to 'the masses' as court shelves groaned under yellowing papers and judges could usually be bought off or influenced with threats of violence. Corruption charges became little more than levers to be used to effect a change of government; one half of the political class enriched itself while the other half, temporarily in jail, waited its turn.

Musharraf had come to power in 1999 after mounting a coup following a power struggle between the military and a civilian government. The army had ruled the country directly for half of Pakistan's lifetime and indirectly for the remainder.

Neither side had very concrete plans for 'the masses', other than to use them for their own ends, as cannon fodder or illiterate voters to be cheaply bought off.

Despite endorsing a homespun 'enlightened moderation' for the nation, Musharraf's support for *jihadis* meant that militant Islam was again on the rise, even if it was kept out of sight, in remote training camps and *madrassas*. But this time, in line with what I'd heard at Bari Imam shrine, with Pakistan caught up in an international conflict, the Islamist surge seemed poised to irrevocably change the nature of the country.

I wondered if Gul felt any sense of responsibility.

'By turning Pakistan into a factory churning out ranks of young fanatics, aren't you dooming your own country?'

'This is a Muslim country', he replied, happy to reaffirm his creed. 'We are sworn to live as Muslims and to take up the cudgels for our brethren.'

God. How many times was I to hear this stuff? There was a dullness behind his voice, which suggested he'd heard it all before too. He leant on his ideology like a walking stick. Wasn't it less to do with religion and more that he was angry because his country, defined only by its opposition to and apartness from India, felt insecure and impotent, and his old Cold War buddies, the Americans, had abandoned him and its support for *jihad*?

Our interview ended, I noticed a lump of concrete on the carpet at the end of the room. 'A piece of the Berlin wall', he said, his words slowing, sombre with self-importance. 'The Americans. They sent it to me' – he was not gulling now – 'They sent it to me for *striking* the first blow for freedom.'

*

A couple of weeks later, Allah Ditta (meaning 'Gift from God') came into my life.

A relation of the Begum introduced him as somebody I might employ as a cook-cum-driver; but his previous work had done little to prepare him, despite his unbridled enthusiasm, for the job. The relation thought that he'd been an army batman, but in fact he'd driven a minibus in Rawalpindi.

In his early thirties, he had a thick mop of black hair, which sometimes, mysteriously, had bits of straw in it. From his smartly trimmed black beard flashed a ready and ingenuous smile. Malnourished, energetic, a bright-eyed Punjabi Muslim about the height of a fence post, he did everything at a jog. His driving ability was poor as his diminutive height prevented him having a clear view of the road and because he tended to fall asleep at the wheel. His defence of the sleeping habit, as I understood it, was that by birth he was of the truck-driver's caste and that he was not sleeping but resting while squinting into the far distance, an old truck-driver's ruse to conserve energy. His poor cooking and general drowsiness meant that my existence was precarious. His eyes were often suspiciously bloodshot. I don't think I ever saw him say his prayers.

At the beginning, instead of sitting in the back of the car as local norms dictate, I sat next to him, and from this began the vertiginous decline of my prestige.

I was struggling to navigate the complexities of the country's hierarchies of class, caste and tribe. For although a Muslim state, it was riven by the Hindu caste system its inhabitants disavowed; thus Rajput looked down on barber and barber on the darker-skinned Christian and lower-caste Hindus, who were traditionally 'sweepers', street cleaners. The North-West Frontier and Baluchistan were overtly tribal with most matters settled by councils rather than the courts and administration inherited from the British. Even the feudal, plain provinces of Punjab and Sindh ran along the lines of tribe and caste. The writ of the government was feeble in most of the country, which hung together loosely on a dog-eared colonial structure of cantonments, district commissioners, railway signalmen and post office clerks. It also seemed to adhere to the empire's old prejudices as laid down in its gazetteers, which were still available in bookshops, where ethnic groups and peoples were classified in such categories as 'Criminal Tribes'. If the Begum heard that I was hiring someone to do a task, she would ask the person's surname, which often denoted their clan or tribe, and on hearing it invariably say something like: 'His lot make good soldiers. Reliable' or 'that tribe is from the edge of Punjab. A notoriously thieving crowd. Handle with caution'.

The Begum, from the hierarchy-conscious Punjab, a province despised by all the others as the most powerful, thought that I had become 'too chummy' with Allah Ditta. 'Don't bring your filthy Western habits here,' she admonished with a shake of a finger.

She suggested that I sit in the back of the car instead of beside him.

Much later on, I acquiesced. People talked about 'keeping a distance' with servants, but from there I could better see Allah Ditta's eyes closing in the rear-view mirror and therefore knew when to wake him.

*

Soon, I found a house. Its main assets included a terrace overlooking the hills and its gentle owner, Professor Malick, a retired widowed English teacher and author of dictionaries, who lived behind it.

Before I left the Begum in Lahore, knowing that soon I would be struggling to set up my own household, she had recited a Persian refrain for my benefit, a key tenet of domestic order: '*Gurba kushtan rose aval*,' or 'Slay a cat on the first day' – and then minions will think that if the leader has done that to a cat, what will he do to us if we step out of line?

I failed to slay a cat; and so we were a household with a torrid routine and rhythm: a perpetual cycle of rebellion, reprisal and spells of short-lived serenity.

At the beginning, to some degree, I subconsciously set out to create a household similar to the Begum's and that of my grandmother's British Raj childhood. From such a misguided notion sprang many of my later domestic troubles.

In Pakistan most foreigners and well-off people had staff, calling them 'servants'. Foreigners employed mainly Christians as they were deemed 'safe' – meaning unlikely to murder an infidel in a fit of religious pique – who on the whole had been handed down from one expatriate to another, becoming blander and subtler with each inheritance. In Pakistani households, servants formed part of the fabric of the family, sharing its sorrows, joys and, sometimes, its riches and murderous disputes. Every so often you read in the local papers about servants murdering their employers. For all their intimacy, the two classes were worlds apart, with only a few enlightened employers offering their servants an opportunity to improve their lot.

Even as a humble journalist I had the means to supplement my staff with a toothless old Pathan guard, unarmed for my own safety, and a shy, impoverished young mother who did the cleaning, Shazia, a Christian.

Allah Ditta, as well as driving and cooking, promoted himself to *major domo*, or chamberlain, and he controlled my door and decided whom I might see and whom not. I was not yet sure of the criteria for entry. One day I'd seen him on the doorstep dismissing a hawker with a low wave of the back of his hand and a muttered curse. The next day

I saw him doing the same to a local journalist whom I had invited to lunch with the hope of employing him as a fixer and whom I then had to call back and placate. Allah Ditta was unrepentant. Later on, his judgement proved to have been correct. When the truth emerged that the journalist was an idle chiseller, Allah Ditta rolled his eyes and shot me a merciless told-you-so look.

Following a garbled discussion in Urdu and Punjabi about how best to decorate the house, Allah Ditta brought in a team of tailors and artists from his native borough of Rawalpindi. The suburban house was transformed into an Orientalist painting of a brothel. A row of tailors, each in a uniform of neat black hair, lacquered moustache and white robes, sat on the floor in front of old black and gold sewing machines, clattering away. They stitched together yards and yards of brick-red Sindhi *ajrak* fabric, block printed with black, blue and white geometric floral designs bordered with fluted arches on pillars. This fabric now covered every chair, cushion, sofa and table.

Allah Ditta donated a vase of plastic flowers and decorated the car with a faux-gilt tissue box and garlands of fresh, fragrant marigolds; the Begum sent over a carpenter who knocked up a *takht*, a raised dais-sofa like her own in Lahore, replete with shapely legs and red covered bolsters sparkling with mirrors.

Thinking that the place needed a further dash of colour, Allah Ditta contracted an artist who whipped up several vast canvases in the style of truck art: a depiction of a Sufi saint at whose feet worshipped a woman whom poor shading had given a hairy upper lip and a portrait of an actress as enigmatic as La Giaconda. It was not clear if she was colossally breasted or heavily pregnant. He also presented me with a painting of a Pathan film hero toting a Kalashnikov in each hand, who was smeared from head to foot with the blood of his enemies.

Whenever passing the painting, Allah Ditta pulled an imaginary gun trigger, smiling knowingly at the Pathan's simple-minded martial spirit.

After several months, I had to relieve Allah Ditta of his cooking duties. The final straw was his leaving an unlit gas ring on all night, threatening our neighbourhood with conflagration. The new cook was a toadying, skeletal Christian with a wracking typhoid cough. His name was Basil. He was a careful bookkeeper and hoarder of sheaves of receipts, which he kept in one of the kitchen's many dusty drawers. He would present himself in front of my desk, wringing his hands, a picture of self-abasement, desirous to reassure that he was at my service for my every need. His *bona fides* included a letter from a Swiss woman who had trained him to cook in the *cordon-bleu* style over a decade before. Switzerland is not overly celebrated for its cuisine, but his omelette stuffed with spiced tomato and his Beef Wellington accompanied by spinach and potato were beyond reproach. His *desi* or local cooking was not so good. I had to order takeaways from the market if I wanted to eat a half-decent curry.

Soon I began to suspect that Basil's efficiency with bookkeeping was a smokescreen to obscure a consistent and highly effective operation to empty my pockets. It was easy to do: he had a deal with the shopkeepers who gave him false receipts for inflated sums. In such a country, where the poor were grossly underpaid, it was natural leakage. And as a practitioner of a trade long known for its creative use of expense receipts, I could hardly take issue with Basil over the morality of his claims.

My other servants were providing a similar level of service: the guard was usually away at his village, the cleaner shifted a trailing cloud of dust from one end of the house to the other and the gardener limited his activities to occasionally removing turds left by the Professor's sweet-natured, decrepit old Alsatian from the lawn.

Occasionally, particularly halfway through my infrequent attempts at dinner parties, I found all the men slumped on the kitchen floor, asleep on flattened-out cardboard boxes, smelling strongly of gin. It made for as homely a scene as a bachelor out here could expect.

*

The Professor lived in an annex behind the house with his two sons. His face, nailed with white stubble, was gentle, walnut and thin, and his distant eyes sparkled with benevolence behind thick-rimmed spectacles. He always spoke slowly and correctly and looked mistily out on to the world as if it was a place that didn't bear close observation. He was the epitome of middle-class decency, a teacher who had laboured a lifetime in the moth-eaten bureaucracy of the state, a kleptocratic elite above him, the illiterate majority below, scooping away at oceans of ignorance with a thimble. Many younger members of his background, frustrated by the failing state, had armed themselves with conservative piety and were placing their hopes in Allah.

The Professor saw things in earthier terms. Often a roguish sparkle would illuminate the gap between his spectacles and his erratically shaven chin.

'All problems facing this country can be traced back to the terrible decline in English standards, particularly written,' he would say apropos of nothing. 'I have written to the education minister and warned him in the gravest terms that he *must* stop the *rot*.' He would then beam his distant scholarly smile.

One day, the Professor handed me a copy of his latest dictionary, *Essential English Usage*. 'I've written it,' he said, pausing to compress his lips, eyes twinkling with satire, 'so that I might become very famous.'

I skimmed through it. Several phrases stood out:

'...the moon's lucent rays silvered the river'

'...she is a voluptuous dancer (Having large breasts and hips)'

'...Portly – having a rather fat body'

As I skimmed on, its deeper currents revealed it to be a Voltairian swipe against infamy.

'Why does the feudal abase his servants in public?'

'Her landlord is a bit of an ogre'

'Who is not aware of the political and financial shenanigans among the political elite?'

The Professor asked if I would mind reviewing his dictionary for my newspaper. 'The paper doesn't usually review such books,' I said.

'But couldn't you put a little something down on paper?' he gently prodded.

Later on he pressed a fresh edition of the book into my hands. He turned it over so I could see its back cover. There was my paper's endorsement of his work '...this steadfast collection of definitions and usages is brightened by wit and literary flair'. He was very pleased.

'You know,' I said, in a confessional tone, 'the review was never actually published in the paper.'

'No matter. No matter at all. That is far from the point,' reassured the Professor.

We gorged on food together at a Chinese restaurant in celebration.

*

One morning, a month or so after I moved in to the house, Allah Ditta brought on my breakfast tray a large brown envelope, freshly ornamented with a dollop of porridge, bearing an Irish stamp: my grandmother had sent some decade-old notes that I'd left behind and asked her to post to me. Opening the envelope unleashed a whoosh of memories.

The notes were about a trip my elder brother and I had made a decade before to the desert fort of an old, cantankerous and highly cultured tribal chieftain in Pakistan's south-western province of Baluchistan. Nawab Akbar Khan Bugti was a living relic of an unblushing age, a chief with absolute power who submitted his tribesmen to trial-by-fire, a tyrant and a contrarian who had retreated from society to live among his people and the books of his library in his remote stronghold.

Beset by feuds with his own clans, other tribes and the government, he had assassinated rivals and ordered his men to attack development projects, railway lines, gas refineries and the electricity grid whenever he wanted to extract concessions from Islamabad. Though his territory was off limits to outsiders, we had sneaked in and spent a week in his company. He was the most extraordinary figure I'd ever met and the experience confirmed in my young mind that real adventure did exist.

Holding those notes brought back the storybook quality of that journey – our covert entry into his tribal stronghold, his armaments, his ledger book of punishments, his punctilious warning over the telephone before we set off to 'tell me if you *do* try to come, or someone may take a potshot', and so on.

I'd asked for the notes to be sent because the chieftain was back in the news and there was a chance to travel to meet him again. And to conclude some unfinished business – for during our visit, he had kept us under house arrest, not allowing us to see the area he controlled, which was something I still longed to do.

Now 80 years old, the Nawab was leading an insurgency against the government. His dispute was not religious, for his people although nominally Muslim were of a secular mindset, but part of a wider, long-running discord between the State and other Baluch *sardars*, or tribal leaders, which arose from the centre's desire to control the immense but sparsely populated province's mineral wealth.

A journey to visit him would allow me to reconnect with my old, broken travels in Pakistan. But as I sat holding the notes, watching hovering dots, jinking and zigzagging round a beehive outside my bedroom window, I had a nagging fear that I would find my memories untrue, that the past would seem unreal, as if those notes had been written by a different hand about a different country. I wondered how that enchanting place of the past squared with the one that now dominated the headlines: suicide bombs killing Pakistani soldiers and American unmanned 'drone' aircraft raining down rockets on militants hiding in the Pathan tribal areas; and I struggled to see how it was all of a piece.

On my previous travels I'd seen the country as a dilettante, seeking things out on a whim, picking up threads and dropping them, viewing the country through the prism of a kind of boyish wonder. But now I had to confront the country as a foreign correspondent, dealing with its conflict and violence, viewing it within the narrow, unforgiving scope of journalism.

Things weren't quite as they had been before. As I'd seen at Bari Imam shrine, they were changing; the old order, for better or for worse, was under threat.

The Nawab was the last great Baluch chief – a remnant of a loose system of control put in place during the British Raj's attempt to administer the frontier of imperial India. He was therefore an emblem of the tribal nature of the country, and, as he would have it, of resistance to the pro-*jihadi* military, of the old Pakistan staving off the new.

And as such, he would be more difficult to reach this time. He was holed up in a cave, deep in the mountains with his tribal army, surrounded by twenty thousand hostile Pakistani troops. Several months previously, the military had bombed his ancestral fort and the surrounding parts of his capital to pieces, resulting in the deaths of over two hundred people, and forcing him and his fighters to flee.

With Pakistan staggering under so many troubles on other fronts, the Nawab posed an existential threat to the country; and he was making a last stand.

The Pakistani military was also facing irredentist claims by Afghanistan on its western border, where its soldiers were bogged down against Pathan tribal insurgents, and fighting a sporadic, covert war against India on its eastern border in Kashmir. Fearing that the state might disintegrate, it was ruthless in quashing Baluch attempts towards the secession of their mineral-rich province – a vast howling desert wilderness that accounts for just less than half the country's land mass.

The government wanted to control the province's oil and gas, which the chieftains regarded as their own, to do as they wished with. At the same time, the *sardars* thwarted development schemes because they viewed them as further evidence of the government's effort to 'colonialise' the province.

Replacing the notes in the porridge-smudged envelope, the possibility of seeing the Nawab again seemed remote. But I began plotting to see how this could be done.

*

In early March, my scheming had produced enough leads to justify an attempt to find the Nawab in his hideout.

The day before flying to Quetta, Baluchistan's capital, I rode – badly – an ungainly bony speckled mare into smoky hill villages above Islamabad.

I clip-clopped past fragrant wild marijuana plants taller than the horse's head. Dog roses, cherry, apricot and apple blossom brightened formerly dull roads. An old man with blue eyes sat on his haunches, rolling out hashish on a flat stone, wisps of hair billowing out of his ears and nose like smoke.

It was the end of spring, an all-too-brief flicker of levity before the summer mercilessly puts it to the sword. '*Kaanji*' (a dark carrot juice) was prepared by locals as a blood thinner to mitigate the worst effects of the coming heat. Sporadic rains had deepened the green of freshly sown wheat. Fish-*wallahs* clattered about the streets on bicycles, advertising the contents of their baskets in singsong jingles. Jacaranda trees, lilac against fresh green foliage, bobbed under the raindrops of a light shower. Open parachutes of yellow petal-lanterns floated over the top of *amaltas,* Indian laburnum trees.

I reached a pretty hamlet. The hills' lime foliage rose behind adobe walls of huts and a small whitewashed domed shrine, its contours defined with freehand strokes of gamboge paint. A munching buffalo, children chasing chickens, hip-swaying women spitting into the earth and men lying on string beds smoking *hookahs*. The simple lines and basic components of Pakistani life, things that had been blurred in the background while I'd been in Islamabad, were now coming back into focus.

I was back in Pakistan, on the cusp of returning to Baluchistan. After several clumsy digs of my heels I coaxed the poor nag into a trot towards home.

That night, packing for the trip, I came across my brother's scrawl again in the backflap of the old guidebook. He had written in Urdu: 'Where are we going?!' I could hear him jauntily repeating the phrase and it brought back all the excitement that then knocked at our young hearts.

BALUCHISTAN:
BLACK SHEEP

Chapter 3
On the Trail of the Nawab

To avoid the prying eyes of intelligence agents I left Quetta with Shahzada – my contact and fixer – a driver and two fellow journalists, through empty backstreets in the gloom before dawn.

On the outskirts we stopped at a solitary stall lit by a naked light bulb to pick up water, cigarettes and biscuits, and a man who Shahzada said would help us make our rendezvous with Nawab Akbar Khan Bugti's people. In the grey light, before the sun rolled itself on to the top of a nearby ridge, we crossed a vast stony plateau from which rose shadowy brick-kiln chimneys, brown smoke rising heavenward from their tips like a prayer.

It was a relief to be on the move and out of the city. I'd spent more than several nail-biting days there in a dingy hotel, waiting to see if Shahzada could contact the Nawab, confined to my room 'so as not to give arousal to suspicious thoughts in the minds of the agencies'.

I was frustrated that I couldn't enjoy Quetta's fresh spring mountain air. I'd briefly visited before. An urban periphery sprawled from its colonial-era centre over outlying plains and up the slopes of jagged ochre mountains. It was a skulduggerous and secretive place and home to the one-eyed fugitive Taliban leader, Mullah Omar and the world's largest heroin trade. Baluch tribesmen used it as a convenient place to settle scores with one another, usually by shooting up hotels, lobbing bombs into each other's houses, and knocking off each other's turbans (grave insult).

Shahzada was a short sardonic man with neat greying hair and moustache, dressed permanently in the uniform of our trade – an armless, many-pocketed khaki vest. Balanced on the edge of my hotel bed, for hours he had recounted alleged details of the baroque sexual appetites of my Western media colleagues ('she oral-sexed her way across the border'. He also explained the delay to our journey by giving details of skirmishes between the Nawab's men and Pakistani troops, and roadside bombs that had exploded on several routes into his lair.

One morning I'd read, with a sense of increasing agitation, a government announcement in the local press stating that the Nawab had left the country.

'That's just their usual bullshit,' Shahzada had assured me with a cynical chortle. 'He's still here.' But the report had deepened my unease about whether I was being strung along.

Sequestered in my hotel room, I pulled out my old notes on the Nawab. In my mind's eye, I saw him as he was on my last visit: 68 years old, sitting crosslegged in his council hall, powerful shoulders and a martinet's rigid backbone, with a long nose curled over a moustache, the tips of which he preened upwards into tusks as tribesmen filed in to his council hall, touching or kissing his feet before subsiding silently before him. He had a penchant for shaving the hair, eyebrows and beards of his enemies; blackening the faces of recalcitrant tribesmen, stripping them naked and tying them backwards on donkeys and parading them through the bazaar.

I wondered how much he would have changed and how he was faring in his mountain cave hideout and whether he would still live up to my expectations of him as a great old tyrant. Before we'd left his fort the Nawab had ordered his tribesmen to parade a large anti-tank gun before us.

'We are at war on many fronts, tribal vendettas and so on. This is a war of attrition. They want to finish me off,' he had said with a touch of pride.

To him the cannon was a thing of great beauty and he hopped around it with a malicious glint in his eye.

'I would be grateful if you did not mention to my enemies that I have this cannon in my possession,' he said, unable to take his eyes off the artillery piece.

Since then the Nawab had upped the ante, not only attacking development projects, railway lines, gas refineries and the electricity grid, but he also stood accused of directing the Baluch Liberation Army, which was engaged in a full-scale insurgency, targeting military personnel and executing Punjabi immigrant labourers in cold blood.

The Nawab's position was particularly piquant because Sui, one of Asia's largest gas fields, lies on Bugti tribal land. His forces sabotaged pipelines or abducted workers, cutting off major cities from gas, when he felt that he was not getting enough dividends. Conversely, the army was accused of indiscriminately bombing civilians and conducting a campaign of torture, disappearances and custodial killings.

Yet, for all the province's history of upheaval and oppression, the shelling of the Nawab's fort was unprecedented. President Musharraf had signalled his intent to finish off powerful rebellious Baluch chiefs, who, however wayward, were once considered part of the country's establishment, and through whom power over the complex province was exercised.

Such was its sensitivity, the army kept the conflict under wraps, denying that there was any military operation at all.

When, finally, the Nawab had given the all clear for us to start our journey, Shahzada sprang a surprise: we were to be accompanied by another British journalist and an American photographer. It was too late to be churlish; and the company and shared resources would be welcome.

*

In the hours that we jolted along together, I got to know my companions. Carlotta, a tough war correspondent, was based in Kabul, where even the hairiest Afghans with the biggest beards treated her as an equal, she said, sometimes mistaking her for a man.

'Some of these great commanders are really as soft as lambs … but they can be very naughty, reneging on deals and changing sides when it suits them.' There were a lot of *naughty* people in the region. Scott, youthful, handsome, reserved, fiddled with his cameras, as photographers do.

In a lull between conversations, I returned to the landscape: plains that are the abode of dust devils and of winds famed for killing livestock, quickly reducing their victims to shiny bones.

Red-eyed and rigid with tiredness we arrived after sunset in an almost empty dirt-and-dust town.

We waited in the car to meet a contact. In the street a boy, his shoulder covered by a shawl of red and blue printed Sindhi cloth, held a sacrificial bull by a nose-rope. Thick folds of creamy dewlap skin fell from its chest like a crushed silk curtain from a pelmet. Its coal-dark eyelids were slits, closed as if the animal were basking ecstatically in the moonshine.

Suddenly, a pick-up truck roared alongside and two men jumped out. They thrust their faces up to the car windows. They were the Nawab's men, Shahzada said. After smiles and hushed greetings, we followed them up the road and again stopped. Shahzada gestured that Carlotta should hide her face with her headscarf and told me to cover myself with a shawl and pretend to be asleep. We rattled on a few miles along a dirt track and approached a checkpoint. Beyond lay the outer perimeter of the Bugti tribal area and all the excitement of a prohibited world. A supine policeman, luckily not a soldier, who would be better trained, raised the barrier and waved through the first car. When it was our turn, another of the guards, a more senior officer, came out from his hut, wrapping himself in a thick shawl. He shook hands with Shahzada through the front passenger window, exchanged greetings, and shone a torch in the back at Carlotta and me. I feigned sleep but I had been unable to lie back and so sat bolt upright with a shawl over my head, looking less like a tired Baluch traveller than a standard lamp. The policeman waved us on.

We drove to a small mud-walled farmhouse surrounded by green wheat fields. There we met yet another guide, a tattered, stoatish, former tribal policeman who was secretly in the service of the Nawab.

That night we bedded down uncomfortably in a row on the mud floor of a farm building. I eyed the sleeping forms of my companions: a police officer, journalists, driver, guide, farmer, his young sons and a couple of goats. What strange bedfellows travel throws together.

*

Early the next morning, the light buttercup-yellow, we drove to a line of eucalyptus trees, where we left our vehicle and made preparations to cross a canal that stood between us and the sanctum of Bugti territory. We found a group of men waiting next to a taut wire strung across the dun waterway and two at a time we floated precariously on a tractor tyre's inner tube from one bulrush-lined bank to another.

A snipe and a kingfisher watched from the reeds as a tribesman, standing on the rim of the tyre, hauled us along by pulling hand over hand on the wire. On the far bank we were greeted by heavily armed, shaggy-bearded 'tribals', all of whom wore abundant pantaloons, polished bandoliers and a turban large enough to fill a laundry basket. The soles of their sandals were fashioned from old car treads; their eyes were lined with kohl and they stroked their moustaches incessantly; some smiled, others, not so free with their favours, glared contemptuously at our unmartial party. My attempt to be friendly with one of them by grinning was met with a stone-cold stare.

They loaded us on to pick-up trucks and we motored off across an escarpment with sand and dirt billowing behind us, passing conical tombs barely discernible amid a sea of shale. A bearded, ragged figure stood looking at us from an isolated dwelling of unmortared stone and straw. It seemed a bare and cruel place to inhabit, remote from our world of comfort and compromise.

As we crossed dry seasonal riverbeds the driver crashed over embankments and weaved around thickets in axle-deep sand at a breakneck pace and we did our best, often unsuccessfully, to avoid smashing our heads on the vehicle's roof. In colonial times, the Baluch were famed as skilled horsemen; now they drove as once they rode.

After a few hours we came to a handful of tribal retainers squatting in the shade of spindly trees, miles from any habitation, with a feast of *kark* (unleavened bread made by wrapping dough around hot round boulders which are then placed in an undergound oven), *sajji* (goat roasted on skewers between two rows of flame), platters of fatty, paprika-orange lamb stew, and plastic bowls of almonds.

After lunch, crossing a section of mountains impassable by truck, we walked for hours and at one point a horse, which, rather small, seemed Chaucerian, was magicked from behind a bush and Carlotta (ex-English pony club, keeper of powerful Wazir horses in Kabul) mounted it. A couple of mules carried our bags.

We passed reminders of the Nawab and his people's hasty exodus from his citadel: mottled leathery camel carcasses and stone huts reduced to rubble, in which we found parts of precision-guided missiles made in Texas and fired by Pakistani jetfighters.

By the time we finished that walk it had already been a long day and so when we piled into trucks waiting for us at an oasis, we were grateful once again for the logistical finesse of our hosts.

After dusk, driving without headlamps over boulder-strewn riverbeds, we could just make out the silhouette of a promontory on top of which was a surveillance post manned by the paramilitary Frontier Corps, a force under the army's command. As we skirted the base of the rock, we passed right under the sentries' noses, scarcely believing that the noise of the engines crashing over rocks would go undetected, certain that at any moment the beam of a searchlight would pinpoint us from above. Surely that would mean at best a humiliating arrest and the end of this journey; and at worst a barrage of gunfire.

We arrived after nightfall at the mouth of a tall chasm, its opening just wide enough for us to trundle along its 100-metre length before debouching into a guerrilla encampment in an amphitheatre of sheer rock. Camels and horses were tethered in the foreground and snatches of a voice or the clatter of a stumbling hoof reverberated above the muttering of guerrillas moving about in the moonlight.

A local commander, appearing out of the gloom, greeted us with a firm embrace and led us over to a patch of flat stony ground sheltered by an overhang of rock where he invited us to sit on reed mats. Yet more lamb and bread was brought and as we ate, the commander and Shahzada exchanged *haal*, a formalised way of sharing news according to local custom. The commander said that five paramilitary troops had been killed in a landmine explosion the day before.

After dinner, tribal attendants poured water over our food-stained fingers. Accompanied by a band of tribesmen, we mounted up and moved off on six camels, tied to each other by nose-ropes. The moonlight fizzed about us as we crossed a high desert plateau bound on each side by blueish mountain ridges. Cast in silhouette our shadows joined up origami-like and glided across the sand as stray currents of the day's now spent heat mingled with the night's cooler air. Up on the camel's back, I sank into a trance of pleasure, soaking up the comforting rhythm and soft crunch of the camel's plodding. Raw exhilaration made me light-headed and I smoked a foul cigarette in an attempt to prolong the giddy sensation.

I hadn't told my consultant that I'd left Spain. I would let him know by and by. After all those days and months tethered to a beeping, sucking dialysis machine and the hopes and fears of waiting for a transplant I was really free again, only praying that these travels would last and that now, more pressingly, nothing would prevent us from reaching the Nawab.

But a few problems arose.

Scott, the photographer, stricken suddenly with a virulent ailment of the guts, was too ill to ride. He straggled stoically on foot behind us. For a long stretch we plodded on, so long in fact that it seemed even to those of us who didn't know the route that something was amiss. Soon, shamefaced, our guides admitted that we were lost; we would have to retrace our steps.

My camel, groaning like Chewbacca, repeatedly buckled beneath me with exhaustion. I decided to walk, which I quickly regretted because we trudged on through the night for a couple more hours, groping our way in a tarpaulin of shadows, stars and rocks.

And then, suddenly, just when the journey seemed interminable, there he was: illuminated in the moonlight with sheer cliffs of rock towering above him, swathed in robes, leaning on a walking stick and supported by two tribal retainers.

It was 3am. He motioned for us to follow him to a cave hewn into the foot of a narrow winding *nullah*, or ravine. This was his headquarters. The cave was furnished with a *charpoy*, a string bed, a cream-cushioned heavy wooden armchair, into which heart-shaped holes had been carved, and a side-table. His luxuries were a small stack of current-affairs magazines, including *The Economist*, and a stock of chocolate bars.

He listened politely to our accounts of the travails we had experienced on our journey.

'You can sleep lying on a camel,' he brooded, curtailing our petty complaints.

He began to talk about unmanned surveillance aircraft routinely flying over his hideout, which I thought was a tall tale in accordance with the local penchant for hyperbole, but seeing our tiredness, he ordered our bedding to be arranged on the pebbles at the foot of his *charpoy* and we all settled down to sleep. Etiquette for cave dwellers is obscure and I wondered if I should bid him 'good night'. I did. He grunted in a grumpy grandfatherly sort of way.

Chapter 4
In the Lair of the Nawab

'WHAT MORE IS THERE TO LIFE than love and warfare?' the Nawab asked over breakfast. Seated on his armchair in the cool morning air, the rest of us gathered around him on the floor, he was still a domineering figure.

'What is better than seeing your enemies driven before you and then taking their women to bed?' he continued in a gravelly voice, savouring his words like a jackal crunching a bone.

We'd woken, crumpled, unwashed, nostrils hardened with dust in a beige landscape, as tribesmen were kindling a cooking-fire. The night had been cold but we had ample blankets, and I was buoyed by having slept under the stars in air that smelt of rock and desert, and by waking up in the Nawab's cave, ringed by mountains and thousands of Pakistani troops, whom the day before we'd managed to avoid.

'Have you killed anyone yourself?' I asked the Nawab, hoping to draw him out further while he was in an epic frame of mind.

'Certainly,' he said. His mouth and nose twitched as if the question smelt a bit off. 'Where else would the pleasure be?'

He carefully cultivated his air of *terribilita*, the awe-inspiring power that had made him a legend in Pakistan. An American ambassador had averred that he would be capable of running any US state and his peers deemed that had he lived in a more red-blooded era he would have rivalled Tamerlane for conquest and slaughter. He was a potent amalgam of the primitive and sophisticated. Reputed to have murdered his first man aged 12 and to have thrown his uncle down a well not long afterwards, he had received a standard public school-type education at Aitcheson College in Lahore (an establishment set up by the British to educate the sons of chiefs); but then in adult life he'd accrued a multidisciplinary store of knowledge that would be the envy of any autodidact.

Now 80 years old and straight-backed with a well-preened moustache, his manicured hands still looked strong enough to throttle a goat. At our previous meeting he had attributed his excellent physical condition to a regime of vegetarian food, fifty press-ups a day, and two and a half hours' sleep each night. Of course, he *had* aged: thrombosis had slowed him and he was a little less robust, but only the armchair and walking stick gave him the air of a pensioner out on a spree.

After breakfast, the Nawab was ready to describe the attack that had expedited his flight from his fort to the hills; but he maintained a studied nonchalance, not wanting to give the impression that Musharraf was capable of causing him excessive inconvenience.

'Six to seven hundred shells were lobbed on my left and right, the ceiling collapsed, three people around me were killed. Some sixty were killed in that attack, including women and children,' he said flatly. 'My library has been cast to the four winds.'

The previous year the Nawab had greeted Musharraf with a hail of rockets as he visited a neighbouring tribal area. Since then the conflict at times appeared to be a feud between two colossal egos.

The president, a stocky, mustachioed and pouchy-cheeked former commando with dyed black hair (left silvery at the temples to denote wisdom) was as plucky as a badger. In response to the welcoming salvo, Musharraf had threatened that 'one day Bugti will die without knowing what hit him'.

The Nawab had replied: 'I will give the dictator a war he will not forget.'

The Nawab now pulled a notebook from his pocket and read out a list of his enemy's order of battle and armaments, and casualties.

'I am leading the resistance and the man with the swagger stick thinks it is an affront,' he concluded. 'We are defending our homeland, our natural wealth.'

Given that he was facing a large, well-equipped force that had shown willingness to use fighter jets against his small tribal army, I asked if he was not leading his people irresponsibly towards destruction.'Let the people suffer. If people want rights sometimes you have to suffer, that is if you are a man, and not a mouse,' he retorted violently. There was a basalt core in his alert blue eyes.

With his usual enigmatic *hauteur*, he denied government claims he was actively organising a province-wide insurgency. 'If various allied groups see me as a figurehead, how can I object?' he drawled, content with his neat evasion.

*

That night we ate well. Woolly black lambs, which had tumbled about on the rocks near us all day, were slaughtered and cooked over a fire. The Nawab, perhaps delighted to have female company, or perhaps sensing that she was the alpha in our pack, addressed most of his supper discourse to Carlotta.

The campfire burning low, we readied our blankets to sleep on the floor, and he scoffed under his breath. '*Haw haw haw*. Tired already? Too much war, eh? Well, I suppose I *must* be at war because you're *war* correspondents.'

*

Not long into the next morning, I found myself becoming increasingly tetchy. I was tired of being in such close proximity to my companions. I had had enough of the Nawab's haughtiness. I wanted a break.

Carlotta had received news from a colleague, perhaps via a satellite phone, that Pakistani military intelligence knew we were here. Possibly they had known all along of our destination and saw our journey as being useful to them in some way, but the Nawab, crotchety, blamed it on Shahzada. He started accusing him of being an army informer – perhaps sarcastically; it was hard to know. 'You can tell your friends...' he said in preface to his occasional, scornful remarks to our guide. Shahzada looked sheepish.

'He cannot even speak Baluchi properly,' the Nawab spat. Shahzada shrank into his *chador*.

Oppressed by the morning's verbal sniping, I left Carlotta pondering whether the cave in fact constituted a cave or was merely an overhang.

Soon I found myself in an open gorge through which ran a cool, clear stream bordered by rocks covered with lichen. Tribesmen bathed their long lovelocks and washed their garments or sat crosslegged in small circles chatting. I was frustrated that I couldn't speak to them without Shahzada at hand to translate. I wondered how they saw their leader and their fight.

The Nawab had regaled us with tales of the Baluch, a warrior race who, with the Kurds, he said, traced their origins back two thousand years to Aleppo in Syria. For the last thousand years or more they had lived in present-day Pakistan, Iran and Afghanistan.

Firdausi, in his 10th-century Persian epic, the Shahnama or *Book of Kings*, sings:

> 'Heroic Baluchis and Kuchis we saw,
> Like battling rams all determined on war'.

Balaach, the greatest medieval Baluch warrior hero, held that 'War is looked upon as the first business of a gentleman and all Baluch are gentlemen.'

The Nawab certainly tried to keep his tribe up to the *beau idéal*.

By now the sun shone directly into the gorge and before the day got too hot, I decided to scale a steep mountainside to find some privacy; but after climbing for twenty minutes I still couldn't find cover among the glissade of shale. Finally, when the tribesmen were reduced to dots below on the valley floor, I stopped on the steep incline, my weight on one foot, out of breath. The hard brilliance of the sunlight created a blur in my sweat-suffused eyes, merging the mountains, desert and sky. Baluchistan shimmered about me like a fairground carousel seen from its centre, ochre, blood, pitch, khaki and Persian blue swirling and liquefying, fragments of rampart, peak and stream floating in isolation, fragments that gave the impression of a buttressed, moated citadel afloat in the sky.

My breathing steady, I wiped my eyes with a sleeve. God, yes, I really was here. My happiness was gilded with something that I realised was vengeance satisfied.

The day my illness was diagnosed and the doctors said it was a life-threatening and life-long disease I felt as if I'd been thrust into a pit. I was 27 years old and in an instant my ambitions sank within me and the world I'd hoped to explore seemed impossibly remote. IgA nephropathy, the consultant said. A nephrotic nephritic, I said to myself now, the words loaded with comic, morbid repulsion. In short, as Mr Micawber would say, my own antibodies had attacked my kidneys. I had kidney failure. The doctors didn't know why.

Kidney failure, according to the medical literature, 'is a major life event'. The description made it sound like moving house, getting divorced or buying a dishwasher. Even so it had not helped me, having never experienced 'a major life event', work out to what pitch of self-pity and melodrama I should sink. 'End stage renal failure is 100 per cent fatal within a few weeks unless treated through dialysis or transplantation,' stated a medical leaflet. It all had a whiff of the body bag. I'd had mini-strokes at the back of my eyes and my sight had started to fade. I was told that my right testicle was 'atrophied', a word I'd previously associated with declining civilisations. I had misguided visions of sitting out the rest of my life in a darkened room hooked up to a dialysis machine which, my having become dependent on it, would kill me if I abandoned it. The prospect of having some unnatural Frankenstein-type operation – a transplant – was equally abhorrent.

My body had failed me. I couldn't trust it or myself fully again, often wondering if it was my fault, some wired-in weakness of spirit or character. This sort of thing didn't happen to Fitzroy Maclean.

But a transplant *had* given me another chance and I *had* come back, I told myself in this little introspective mountainside harangue, and I'd shown life, 'fortune's spite', god, whatever, that I was not to be thwarted. My mother would have been pleased to see me in these mountains. Living life. It was in high places on days like these, remote from everyday things and a little nearer to notions of death and heaven that I felt close to her; I remembered her voice and face more clearly than, as the days passed, I otherwise did.

I heard a strange, bird-like trilling carried on the air above me. During this chat with myself I'd lowered my *shalwar* to have a purge. There, standing on a ridge, a barelegged shepherd-boy was laughing and biting the collar of his knee-length grubby shirt. I hoisted up my pyjama trousers. We stared at one another and he then ran off to a group of women barely discernible in the sparse shade of a solitary thorny tree.

Disturbed, my moment of introspection ended, I looked over at the shadows in which the boy now stood. The group of tribal women pricked my curiosity but I knew that my attentions would be unwelcome. Above all, I wanted to know what they were chatting about. A footnote in an anthropological work that I'd recently read recorded the conversations of Baluch womenfolk in nomadic camps:

A dispute between two women:

'By my father's bad smell. I'll squeeze out your crap. You black wild pig.'

And a woman to her nephew who is asking for water:

'Can't you see my hands are busy. Do you want me to piss in your face?'

It was a rough life, the one these Baluch lived. The same ethnography contained a description claiming that in some cases of 'honour killing' the offending woman was sentenced to hang herself, using her tent as a gallows, a feat made all the more appalling by the fact that their abodes would have been so low she would have to bend her knees to end her own life. But this account was at odds with my grandmother's story of meeting a Bugti lady at a society gathering in Punjab. As elsewhere in the country, the upper echelons were largely spared the grislier parts of the exacting code. It was poor, and sometimes middle-class women who, considered as domestic slaves, chattels, worse than animals, fell victim to the country's 'honour' killings, acid attacks, gang rapes. These traditions from the Old Pakistan were seldom, if ever, prohibited by militant Islam's new wave of leaders.

I walked on and up on to another ridge, looking across the humped backs of the reddish mountains, scarlet in shadow, outcrops blown into Daliesque stalks and baubles. In the distance a caravan of camels and a flock of sheep spilt out on to the plains from a hidden ravine and I wondered how long such things would last.

The Baluch and their way of life were under threat, not only from the Punjabi-dominated centre, which was attacking the hierarchy on which the structure of these tribes depended; but also from Saudi-financed *wahabi* mosques, which were proliferating in those areas of the province not under the control of strong chiefs. Pakistan's sectarian violence was funded in part by Shia Iran and Sunni Saudi Arabia, who were fighting out their regional rivalry through local proxies. Sunni Baluch tribes straddling Iran's border, already hostile to Tehran's Shia chauvinism, would be a greater thorn in the ayatollah's side, perhaps Saudi *wahabis* had surmised, if they were to adopt a more militant form of Islam.

Perhaps the Baluch's only chance of preserving their way of life was to break away from Pakistan. At Partition, Baluchistan had been a reluctant participant in the new country; some tribes had launched a brief armed resistance against its inclusion. The Nawab's war made me wonder how serious a threat to Pakistan that disgruntlement was. With all the country's current troubles and the fibres of the old order fraying and unravelling, would Pakistan last? The Begum's warning, that I should return here before the country changed beyond recognition, was starting to seem portentous.

Slipping and sliding back down towards the Nawab's camp, I remembered that a decade before in Lahore I'd watched an American senator poring over maps of Baluchistan with Pakistani officials, discussing building gas and oil pipelines that would run from Central Asia and Afghanistan through the province to its coast. But

Washington, for all its attempts to get a grip on the region, seemed to be losing out to a more local power. Baluchistan's port of Gwadar was now being developed by China, which hoped it might connect Kashgar with the warm waters of the Gulf. Pakistan's efforts to quell the rebellious province were partly motivated by this Chinese investment.

*

That afternoon, a surveillance aircraft flew high above us, its wings winking silverishly in the heat-faded sky. Everybody scrambled into the cave – apart from the Nawab. He raised his straw hat to it, beckoning his foe to join him. 'I am in no condition to be fighting as you can see, but I am glad to be in the field,' he said after the aircraft passed, his face animated by the incident.

Talk of moving camp ensued; he was in favour of staying put but his grandson, Bramdagh, his commander in the field, was bold enough to disagree, saying our position had been compromised. They came to an agreement: we would shift in the morning.

'We will not have to set off till 8am,' pronounced the Nawab, 'because the Pakistan army is so decadent that it doesn't get up until 10am'.

Later that day, still in ebullient mood, he asked me:

'Have you read *Rebellion, Resistance and Death* by Albert Camus?'

'No,' I replied, 'I'm afraid not'.

'You must know that bit from Bacon about revenge being a kind of wild justice?'

'No, afraid not, Nawab sahib'.

I later looked up the section of that quotation that he had omitted: 'which the more man's nature runs to the more ought law to weed it out'. I had heard his views on justice before.

The Nawab brooked no dissent within the ranks of his own tribe so when, a decade previously, a Bugti clan leader had joined the then prime minister Benazir Bhutto's political party, he'd had the leader's son assassinated at an election meeting. That clan, whose allegiance was valuable because they owned the lands around the Sui gas field, reacted by killing the Nawab's most cherished son, Salal. In retaliation he attacked the clan *en force*, driving 4,000 of its members from the area, and sent hit men to pursue them to the farthest corners of Pakistan. I'd met the clan leader, a greybeard with a narrow face and watery old eyes, and asked him if he wanted to kill the Nawab.

'Yes,' he replied gravely. 'I have already killed his son.'

Conducting a long conversation with the Nawab was testing. With him on the one hand singing his glorious swan song, and on the other, Carlotta and me ploughing our furrow of war and the region, he began to grow irritable. Finally the narrow gauge of our journalistic questioning ignited him.

'Have you *no* conversation at all?' he barked as witheringly as a *grande dame*, brushing invisible specks of dirt off his clothes. 'All you can talk about is this infernal "war on terror" business.'

The acoustics of the rock reverberated remorselessly with the nakedness of this truth. In reparation I offered up, in quick succession, a couple of tidbits from my small knapsack of ready-to-go sweeteners for tyrants: La Pasionara's exhortation to Republicans in the Spanish Civil War to 'die on your feet or live on your knees', and King Boabdil's mother's reproach: 'do not cry like a woman for what you did not fight for like a man'. He grunted low-spiritedly. It was a temporary sating.

*

The next morning, after breakfast, donkeys and camels were loaded. A tribal vassal guided the Nawab by the arm as he sought privacy to relieve himself behind a rock. The servant foreshadowed his master's every step by whispering loudly '*Biss, Biss Biss ... Bismillah*' (In the Name of God), an incantation intended to ward off any calamity that might befall him on the uneven ground.

Then tribesmen placed two slabs of stone next to a sitting camel like the pedestals used by dignitaries on state occasions to climb into carriages. The Nawab, with some majesty, processed from behind the rock towards the animal. He paused and, ever the Baluch buck, turned to say to us:

'Don't take pictures until I am sitting.'

Once astride his camel, he quoted from the John Donne poem 'No Man is an Island', the part about 'for whom the bell tolls'. Relishing the drama, he repeated his jibe of a few days before:

'Are you war correspondents? Yes, as I remember you are. So then, we must be at war.'

After a couple of hours we arrived at a new camp, which was less a cave than a widening in a cramped ravine. We sat at its edges under rocky overhangs, with the central space open to the elements.

Every cave creates its own atmospheric dynamic. This one was more intimate and informal. The Nawab, growing ultra relaxed, lay back and chatted. Dressed in a corduroy jacket with elbow patches, looking as comfortable as a farmer at the country races, he spoke of Baluchi traditions and lore and a clan that has 'spiritual powers that staunch bleeding wounds'. Growing more garrulous, he embarked in immaculate English on a disquisition on the intricacies of camel copulation. Relishing his anatomic precision, he declaimed on the narrowness of the *urethra* with pedantic exactitude. 'A camel enjoys thirty to forty she-camels in his harem, taking half an hour to pleasure himself.' I imagined he saw something of himself in the male camel.

*

After a day at the new camp it transpired that despite our conversational deficiencies the Nawab was either not willing to let his audience go or too polite to raise the subject of our departure. We'd gleaned enough for our reports and wanted to head back to meet newspaper deadlines, but we had to force the question of arranging our journey home. The Nawab, at first, seemed not to hear it, but after a few attempts to raise the matter we gathered from his nephew that he was organising our escape from Bugti land.

On the eve of our leaving, milling about with some of the young fighters, one of them asked me if I'd like to stay and fight with them. Momentarily, my chest tightened and a buzz of adrenaline-fuelled madness surged through me, something I'd not felt since my early twenties. But the moment fled as quickly as it had come. Aside from my doubts about the Nawab's cause, how would I get my medication? Could I take the extremes of hot and cold?

That night, as I bedded down on the hard ground in front of the campfire, I admitted to myself what I had long secretly known: I was no longer the person who had started these travels years before. The intensity of that first encounter had passed; I was more calculating, less innocent, more cautious; and the country itself had changed. But, as the embers of the fire turned to ash, I grinned to myself. For Pakistan was still exciting; and was revealing to me some of its hidden places. I gathered the blanket tighter about me, and slept.

*

Our final hours with the Nawab were filled with a mixture of misgiving and relief. He fussed a little more than expected over the details of our journey and I wondered if he might just – in his odd way – miss us. We'd seen glimpses of his softer side: he admitted that he had made up the story years before about killing his first man at the age of 12 purely to excite the gullibility of a visiting female writer; and at times, he had appeared to leave open the possibility of reconciliation with the government.

He was powerfully contradictory. He thought of himself as having always been 'a rebel'; he delighted in telling of his youthful escapades, such as derailing a train at Simla during the Raj, and turning his back on a visiting American dignitary; and he was proud that in society circles he was perceived as an *enfant terrible*. And yet, in the past, whenever it had suited him, he had served in senior government positions and backed the state against the Baluch struggle for autonomy; and he belonged to the country's elite.

We mounted our camels after breakfast. He, his grandson and nephews had come out to see us off. 'The government says with glee that Bugti is at an end,' growled the Nawab. 'Of course everything comes to an end. I am 80 years old but the younger generation carries the flag.' He was relishing the prospect of a showdown, a grand finale. It would exonerate him, lay the old ghost of past infidelities to the Baluch cause to rest, and give him the dramatic exit his ego merited. He had told Carlotta that he had 'had a good innings', adding: 'It is better to die quickly in the mountains than slowly in bed.'

He, his nephews and grandson waved us off cheerily. The camels set off up an incline so precipitous that I thought that the saddle, and me with it, would slide off. I glanced back. He was a piece of work, a cruel and bloody-minded tyrant, but there was something admirable about his desire not to go 'gentle into that good night'.

On the way back we traversed the same escarpments and desolate ravines. Again, groups of armed tribesmen met us at intervals, laying out food on a chequered yellow and black *pattu*, a light cotton shawl usually worn slung over a shoulder. As night fell, there was a flash and boom of mortar fire not far off, which warmed my belly with fear. Scott and Carlotta, who had been only feet away from a suicide bomb explosion a few weeks before in Afghanistan, paid no attention.

*

Five months later, a journalist friend telephoned late at night.
'They've got him. They've killed him'.

'Oh God, bin Laden?'

'No, no. It looks like they have killed your old chum the Nawab.'

The sequence of events gradually emerged: a commando operation had been launched against him in one of his cave hideouts. The Pakistan government claimed that, having surrounded the Nawab, an unarmed group of officers entered the cave to negotiate with him. The Nawab fired a rocket, which brought down the cave on all of them, killing him, several officers and a handful of troops. One of his aides confirmed the outline of the story, but denied that the soldiers were unarmed. He added that his chieftain had decided that he would rather die fighting than surrender to the security forces, and he had asked his tribesmen 'to leave the cave and let me fight them alone'.

The Nawab had died in the manner of his choosing. Baluch ballads now commemorate his deeds.

PUNJAB:
THE LAND OF CHUMMCHA,
CHAUDHRY AND CHILLI

Chapter 5
Ground Realities

BEFORE THE GREEK ARCHITECT laid out Islamabad's grid of streets in the 1960s there was nothing here but a small village of field-hoeing peasants and baleful-eyed buffaloes ruled by a stubbly worthy who spent his day straightening his back on a string bed. No mighty river runs through it; no great king has ennobled its soil; and if it were not for the proximity of the jungly slopes of the Margalla Hills, it wouldn't be on the map at all. It could be razed and nobody would greatly object, least of all me, I thought, as – seated in a flimsy wicker chair on my terrace – I waited patiently for my most punctual visitor: a fruit bat who lolloped into the branches of a plane tree every evening just after the sun and the servants disappeared and the purplish silhouette of the mountains oblivioned the barely living capital.

It was spring again, in 2007, almost a year after we had left the Nawab in his fastness, and my mood was coloured by the day's events.

That morning, during a walk to the post office, I'd seen an old man crack his wife's head open with a walking stick. As she clutched her injured crown, thick scarlet blood seeped between her fingers. Nobody in the street responded; so I'd walked up to him, acid with revulsion, uncertain of my next move. The man shouted at his wife and raised his stick over her head again, then lowered it, having reaffirmed his right to hit her. Muttering gummy curses, he walked away, his wife following miserably behind. A few minutes later I passed a pimp shouting at two prostitutes, whom he pursued with insults as they click-clacked on high-heels away from him down a street where droves of religious students with wispy beards and calf-length trousers strode with angry-browed purpose.

Small incidents and sights; but they mingled in my mind with more troubling reports. Forty thousand young men in Pakistan had been brainwashed, trained and made ready for *jihad*; increasing numbers of men and boys, mostly from the Frontier, were strapping explosives to their chests and blowing themselves and others up in suicide attacks. A missile, fired from an American drone aircraft, had hit a *madrassa* on the frontier, killing seventy or eighty people; shortly afterwards a man had walked on to a military parade ground and detonated explosives concealed under his *chador*, killing himself and forty or so young recruits.

Over the past year, I'd spent several months on assignment in Afghanistan, where low-scale Taliban activity had flickered back into a full-blown insurgency with which Pakistan was intimately involved. Video footage had shown a Pakistani Pathan father holding the beard of a neighbour while he encouraged his 12-year-old son to cut off the man's head with a knife. The incident was part of a complex web of intra-tribal feuding: one faction had supposedly given information to the American-led coalition over the border that had led to the death of the commander of another faction.

My fears for the changing nature of the country and the urgency of my desire to see all that I could of its old ways had been heightened by another event. Islamic militants had detonated a bomb at a meeting of Sufi-minded clerics, Barelvis, killing over sixty people. Not a Sunni–Shia attack, but Sunni on Sunni. Militants were now directly targeting the country's pacifist, mystical core.

It was not only militants who'd become 'barbaric'. Pakistani journalists had been killed in the most brutal manner for reporting on things that sections of the military wished had remained hidden. Carlotta had experienced the vicious way in which the military was increasingly prepared to defend its interests. Military intelligence agents had broken in to her hotel room in Quetta and snatched her cellphone, computer and notebooks. One of them punched her twice in the face and head and knocked her to the floor, leaving her with bruises on her arms, temple and cheekbone, swelling on an eye and a sprained knee. The attack had only girded her courage and journalistic zeal.

Other developments hadn't boded well for the future: America and Britain were plotting to shoehorn an exiled former prime minister, Benazir Bhutto, into a power-sharing agreement with a reluctant Musharraf.

The bluff man-of-action had survived two assassination attempts by Islamists, had two dogs, danced, entertained girlfriends and drank whisky, so he was not one of the 'bad guys'.

But Washington occasionally leaked details of its intelligence reports to the media suggesting that Musharraf was also offering tacit support to the Afghan Taliban. On the one hand Pakistan was being cajoled into supporting the West's efforts in Afghanistan; but on the other, Pakistan wanted to retain its influence there through its Taliban proxies. It was a precarious balancing act: the tribes on the frontier, with their highly developed sense of revenge and religion, would not tolerate for long having their family members killed and their houses bulldozed by the army. Adding to the layers of intrigue, India was accused by Pakistan of arming its enemies. These were some of the 'ground realities', a term used by Pakistani officials to describe events and circumstances beyond their control.

At that time, I'd begun to see Pakistan through different eyes, those of a foreign correspondent, but still the country was imbued with the rose-tinted colours I'd seen in my youth, and the country's blackening atmosphere seemed rather superficial. There was an optimism that things would bounce back; that equilibrium would be restored.

And that evening I, at least, was lifted by some good news. My brother would join me after a week and we would resume our old travels together.

*

In the week before my brother's arrival, there was a lull in the news. Basil placated me by ferrying in cups of tea and dishes of spicy omelette and *paratha*, and continued to empty my pockets. Allah Ditta, who had put on weight, had a more confident air. He'd taken to stroking his beard in the manner of a sage and entertained me with tales, theories and strange stratagems.

One morning, as I sat at the dining table reading, there was a rustle at my feet, then a slithering sensation running round the back of my legs. I froze and very slowly looked down expecting to see a snake. But the sensation was of Allah Ditta's black beard playing against my ankles. He had climbed under the table and was about to put my shoes on and lace them up. It was his way of prompting me to leave for an appointment. I looked guiltily about to see if anybody had witnessed this act of servility. No one had, so I allowed him to continue.

A few days later, he came to me with a carefully prepared request. Standing barefoot, arms folded behind his back, he said that he would require an advance of money to buy a small plot of land in his hometown. I asked him how much it would cost. He placed one hairy bare foot on top of the other, tilted his head towards the roof, consulted a calculator on the inside of his flickering eyelids. It would not cost more than several hundred pounds sterling. How would he repay me? By 'cutting' his salary (the word was always accompanied by a scissors gesture). The deal was done. Gift of God's springy step became springier.

*

For a few months now a teacher had come to the house several times a week to give Allah Ditta and me lessons. The arrival of Ustaad, a tall, dark man with a black bushy moustache, was the occasion for Basil to set out dishes of melons, mangoes and grapes, or whatever fruit was in season, on the dining-room table. At times he handed round bowls of *chaat*, chillied banana and pomegranate seed. Then Ustaad, seated at the head of the table, tried to teach Allah Ditta to read and write, and me, Urdu. The two aims were incompatible, so chaos ensued as the suffering Allah Ditta read aloud in the high monotonous voice of a young schoolchild and I stammered my way through verb endings.

Although Allah Ditta was indifferent to the classes, his wife was happy with the idea that he was improving himself and as a token of gratitude sent a photograph of their two young boys and a container of curried meat.

Ustaad spent half the lessons rolling his eyes with impatience at Allah Ditta, who looked more dazed and sleepy than ever. I also found it difficult to stay awake. The other half of the lesson, Ustaad gossiped about the European households in which he taught and informed me of the movements of other journalists, who were also his pupils. For this I was wide awake.

Ustaad was easily diverted. You'd only to say the word *gupshup* (chit-chat) and he was off, his laugh starting in a bass staccato and ending in a high-pitched shriek. During one class I asked him about polygamy.

'Ooooh God! No! This is the very worst ... I would say ... *calamity* that can happen to a man'.

'Why?'

'Well, *theek hai*, three wives are a worst nightmare,' he said, dissolving in gusts of laughter. 'Let me tell you, my wife and I, we *enjoy* watching the house opposite ours. A man lives there with three wives and there are always great shouts and screams and we see this poor fellow running from one side of the house to get a bashing from one wife, and then to the other side to get a bashing from another and then out to the garden where another is screaming at him. It is *the best* entertainment!'

In the natural course of his conversation Ustaad conveyed some of the local gestures and wisdom: a shared joke was celebrated with 'the *desi* low-five', executed by two people imparting the subtlest of touches of the palms of their hands, one on top of the other. If the joke was particularly good, it warranted a flourish that began at the crooks of each other's elbows. The beckoning sign is an upside-down version of its Western counterpart. The West's raised little finger meaning 'he's got a small penis', here means 'I must go for a pee'. Shoes left one on top of another portend that the owner may soon be off on an unexpected journey. And here an owl is not wise, but very dim; and white is the colour of mourning.

The virgin Western ear alights on certain common words to which it is attracted by familiarity: *Aitcha* (good, okay)! *Zabardast* (great)! *Bulkul theek hai* (absolutely good)! *Tukriban* (roughly, about), *Bohut* (many or much), *Shabash!* (well done)! While Urdu with its many Persian borrowings is refined, Punjabi is a language that lapses into profanity regularly. Soon the ear attunes to the regular declamations of *Choot* (female genitalia)! *Bhain chod* (practitioner of incest with sister)! *Gandu* (sodomite)! *Lund pay charhna* (sit on a male organ)! and, less bawdy, *Soor Ka Baccha* (son of a pig)! *Khotay ki dum* (tail of a donkey)! Ustaad and I took great delight in shouting these at each other at the tops of our voices, until he would crease up, complaining 'No, no, no, we mustn't. This is very bad.'

*

One afternoon, I found the Professor dawdling on my doorstep like an Emperor Penguin that had lost an egg. He'd come to show me a carefully preserved copy of *Time-Life* magazine featuring a black-and-white photograph of pairs of horned white bullocks pulling carts with immense solid wheels, loaded with robed and turbaned figures, rolling past a line of spindly trees. The image was as clear as a picked bone: calcifying heat, creaking carts, death-stalked refugees; it was a biblical-era tableau captured by a modern medium.

'You see this is Partition,' the Professor said, already backing away, not wanting to intrude, 'so, I thought you should see this.'

A week or so before I'd asked him about his family's experience of Partition, and looking into the distance, he had not replied, and I'd not insisted, thinking his family had suffered.

The photograph showed unnamed peasants emerging from the darkness of their ancestral villages in Punjab, part of the mass exodus when Muslims crossed to Pakistan, Sikhs and Hindus to India, few knowing their destination, the largest mass migration in history.

The Professor shuffled off to his house and left me standing there, holding the photograph. On that pleasant spring morning, Allah Ditta and Basil chatting in the background and the trees heavy with fragrant blossom, it was difficult to imagine the savagery that Partition had unleashed.

Independence, which took place at the stroke of midnight on 15 August 1947, was accompanied by Partition, a decision by the British to divide India into two nations on the basis that a separate state was needed for the Subcontinent's Muslims, whose leaders feared they would otherwise be dominated by the Hindu majority. It prompted fourteen million refugees to cross the new border between India and West Pakistan and in the ensuing communal violence, between four hundred thousand and a million people died. National and local leaders had stirred up ancient animosities: big men and young men reached for spears, axes, knives, clubs and guns and attacked their neighbours. Women were stripped naked, paraded, raped and burnt alive; they were tattooed, branded and mutilated; ninety Sikh women committed suicide by jumping into a well to avoid being taken by a Muslim mob; Sikh fathers hacked daughters to death in front of their families rather than hand them over to Muslim gangs; heaps of putrescent corpses shimmered with flies. Men bashed babies against walls and roasted them on fires.

'... both sides killed. Both shot and stabbed and speared and clubbed. Both tortured. Both raped,' observed Khushwant Singh in his novel *Road to Pakistan*. Many had thought that Partition would just be a line on a map; that people would come and go as if nothing had happened. Instead it became an iron curtain dividing families, pitting two nations against each other in a blood feud. Within months they were at war over Kashmir, a Muslim-majority Hindu-ruled state, bordering both countries. A Pakistani poet, Faiz Ahmed Faiz, wrote, 'This leprous daybreak, dawn night's fangs have mangled, this is not that long-looked-for break of day'. It was the last hurrah of the British in India.

Memory of these facts is unspoken but still present, embedded in the DNA of the nation.

*

I'd run out of alcohol, so set off with Allah Ditta to secure the necessary 'permissions' to procure more.

Much of the country's officialdom runs on Johnny Walker Black Label, despite Pakistani law, which forbids the Muslim population to drink alcohol. In fact, the ingenuity of thirst had given rise to various booze outlets: the colonial-era Murree Brewery produced enough beer and whisky to keep the Islamic Republic rolling; black marketeers sold foreign brands; and a store, operated semi-officially by a cabinet minister's son, was discreetly open for business.

In a stuffy Customs and Excise office at the airport, I sat silently waiting for an alcohol ration book, while a bureaucrat, bald pate hovering over a brown file, pen in one hand, smouldering cigarette in the other, sat at his desk under a portrait of a narrow and sunken-faced spectre. I had time to examine the image: an emaciated apparition, wearing a tall Astrakhan hat and high-collared *sherwani* tunic, with a grim stubborn mouth and eyes that glowered through twirls of the bureaucrat's cigarette smoke. The portrait was in every office; and overly familiar with it, I no longer looked at it closely, seeing it as blankly as I did the models of the mountain in Baluchistan where the country had first tested an atomic bomb, which adorn roundabouts across the country. But now, forced to wait, I gave it more thought.

The least remarkable thing about Muhammad Ali Jinnah, the Quaid-i-Azam ('Great Leader'), once one accepts that much of the Muslim world runs on Johnny Walker, is that he ate pork, drank whisky and smoked fifty Craven A a day. More notable is that through sheer bloody-mindedness he created a nation-state. His portrait makes for uncomfortable viewing because he looks so ill; and indeed he was. Wracked with lung cancer and tuberculosis, he died shortly after Partition.

I asked myself, as Jinnah retreated behind another bank of cigarette smoke, whether Pakistan's existence was not an accidental by-product of his determined ego and his thwarted ambition. Some scholars posit that he began by using the idea of Pakistan as a bargaining chip to win Muslims greater rights in a united India, and that he didn't really believe in the idea.

His beginnings did not point to his destiny as the creator of such a state. He was born to a middle-class Gujarati-speaking family of provincial merchants from the Shia Khoja minority. As an urbane, aloof and anglicised politician, mad about Shakespeare, he had cut a dash in Bombay's cosmopolitan society. Yet he always argued, and then fought for independence from Britain.

At first, he was a champion of Hindu–Muslim unity. But then he was cold-shouldered by his fellow lawyer and stylistic antithesis, Gandhi, rebuffed by religious Muslim factions and suffered a series of setbacks, including losing popularity to Gandhi and a stint in political oblivion. But that face above me was not one to be defeated. He relaunched himself: espousing the 'Two-Nation theory' which held that Muslims and Hindus couldn't co-exist, he galvanised diverse squabbling Muslim groups and agitated for the creation of Pakistan. With the epic vanities of Mountbatten, Nehru and Gandhi arrayed against him, the game of independence, with all its high drama, deceit, horse-trading and communal violence, which Jinnah played with masterful ambiguity and *sang-froid*, became an end-game and Pakistan was its accidental prize.

His jubilant followers had hailed him as the 'Pakistani Moses', but he denigrated his winnings, complaining that he had been handed a 'moth-eaten' country.

The portrait depicted the bare bones of a man that others had since fleshed out with sanctity. Although Islamists had always hated him because of his moderation and secularism, most Pakistanis saw him as a sainted figure, blessed with the sort of virtues that are praiseworthy in others but undesirable for oneself. The country he created and the man himself were incongruous: he was a modern, liberal, stiff, secular, not very religious type of Muslim of Shia origin and his creation was a feisty, backward Sunni Muslim state dominated by Punjabis and Islamists.

Jinnah had told his freshly minted Pakistani countrymen: 'You are free; you are free to go to your temples. You are free to go to your mosques or to any other places of worship in this State of Pakistan. You may belong to any religion, caste or creed – that has nothing to do with the business of the state.'

But his message was not heard. Less than a decade after his death, the country became formally titled as an 'Islamic Republic'.

The *clump clump clump* of a rubber stamp distracted me. At least Jinnah would have approved of this transaction: the country hadn't become completely dry.

Perhaps it was for the best that he'd died so soon, allowing him to become a national relic, before the disappointment of what was to come. Yet in that portrait he still presented a sorrowful sight, a disembodied metaphor for rectitude and willpower.

My meditation was brought to a close by 'Now, Mister Willy-Kinsson, here is your licence to drink', and the treasured booklet was handed to me. Allah Ditta and I went down to the customs warehouse and loaded up bottles of Murree beer which clinked all the way home, where they brought an entrepreneurial gleam to the eyes of Basil.

*

A week or so later, I climbed the stairs of my sequined and bolster-cushioned house, passing the painting of the enigmatic plump actress on the wall, and there was my brother, Chev, his fair head gilded by sunshine as he lay on a string bed reading our old guidebook by a large window that looked out on to the terrace.

'You can't hang about here like a mixture of a wannabe Lord Byron and Lord Fauntleroy waiting for the next cup of tea or bout of diarrhoea. Pick a spot on the map and let's be off,' he said.

But he wasn't making haste; he never does. He's of the laissez-faire school of thought.

'I let misself in,' he continued, parodying an accent somewhere between Edwardian Upper Class and Cockney and pointing to a pot of tea on a tray next to him. 'And 'vailed misself of the servants, see.'

Tall, a head taller than me, Chev is good-looking, his eyes unsentimental, sometimes stern, but not narrow enough to be self-seeking. They're preoccupied, distant, for he's reserved, even shy. A photographer, he's happiest observing things at his own pace; preferring solitude to the crowd. He's a goat, not a sheep.

His presence was reassuring. He's always stuck by me, whatever my failings. He doesn't mind sharing a bed with me, as long as there's a pillow between us lest I grow amorous in my sleep. And he's good at pointing out if I have food round my mouth before I interview people.

He shared my passion for the old, submerged tropes of Pakistan. He'd come out this time keen to see an obscure Sufi festival on the edge of Punjab.

'You know, that one we heard about years ago. The country fair with women whirling dervishes falling into ecstatic trances and poetry recitations.'

Punjab, yes Punjab would do very nicely for our trip. We mulled over maps and plotted a route that ran from Islamabad to Lahore. *Lahore! Lahore Lahore ai!* Pakistanis say excitedly when approaching its gates: the Badhshahi mosque, Akbar the Great's fort, Kipling's Wonder House, the old city and the tomb of Lahore's great saint; yes, perhaps; but what they are really looking forward to is its wicked food and bad lives; and so were we. And from Lahore we would go south west to the ancient citadel of Multan and across the Indus towards the mountains that separate the plains from Afghanistan and Persia, and on to the festival. All this should take us on a path bright with the names of Alexander the Great, Genghis Khan and Tamerlane, where we could call on feudal lords and living saints and get a glimpse of the treasures of the Persians and Greeks – and of the Begum and our grandmother.

*

The next morning, Allah Ditta packed the car. His own baggage was a plastic bag containing a spare set of clothes. Once we were on the road, Chev, sitting next to him, observed Allah Ditta's driving with increasing horror.

We made a day of the journey, stopping off at Ketas, near Kallar Kahar where, reflected in a malachite spring pond sacred to Shiva the Destroyer, we clambered about a ruined temple among abandoned domes, balconies and arched windows, where now no Hindu pilgrims gather as they did in the past, the place silent after the purges and purifications of Partition. Ghosts were present where there should have been life: Hindus, Sikhs and people who after centuries of living together had fled, leaving only the husk of a time-wrought hybrid culture. Partition had left parts of this old land ethnically cleansed: as if a river had been diverted and left the puzzling remains of a civilisation by its dried-up course. As we departed the empty temple, I was assailed by a melancholy and unanswerable question that recurred throughout these travels: what would have been if Pakistan hadn't been brought into existence?

We stopped again soon afterwards to watch proprietary peacocks strutting in front of a Sufi shrine at a spot favoured by the young emperor Babur (AD1483–1530), the first Mughal. Babur had passed here on his first conquering campaign from Afghanistan and later laid out a garden that has long since disappeared. I'd dipped in to an old translation of Babur's magnificent diary, and learned that near here he embarked on riotous boating trips accompanied by minstrels, and indulged in wild drinking parties:

'Very drunk I must have been for when they told me next day that we had galloped loose-rein into camp, carrying torches, I could not recall it in the very least. After reaching my quarters I vomited a good deal.'

He described one such party being divided between a faction of araq drinkers and another of confection eaters (opium mixed into *mitthai* or sweets and dried fruits such as plums, tamarinds, apricots and sesame). The mixture of styles did not complement one another, and the topers taunted the confectionists:

'Try as we did to keep things straight, nothing went well; there was much disgusting uproar; the party became intolerable and was broken up.'

The plains, in which now and then a mud village of primeval simplicity appeared by the side of the road, can have changed little since the young emperor, full of raw Central Steppe spirit, galloped into camp, reins bouncing about his horse's neck, high on booze, drugs and his conquest of this foreign land.

Travelling on this road a few months before, I'd experimented by drinking a glass of a local concoction, hashish-laced yoghurt, before Allah Ditta and I took the motorway from Lahore to Islamabad at night. My mind had flown about like a rapidly deflating balloon and when we'd been stopped on the road by two shadowy figures, their faces covered by headscarves, I feared the worst. Allah Ditta had been ordered out and knelt down in front of the car. Then one of the figures had approached me and gabbled in a language I'd never heard. Was this a Chechen or one of the Uzbeks who were reportedly fighting alongside the Taliban in the tribal areas? I'd frozen with fear. But on seeing my anxiety, the phantom removed his cloak, revealing the uniform of a highway policeman, complete with striped black-and-yellow cravat. He slowed his speech and it gradually became clear that he was speaking poorly enunciated French, and was saying that one of our headlamps was broken and that we would have to pay a small fee for him to mend it. It transpired that he had just returned from a training course on *les autoroutes de France*.

I told Chev the story; but he was more concerned with Allah Ditta's siestas behind the wheel. Indeed, viewed from the backseat in the rear-view mirror, our driver's eyes were as spaced out as a Rouault Christ.

Chapter 6
The Demi-Monde of Zeenat

THE BEGUM WAS ORCHESTRATING a spring clean from a lawn behind her house. Servants had carried out cushion-laden *takhts* and reclining teak and rattan garden chairs on which the Begum, my grandmother, who was here for her yearly visit, Chev and I sat for breakfast. Crows cawed on branches above us, and the morning air was lightly spiced with wood smoke and the fragrance of blossom. Local varieties of roses, calendulas, narcissi and jasmine were in bloom.

The innards of the house were being moved outside. Sweating, laughing and cursing under their breath, Mehmud and his colleagues dragged mounds of *kilim* rugs, mattresses and steel dispatch boxes full of clothes for sorting into the garden. This was the time of year when hawkers on bicycles went door-to-door with sacks of cotton, and mattresses would be restuffed or plumped up, while clothes and rugs were aired, cleaned and mothballed.

The Begum and our grandmother had shared much since they had met fifty years before in Malaya, where their husbands were posted. Both strong-willed, the main difference between them was one of style: our grandmother's steel was scabbarded in velvet, the Begum's permanently unsheathed for war.

Breakfast trays removed, they took up pens and paper and began an inventory of the household. The Begum issued further orders: in preparation for the hot season, contraptions called desert coolers, which work by fans blowing air over pans of water, were installed with new filters of '*khuss*', a musk-scented straw; summer clothes were brought out of stores and aired; shawls and sweaters packed away carefully with packets of red *mirch* (pepper) and mothballs and shut in camphor-wood boxes; and more huge silver and black tin trunks, sent for from Anarkali or Bori Bazaar, arrived on the backs of donkey carts, no doubt joining other such vehicles obstructing traffic along the way.

At lunch, they gossiped of mutual friends and recent events, occasionally breaking off to explain to Chev and me the meaning of some strange custom.

'If two women forge a strong friendship,' said our grandmother, clasping her hands together, 'they exchange headscarves, *dupattas*, and are known as '*dupatta* sisters'.'

Afternoon naps concluded, we gathered again in a sitting-room. It was time for the Begum to settle accounts. The servants paraded in front of her; one by one they handed over receipts; figures were scrutinised, added to columns and totted up, only curling toes betraying secret apprehensions. Then the cash box was pulled out and the Begum produced a large key; servants filed up to receive their wages, stepping forward with one hand over the other like a Catholic receiving the consecrated host, then stepping back, a wad of rupees pressed against forehead, in a sign of gratitude and respect. Money and drinking water are received in Pakistan with both hands.

The Begum's family was one of the last, if not the last, in Lahore to keep up an old mansion and abide so strictly to custom. She represented the end of an era steeped in the influences of the British and Mughal empires.

After the staff had gone, our grandmother asked the whereabouts of a servant who was nicknamed 'Bigli' ('Electricity') on account of the speed with which he did his job.

'He was a bit too quick on the draw and cleaned up some things that weren't his,' the Begum replied, frowning. 'So I've sent him back to the village.'

In the evening, after supper, as we sipped cups of green tea in which floated cardamom seeds, the Begum asked about our 'programme' for the next day. We explained we wanted to delve into Punjab, starting with Lahore.

'If you wish to know Punjab,' she said, unfurling the palm of her right hand, 'you must understand the phrase *charte surej ki puja karna* – "you must worship the rising sun" – which we use to explain our unfortunate habit of flocking to fawn at the feet of whomsoever comes to power.'

Chev pointed out that this was a universal affliction.

'Universal it may be,' replied the Begum, 'but like so many other vices, here it has achieved perfection.'

Before long the conversation returned to my marriage prospects. Chev, luckily for him, had recently got engaged.

'Have you found a wife yet? We must find you a wife,' said the Begum.

'You don't seem to have met anyone of your *jaat* [caste],' our grandmother added.

'These things don't matter any more,' the Begum disagreed. 'I think what he needs is a good Pakistani girl. They don't give you the same headache as your Western girls. What about a divorcee? Her parents won't be too fussy about marrying her off to a *gora.*'

It was time for bed.

Until dawn, in a semi-conscious state, I could hear a vigil at a nearby Sufi shrine, a soft, melodious, mesmeric chorus of men's voices, chanting the name of Allah, a sonorous soothing balm, thrumming the night.

*

In the morning, Chev and I walked into the Old City before meeting a friend, a provincial official with a line in bawdy Mughal tales, who had agreed to give us a tour of the fort and a flavour of Lahore's golden era.

I hoped to pick up the trail of Pakistan's fading traditions, in which tolerance was prized. It had once been the seat of Babur's grandson, the Great Mughal, Akbar, a Muslim ruler who had sought ways of co-existence between different faiths: he negotiated a truce with Hindu rulers; married a Rajput princess; employed Hindu generals and advisers; abolished a tax on non-Muslims and permitted forced converts to Islam to apostasise. Famously, he had held a series of inter-faith debates attended by Zoroastrians, Hindus, Jains, Tibetan Buddhists (perhaps), Sikhs, Jews, Christians, hardline Sunnis and Shia mystics. He was a bruiser and a pragmatist but also a thinker. I wanted to reflect on his legacy.

High above the Old City, in a washed-out blue sky, kites bobbed and glistened like seahorses in the deep. It was Basant, the spring festival. For weeks now, kites had ruled the life of every boy and man as if they had been afflicted by an aerial mania. Children darted unexpectedly in front of and between moving cars, faces upturned as they tried to control scarlet, gold, puce, tar-black kites, battling one another's paper-and-wood avatars on soaring gusts of wind, the daily dreams and tussles of the street given flight.

They were not the only ones to take advantage of the sweetest, gentlest season. Women, wearing saffron and turmeric-coloured clothes, walked in groups among street stalls churning out similarly coloured foods: yellow *achaari* potatoes, *sooji ka halwa* – orange halva semolina, and *zarda* – yellow rice sweetened with raisins and nuts.

In the streets, eyes were everywhere: the intense eyes of young men racing on dented 125cc Pak Hero motorcycles homed in on the backseats of *tongas,* horse-drawn traps, from which, with discretion, girls returned their glances; and the omniscient eyes of matronly women, sitting side-saddle on the back of sturdier motorcycles with arms wrapped about their husbands, sparkling sandals dangling from painted toes. On seeing *gora* faces, scruffy boulevardiers sitting on stools in teashops flashed the whites of widened eyes, and with raised hands, thumb and forefinger flipping back and forth, mouthed, '*Kya hua?*' 'What's going on?' Everywhere, animal droppings, rubbish; shafts of sunlight illuminated swirls of petrol fumes and dust. Everything appeared improvised, flying by the seat of its pants.

We plunged into the Old City – a warren divided into large *quartiers* selling different wares – and soon were lost among dirty streets lined with crumbling buildings, passing what appeared to be half of a once-glorious old city gate but which now formed half of a small shop. We ambled down shoulder-width paths to the bustling Azam cloth market where scarlet cotton had been cut into strips and draped down the sides of tall thin buildings. The streets were so narrow that we were in constant peril of being bashed from behind by cartwheels.

Burly Lahori men swaggered three abreast through a wringer of hawkers proffering baskets of jasmine and red roses, and earthy-tongued, betel-chewing vendors doled out the old city's corrupting dishes of spicy chickpeas, and glutinously thick *daals,* or *pathora,* a blend of both. Kebabs, kidneys, trotters and battered fish simmered in skillets of grease before being fished out, garnished with coriander, chillies and ginger and served in folds of *naan* bread or the pages of old telephone directories. Flat yeastless bread was stuffed with cheese. Artisans magicked treats into being by ladling streams of batter into oil. These golden *jalebis* emerged as complex patterns like mandarin script, before being coated in syrup. Thick buffalo milk was transformed into pistachio-rich ice cream. Inside narrow shops, jam pots and plastic bags were filled with mysterious contents – the stuff of love, aphrodisiacs – here a bag of Gujranwala sparrows, there a tray of Lahore's fabled goat testicles.

Chev lagged behind, snared by smiling shopkeepers, beckoning him to see their wares, and followed by a troupe of giggling children, who were cuffed and shooed away by adults concerned that the foreign guests should be able to proceed unmolested.

The buildings had a squalid, lived-in air; skeletons of *jerokahs* (carved wooden balconies) faced each other across subfusc alleys like ageing courtesans. Everywhere were signs of small lives: laundry hanging from mouldering plasterwork embellishments, flowerpots on carved stone canopied balconies and hidden shrines glistening with Sikh and Hindu gods, survivors from the old India.

We walked up the rickety staircase of a dilapidated house, and found a shy, poor family living in the curtain-divided ruins of a long forgotten *haveli*, a type of grand mansion built around a courtyard in the Sikh period, and we backed out, apologising for our intrusion.

The state of the streets tallied with the description left by Alexander 'Bokhara' Burnes in 1831: 'The houses are very lofty; and the streets, which are narrow, offensively filthy, form a gutter that passes through the centre.' Burnes, Scottish explorer and traveller, was a player in the Great Game. Employed by the East India Company, he sailed up the Indus, surveying the river as he went, and then on up the Ravi to Lahore, where on behalf of King William IV he presented six English dray horses to the city's shrewd Sikh ruler, Ranjit Singh, who recognised the gift for what it was: a prelude to invasion. But he accepted it all the same. I often thought of those shaggy, huge-hoofed, sturdy-legged horses clomping massively through these choked lanes, almost as alien to Lahore as elephants would be in the streets of London.

We soon found ourselves at Mariam Zamani mosque. Built in 1614 by Akbar's son in honour of the Great Mughal's Hindu wife, the mosque is hidden in humble obscurity behind a market selling rusty wheel rims. Entering the ancient place to find some peace, we plodded down steps to an ablution pool and fountain set in a hushed brick-walled courtyard. We sat leaning against a pillar under a fabulous heavy central dome from which radiated the ninety-nine names of Allah twinkling in gold next to lapis-blue floral motifs in a richly painted stucco sky. On one of the arched entrances into the mosque itself, part of an inscription reads: 'The faithful is in a mosque as a fish in water.' I was far from faithful, but there was an atmosphere of ease and reflection. It had the air of a beloved thing, not looked after by the state, but cherished by local people.

*

We got lost again in the Old City and were late for our meeting. By the time we found Jan Maqbool Abbasi, maverick bureaucrat and arch-conspiracy theorist, he was pacing up and down on top of the fort ramparts, tapping his watch, impatient puffs of smoke rising from a large briar pipe.

We apologised and thanked him for seeing us on a holiday and, good humour returning to eyes darting above a short greying beard, he led us off at a brisk pace along the saltier shores of Mughal history. He had recently been appointed, he explained, as Director-General of Archaeology in Punjab, and his new office provided a suitable milieu for his interests: it was built in the same compound as a mausoleum that, according to legend, is the tomb of Anarkali ('Pomegranate Blossom'), a dancing slave-girl who was imprisoned between two walls by Akbar the Great for, in Maqbool's words, 'having hanky-panky with his son'.

'Let me tell you about the story of Akbar. It has all the ingredients for your purposes,' he continued, stalking across the massive brick ramparts, Captain Black tobacco smoke and tidbits of Mughal gossip wafting to us over his shoulder. In Maqbool's rendering, there were few Moguls who did not contract syphilis, or indulge a lust for alcohol, opium, debauchery and cruelty.

I'd told him during an earlier telephone conversation that a Jesuit priest had visited the Great Mughal's court in Lahore in 1595 and asked if he could show us what he would have seen here.

After clearing his throat and relighting his pipe he launched into a relatively sober description of what the Jesuit would have witnessed: the highpoint of an empire and an Emperor who had become one of the most powerful figures in the Islamic world, on a par with the Ottoman Sultan and perhaps greater than the neighbouring Shah of Safavid Persia. He was *far* richer than both, Maqbool added with pride. Akbar the Great's domain stretched 1400 miles, west from Lahore through mountain defiles to Kabul and east across desert and jungle to Dhaka in present-day Bangladesh. 'Your good queen, Elizabeth I of England,' Maqbool continued, 'wrote in a letter to him praising His Imperial Majesty's *humanity*.'

Chev had become the centre of a scrum of Pakistani sightseers, who thought him far more interesting than Mughal architecture.

He seemed happier talking to them than listening to the history lesson but Maqbool fished him from the crowd and guided us past intricately arched and carved pavilions and palaces and across courtyards to the eastern side of the Fort. Here we came to the wooden door in the forbidding Majlis Gate through which the Jesuit, Father Jerome Xavier, wearing a black soutane, a dark blue cape and a black lambskin fez, had first entered the city.

He was the Superior of the third Jesuit mission to Akbar, and, having joined a caravan of four hundred camels, had made a precarious six-month journey from Goa, an estuary island that Portuguese colonists had seized eighty years before. Akbar had invited the missionaries to his court as a gambit to establish diplomatic contact with the Portuguese, but also to satisfy his intellectual curiosity about European thought and culture.

Jerome was the least bigoted among a bunch of zealots, one of whom wore a horsehair shirt, regularly flagellated himself and often wrote about his desire to be martyred. Jerome's correspondence shows a charming reluctance to proselytise. His superior often berated him for translating Cicero into Persian instead of hunting for souls. He confessed that he never converted a Muslim by means of persuasion or reasoning. Those who did so, he said, were only after material gain.

Officially, however, for the Jesuits, the encounter with Akbar presented a chance to land a coveted prize for Christendom in the East: the conversion of a Muslim emperor.

'This was the largest city in the world,' puffed Maqbool. 'The Jesuit saw the capital of the Mughal empire not only at the peak of its power, but also at its cultural apex.'

We looked about. Delicate murals decorated the honeycomb of palaces and pavilions in a fusion of Hindu and Islamic traditions, a style that had been the foundation stone of Mughal culture. To Father Jerome's eye the aesthetics would have contrasted starkly with the immense, gloomy and austere granite monastery-palace-mausoleum of El Escorial, outside Madrid, which had been built by his own king, Philip II, at the pinnacle of Spain's world power a decade earlier. At Lahore, there was no bleakness, only lavishness of decoration and precision in architecture, an expression of the Mughal's flowering confidence in the Indo-Islamic order they were creating.

The day after the arrival of Father Jerome and his entourage – which consisted of two other missionaries, an interpreter, and a Portuguese painter (for Akbar was a seasoned collector of European art) – Akbar greeted him, '*com muita fiesta*', as the Jesuits described it, with much pomp. He summoned them to sit near him, later visiting their chapel where, 'like a Christian prince', he knelt with his hands clasped in prayer. The Emperor often wore a reliquary that portrayed the Virgin on one side, and the Agnus Dei on the other. He presented an extraordinary enigma to the Jesuits.

In some ways Akbar was an odd participant in inter-faith discussions. A stocky figure, he was reputed in his youth to have made towers from the skulls of his enemies and to have mounted and tamed rampaging bull-elephants. He enjoyed a sporting life of polo, elephant-fighting, buffalo-fighting, stag-fighting and hunting with cheetahs. The Jesuits said that the Emperor was primarily interested during his debates in seeing the *mullahs* trounced. And this I could only applaud, for I had spent many hours crosslegged, listening to conservative mullahs' brain-numbing theological twaddle.

Pakistanis lionise Akbar as a great Muslim leader, but in truth his legacy is unpalatable to Pakistan's official view of itself as an orthodox Sunni state. For although much of his tolerant policy can be seen as a pragmatic solution to his chief problem – how to unite such a vast, complex and varied society – there is some doubt over whether he even died a Muslim.

In his later years, he created an elite religious cult of which he was the centre: he borrowed dogma from Sanskrit literature, turned to the sun, instead of Mecca, to say his prayers, worshipped fire, venerated the Virgin Mary and Jesus Christ and cultivated his image as a reincarnation of Rama and Krishna.

To make things worse in the eyes of his conservative Muslim critics (one contemporary scholar expressed surprise that he had not been assassinated), he didn't believe in the existence of Satan; he found Arabic religious commentaries on Islam muddled and contradictory; and he questioned the story of the Koran's genesis, doubting its heavenly origin and treating it as a historic document in a way that Islamic scholars five centuries later are only beginning to dare to consider.

The Emperor was often heard to exclaim on religious matters, 'Who is certain that he is right?' The Jesuits called him a philosopher-king, a searcher.

We climbed back on to the ramparts and looked out over the modern tangle of telephone and electricity wires webbing the Old City. Evening approached, shading the streets below in cinnamon.

Earlier in the day, I'd heard bells ringing from one of Lahore's churches, as they had from Christian places of worship in Akbar's time. I remembered how as soon as the Emperor had left the city, his governor had clamped down on the Jesuits' freedom of worship.

Tolerance and intolerance had long battled it out here. Akbar's Sufi-minded great-grandson, Prince Dara Shikoh, had lost the throne to his brother, the austere, conservative Aurangzeb. Now, once again, a puritanical streak was in the ascendancy.

*

Zeenat loomed large in our lives for the next week or so.

'Oh *God*. You really know *nothing*,' she said, minutes after we first met at a party, her tobacco-enriched voice transforming the word 'god' into a groan. 'Here, take this.' Long dark-mulberry fingernails produced a business card from a pocket in the side of her fitted yellow silk *kameez*. 'I will show you around and you will not write *rubbish* about my country.'

The card read: 'Zeenat Khan, Co-Director, *x* Advertising Agency.'

We were sitting on cushions in the corner of a renovated Old City *haveli* belonging to the party's host, a socialite and patron of the arts. Slightly away from us, a hundred or so smartly turned-out men and women, dressed in yellow and turmeric silk *kurtas* and tight white cotton trousers, thronged a courtyard strewn with rose and jasmine petals and lit by hundreds of lamps and candles glimmering on a circle of balconied floors above. The women, gleaming black eyes and long black hair, created an atmosphere of beauty, a quality that was present in general but hard to pin down in particular.

Zeenat reached over to retrieve a glass of whisky hidden behind a wooden box beside her. In her late twenties, she was not tall; her dark eyes were not that large; her nose, a little bulbous; her cheeks, slightly rounded; and her mouth, pert but small. Yet, she had a mane of jet-black hair, an ample bust, brilliant eyes and trailed a pungent atmosphere of cigarette smoke, musky scent and pheromones.

Her mobile phone rang.

'Hillooo Billoooo,' she cooed in lilting English. Dark cherry lips pursed in anticipation of a witticism. She wafted a cigarette with the other hand theatrically as she opened her offensive: 'Where have you been ... I have been missing you ... I need you here with me ... you are the *funniest* man Billoo ... how can I live without you ... *aitcha* I will see you tomorrow *inshallah* and you will do my business ... Yes, yes you can take my case to the minister.'

A mulberry fingernail ended the call with a tap.

'*Chalo*, let's go,' she purred to me and Chev. 'This party is suck*ing* ... and these people, such *fakes*.'

We drove in her car to an international hotel where she had taken a suite of rooms. Her bedroom was soon filled with her 'disciples', all men, who sat crosslegged below her on the floor while she held court, mostly abusing them, from the end of a large bed. 'Ali *sahib*, you really are the most *dunce* person in this city.'

The men watched her like villagers at an outdoor theatre, throwing her questions about politics, issues, gossip and lapping up her long, rambling and self-indulgent answers. She was trying to carve a career in local politics; and her handmaiden, an old, working-class political activist with a face like an Apache chief, was arbitrating the discussion.

'You see, these are my *chummcha*, they call me "Leader",' Zeenat said to me. The word literally means a spoon, but denotes a sycophant or lackey, a staple character of the Indian Subcontinent, who grows infuriated when not treated by his lord with disdain.

Chev and I got up to leave, promising to get in touch with her soon.

*

The next morning, the Begum was adamant that current affairs should not obscure my perception of Pakistan.

'To understand this country you must see more saints' shrines,' she commanded. 'You know, actually, we often say,' she paused, adjusting her *dupatta* about her shoulders, 'that kings bowed down to Sufi saints, and whereas weeds grow on royal tombs, the graves of the saints are always well tended.'

Looking around the room for further evidence on the subject, her eyes alighted on Salal, a poor and ancient cousin slumbering in a chair. He was her much-loved *major domo*, a courtier, a firewall between the Begum and the servants, a family historian, poet and former cinematographer who was never without his stamped silver box of confections. Tall and thin with a large curved nose and stooped narrow shoulders, he was dressed in a waistcoat with a high collar that touched the bottom of his pendulous ears. Realising his attention had been summoned, his small wrinkled eyes opened and, slowly turning his head in the manner of a turtle, he said: '*Yesss*, I am a *pir* with a following.'

The Begum ordered him to elaborate.

'Oooh yes,' he muttered, pulling himself up in his chair and raising a flat-palmed hand of spatulate fingers as if pleading the Fifth Amendment. 'Why not?'

His father, he said, had also been a *pir*. He had been a railway man; when he held up his lantern people came to him and he gave them his wisdom and a section of the Koran to read.

'After he died we received *chummaq* [offerings of money] for his shrine, and I have inherited his honour,' Salal concluded, sinking back into the chair.

Being a saint was no big deal if Salal's testimony was anything to go by, but it conferred some esteem and profit.

*

A night or so later, we took the Begum's advice and Zeenat's offer to act as our guide, and visited the tomb of Data Ganjbaksh ('Lavish Giver').

We met Zeenat outside the shrine, her eyes glinting under a shawl and chaperoned by her stony-faced *duenna*. Light bulbs strung above hawkers' handcarts and levitating sparks from braziers intensified the blackness of the night. At the entrance to the shrine, meat and rice were doled out from giant brass *degs* (pots) to poor pilgrims who received it in their headscarves or the lap of their shirts.

Chev and I slipped off our Western shoes, which appeared ever more cloddish beside stacks of sandals, and our stocking feet accompanied Zeenat's and the handmaiden's bare ones over sleeping pilgrims shrouded from head to toe like rows of corpses. We moved on towards the tomb, Zeenat in a serious mood, explaining her love for the saint.

'He really is the spirit of Lahore, which is known in Punjabi as "*Data di nagri*", the City of Data,' she said with a magisterial waft of a hand over the scene.

The saint lay under a mound of raised plaster in the shadow of a tall headstone; his tomb was draped with brocade and embroidered shrouds, overlain with strings of pearls and yellow and red petals. Pilgrims touched, kissed and prostrated themselves before him, murmuring prayers. Several sat crosslegged by the tomb reciting from the Koran, their heads swaying like *punkahs*, old wooden fans. Men cried and embraced their friends; from a window in one of the octagon's sides, women, their heads covered, crowded to view the tomb.

We were hugger-mugger in the crush, pressed on all sides by mostly poor people who acknowledged us with welcoming smiles. I thought of how such passionate reverence earns reproach at Mecca where scuffles persist between Arabian custodians and Asian pilgrims, who express themselves in a way not too dissimilar from the *puja*, the ancient devotional ritual of their Vedic forefathers. I relished the warmth of this remnant of that old and mixed culture.

'People speak to Data *sahib* with the affection of an old friend,' Zeenat said after chatting with a woman drawn to her outside the tomb. 'During the 1965 war against India, this woman has been saying, green men jumped out of his tomb to catch Indian bombs'. I looked to see if she was joking. A hint of merriment had entered her eyes but she waved a hand to stop any interruption and then closed her eyes, raising both hands in front of her, palms upturned, in prayer.

As we left the shrine, an old caretaker, seeing Zeenat, hobbled up and asked if the *goras* were Muslims. She laughed, her pleasure in his question not just seeping into her eyes but every part of her, and she clutched her body with both arms to contain her mirth. She explained to the old man that we wanted to know about Data *sahib*, adding that we would soon be converted now we had come into contact with the saint's *baraka*, power.

The unaffected way she spoke to the old man and her laughter, which continued in small convulsions as she beckoned her driver, disarmed me.

*

That night we went with Zeenat to a party she had organised at the last minute in the office of a run-down warehouse on the outskirts of town. Before it started, she ordered her handmaiden and driver about on various chores until the setting was to her satisfaction: candles were lit, petals strewn, *bhangra* music blared and booze was delivered in brown paper bags from unlicensed outlets.

Her friends arrived: a lean, urbane provincial politician with an oiled moustache; 'Chaudhry *sahib*' – a thin and liverish minor 'feudal'; a squiffy-eyed Wildean man with a scar on his forehead who introduced himself as 'an outrageous faggot and follower of fashion'; a squat, wavy-haired waste-disposal company owner; and an even squatter mill owner, whom Zeenat presented, arm linked through his.

'Here is my greatest love, the most handsome man in Lahore, my saviour and whom I respect for his courage and ... *decency*.' The last word had seemed a stretch even for her.

Older than Zeenat, in their forties and fifties, they all entered with swaggering confidence, abusing each other familiarly with shouts of '*bhen chod* [sister-fucker]!' and '*gandu* [poofter]!' which they followed up by shaking both hands, touching their hearts and then wrapping an arm over each other's right shoulder.

The evening bore the usual hallmarks of a decadent Pakistani gathering. Vast joints of hashish were rolled; vats of whisky sloshed down throats; and plans made for a journey that never took place.

There was much bragging, servility and sycophancy.

'Mahmud *sahib*, you are the best man in the business. No, I insist you have no equal. You should run this country. In all seriousness, why let these second-raters do it when you are a thousand times, no, one million times the best.'

And small, largely fabricated (as Zeenat later explained) victories were celebrated.

'I had that bastard picked up. I abused him thoroughly.'

They had their enemies 'picked up' by their police contacts; involved themselves in murder cases and feuds; had people pistol-whipped; and praised each other's successes with their group phrase, 'Totally decadent *yaar* [dude]'.

Chev and I joined in with the unfettered, sweaty dancing. They had some panache, preening their moustaches as they strutted and whirled with warrior-like intent in their hashish- and booze-scorched eyes. The 1990s Daler Mehndi hit, '*Saade Dil Te Chhuriyan Chaliyan*' ('Knife Cutting Through My Heart') was played frequently, often at my request.

The mill owner transformed himself into an energetic Don Juan, and with strands of his straggling Latin-master's hair bouncing on top of his otherwise bald head, he leapt into a half bunny-hop, half *bhangra* dance in front of Zeenat, his arms in the air and eyes wide in martial fashion, before collapsing in prostration at her feet. With great noblesse, she stooped to raise him.

Then, Zeenat's muslin green-and-white *dupatta* caught fire on a candle and foolish with Dutch courage, I snuffed out the flames with bare hands, an action that left me unharmed and puffed up with my own heroism.

Soon, too much whisky had been taken, and there were shrieks and chairs knocked over: a dispute between the follower of fashion and the waste-disposal man had broken into a fight which, less an affair of fists than slaps, quickly abated when Zeenat's servants brought in mounds of *biryani* and people settled down to eat.

After midnight, the guest of honour arrived: a thickset bob-haired gangster followed by a retinue of *goondas* (thugs) and dancing girls from the red-light area. He wore piratical earrings, gold chains overlapped on his powerful chest, and ruby and amber stones the size of cape gooseberries encrusted his fingers. Draped in a red knee-length watered-silk tunic, his kohl-rimmed eyes flickered coldly as he withdrew a silver revolver from his undergarments and placed it next to a bottle of Johnny Walker. His malevolent aura and underworld gravitas were enhanced by his circle of obedient highly painted molls, who rolled and lit his hashish cigarettes, their faces alert to his every wish, which he communicated by the smallest gesture of a hand.

We cleared more space and his troupe performed a *mujra* dance, our fellow guests showering them with money as they thrust breasts and convulsed hips. Zeenat, riled that her status as the centre of male attention was in dispute, leapt among them like an *espontánea* into a Spanish bullring and saw them all off until she had the floor, and all the men's eyes, to herself.

The night ended with dramatically declaimed verses of *ghazals*, poems about honour, drink, death and love, greeted with applauding shouts of '*Wah Wah!*' and '*Shabash!*'.

The other guests left and Zeenat played an old Nusrat Fateh Ali Khan song, '*Yeh Ho Halka Halka*', sinking into a deep trance, head bowed over crossed legs, a hand raised aloft holding a smouldering cigarette with which she traced the path of the spiritual song to *ishq*, the high of divine love.

Cleaning up the debris after the party, Chev and the servants momentarily out of sight, Zeenat and I bumped into each other, both carrying clusters of empty glasses, and kissed. Her mouth tasted of smoke, booze and *biryani*.

*

Chev and I spent the next week in voluntary captivity in a residence Zeenat had requisitioned in the suburbs.

She had a collection of motley servants, chief among whom was an ancient orange-haired and toothless Babaji, who customarily produced six or seven neatly rolled hashish-and-opium cigarettes, which would last her until lunchtime, and – on account of being able to jam metal objects into live electricity sockets without killing himself – appeared invincible.

During the day, having scanned the newspapers for mention of her name, she worked the phones and barked orders at her handmaiden and servants as she pushed for political patronage.

She spoiled us: setting up a photographic shoot of traditional wrestlers in the Old City for Chev; summoning officials to her house for me to interview; calling a barber to shave us as we sat in the garden and a man to massage my limbs; and she made sure we had all we could possibly want in the way of food, which she tasted first for quality and freshness before allowing it to be served.

One day, she drove us on an excursion out of town to a Mughal deer park and pavilion, and as she motored along behind the wheel, she managed to unpack tobacco from cigarettes, burn hashish, mix it with the tobacco and repackage the blend in a sheaf of joints that she smoked en route. All the while she revelled in explaining to us her country, which warts and all, she found amusing and astonishing. Apart from the Begum, she was her country's best guide because she had a rare gift for seeing it from outside. Her hoarse, liberated childish laughter suffused it with magic and love.

At the picnic, her *duenna* became less stony-faced. It transpired she was an avowed communist who had compromised her principles by joining the Bhutto dynasty's feudally owned but, in theory, socialist-leaning party. She proudly told stories of her participation in the riots and protests of the last decades. Land reform, she said, was the answer to the problems of the disempowered masses, but it would never happen because the army owned vast farms from which it fed its soldiers and kept its coffers full.

Once or twice, Zeenat rolled a piece of curried meat in a scrap of *chapatti*, and, pincered between mulberry talons, popped it in my mouth. Chev struggled to suppress his laughter.

*

One evening when I was alone with her, she told stories about her life. Her mad and maudlin father had inherited and run down a small textile factory on the outskirts of the city; but out of this decrepit scene she had sprung, full of rebellious mischief. At the age of six, she said, she had stolen her father's car and driven alone into the anarchy of the traffic-choked centre of Lahore. She became a quick-witted, ambitious and irreverent young woman, and although middle-class, in her early twenties she had penetrated, through pure nerve, the catty upper echelon by marrying a 60-year-old industrialist, whom she had recently divorced.

As the evening wore on, now raddled with booze, she began to detail her complaints about her marriage. 'He locked me in a room so that he could have his orgies. He would sit on the pot first thing and smoke seven joints before he could shit … I furnished all that house, and he said it was national heritage handed down by his ancestors. Such bloody *bakwas* [bullshit] … when I went for politics, he said he would kill me. We then divorced … He sent a man to shoot me and I sat down with that damn assassin and I talked to him, and he said: "Sister, you are my leader. I cannot kill such a woman. I am now your follower."'

Then she railed against the class she had breached. 'Who are these people? These feudals? I know them. I do not give a fuc*king* for their shooting of damn mallards and partridges. They can all go to hell … But I will always greet them well … What are you laughing about Bard *sahib*? You are a non-serious person. One day you will write my story.'

Although she was a maverick, there was something of her story that spoke of middle-class frustration, the limits imposed on people of her background by a stagnating, self-regarding elite. As a woman from such a background, her political ambitions were also curbed by deeply ingrained chauvinism. Men in power would allow such a woman, one without an influential family, to proceed so far on the strength of her wiles, but then with the inevitable fall from grace, she would be damned. Later on, I would occasionally hear her social betters dismissing her with contempt, but she had more wit, pluck, originality and – in an unorthodox way, in the way she knew she was not better or worse than anyone else – more integrity than most.

That night she laughingly lamented, with tears in her eyes: 'Can't you see why this country is driving us mad?!' One of her servants was milling about lighting candles, rolling joints, so I didn't put my arm round her, but she had stirred in me love and admiration.

For all her rebelliousness and kicking against the elite, she was an anachronism, a creature of the Old Pakistan. She was quite different from the majority of her age and class, who tended to look at their country in a more critical, detached way.

She had Pakistan's energy, restlessness. But her wildness made her vulnerable. Her nomadism was sustained by an ability suddenly to produce keys to hotel rooms, houses and flats, which – like many other aspects of her life – was never fully explained. It appeared she had a string of sugar daddies – a military man, the bunny-hopping mill owner and a cabinet minister who had flown her around in his private jet, and who, I later heard, had beaten her up.

*

One afternoon Zeenat surprised me with a gift: a copy of a book on Sufism written by Data *sahib*, who, until then, I had imagined was largely a figment of the local imagination. The saint grabbed my attention right away with a rant against hypocrisy, which he said had been given the name 'fear of God', and his distaste for the worldliness of life, which he demonstrated by invoking the words of a contemporary, an Iraqi poet, al-Mutanabbi: *'God curse the world! What a vile place for any camel-rider to alight in! For here the man of lofty spirit is always tormented.'*

His full name was Abul Hasan Ali ibn Uthman al-Jullabi al-Hujwiri al Ghaznawi, and he was one of the earliest of the saints who contributed to the spread of Islam on the Indian Subcontinent. He was a man of peace, but one who worked in the advantageous aftermath of the 11th-century Muslim conquest of northern India by Mahmud of Ghazni – a figure to this day loathed by Hindus and venerated by Muslims. Those who seek a guide to Sufism, said the book's foreword, written by a Raj-era scholar, must do three things: pray for guidance, visit the tombs of great saints, and read this book, the *Kashf Al-Mahjub* ('Revelation of the Veiled') which, the saint said, would help 'uncover the veils that obscure the path to God'.

Lying on one of Zeenat's sofas, reading his prose in a haze induced by one of Babaji's confections, I glimpsed behind the lines of his prose a humble soul. Travelling as a wandering apprentice mystic on his long journey to Lahore, he stayed as a guest at a Sufi cloister in the Persian city of Khorosan, where his fellow ascetics took against him, serving him crumbs of mouldy bread which he was forced to nibble in solitude while 'drawing into my nostrils the savour of the viands with which they regaled themselves ... all the time they were addressing derisive remarks to me ... and when they had finished their food, they began to pelt me with the skins of melons'.

The saint had an attractively flawed side to him: he had an unpleasant experience of marriage; was in love for years with a woman he had never seen; and fell into debt.

I flicked on through the book. He was a man trying to pick his way cautiously through life, not becoming attached to anything that diverted him from the path to God, even if it meant that instead of interrupting a meditation, he would allow a dog to eat his food.

He was beginning to lose me, but I ploughed on.

He advised that an aspiring Sufi should 'tread carefully, his head bowed ... but not too slowly because then his gait would resemble a proud man' and to eat like a saint, not a soldier; to remain celibate;

and to be prudent in speech for 'speaking is like wine: it intoxicates the spirit and those who begin to like it, cannot stop once they have started'.

Hmm. Not my thing at all. But then more promisingly, the saint struck out against conservative killjoys.

It is fine, he said, to throw off your clothes under the intoxicating influence of religious ecstasy; and you can dance when 'that agitation is neither dancing nor foot-play nor bodily indulgence, but a dissolution of the soul...'

Then I came across a passage about the significance of a dervish's cloak. He said all the mysteries of the universe could be found in such a patched garment, containing as it does the earth, sun and moon and all the stages of the path to truth.

The country itself seemed like a patchwork of peoples living along threads of rivers and in the folds of mountains, imagining the universe in myriad ways. I saw myself traversing the cloak, grappling with it, trying to understand it, sometimes getting lost in it.

As I read on the book revealed its purpose, one that had a relevance to Pakistan's present. It is a treatise on how to bridge the differences between orthodox Islam and its Sufi counterpart. Over the centuries, the majority form of Islam on the Subcontinent – folkloric, syncretic, Sufic – had faced challenges from reformist incarnations of the faith, but its great reservoir of believers had remained undiminished. But in Pakistan, conservatism was now beginning to drain away traditional Islam's power, shaming it for its want of purity, making it lower its head. I wondered if on our journey into rural Punjab, one of its strongholds, we would see any sign of Sufism in retreat.

*

We spent our last night with Zeenat at another of her demi-monde parties, which ended with the three of us setting off to the red-light area in search of food.

We found a motorised rickshaw parked next to a roundabout and its *betel*-chewing driver ran a dirty rag over its gleaming metal handlebars before motioning us to climb into its mirrored interior. Once inside, he kick-started the machine and we flew with billowing exhaust into the honking, polluted traffic towards old Lahore. Zeenat rested one of her mulberry-fingernailed hands on my knee, the other, as I later learned, resting on Chev's.

The red-light district, *Heera Mandi* ('diamond market'), lies near the fort in the shadow of the three massive onion domes and four soaring minarets of the Mughal red sandstone Badshahi Mosque. In daylight the district had little allure, being a grubby, deserted enclave, its real purpose only hinted at by passing transsexuals and transvestites, *hijras*, noticeable from their strong jaw-lines and white face powder struggling to mask stubbly chins. But at night it became its raffish self.

We hauled ourselves from the rickshaw and ate dishes of *daal* and thick leavened bread at a stall before strolling past begrimed and candle-oil-blackened Shia shrines that glittered with ceremonial axes and swords. It was here that many of the prostitutes stopped to offer prayers on their daily rounds. I asked Zeenat if we could see one of the dancing girls and so we climbed a dank staircase, up to a corridor where men, whose dark brown hairy backs bulged from white vests, sat on the floor eating from scratched plastic dishes.

In a small room with bare concrete walls lit by a single light bulb, a young woman was produced, dressed in a gauzy mauve chiffon slip over a lighter mauve cheap silk vest. She smiled a smile that insinuated all of her small body. Hastily applied coarse lipstick underlined her childishness. A tinny song played from a battered cassette player. Overcoming some initial coyness the girl sprang into a dance with coltish energy, whipping about her thick black hair and miming come-hitherishness by drawing her hands seductively across her eyes, palms outwards, fingers forming a V.

Zeenat relaxed when she realised the girl would tax neither Chev's nor my affections and encouraged us to follow local custom and flutter rupee notes confetti-style over her head. The plump perspiring madam took us to another room barely large enough for its queen-size white double bed. She said that the girl was a virgin and therefore available only for 'marriage' at two *lakh* rupees. Zeenat explained all of this matter-of-factly, for although she sympathised with these women's individual struggles, she saw the profession as part of her city's culture. 'I run my own woman's NGO,' she said by way of exculpation. Vulnerable Pakistani women were disposable assets. Chev was muted by the grimness of the young woman's fate.

At the threshold to her house, Zeenat quoted a couplet from Ghalib, a great 19th-century poet from Delhi whom many Pakistanis recite with passion and at length:

Na karda gunah ki bhi hasrat ki milay dad
Ya Rab agar un karda gunahon ki saza hai

Do give me praise for regrets of sins uncommitted
If there is to be punishment O Lord for sins committed.

*

We parted from Zeenat promising to meet again in a few weeks' time; and she repeated in my ear a demand of doubtful seriousness that I should marry her.

A couple of weeks later, she phoned. 'I have returned to my husband'. There were muffled angry shouts from a man in the background. 'I will always greet you well and respect you.' The phone went dead. I was reminded of the phrase she had taught me – *Raat gai tho baat gai* – a typically rhyming Punjabi refrain used for jilted lovers, which roughly translates as 'the evening has gone, so have I, and so *Adios*'.

Chapter 7
My Feudal Lord

Roaring into Punjab, Chev and I were travelling in unusual fashion, seated rather formally on some dining chairs, exposed to the elements on the back of a 'jingle truck', which the Begum had hired to carry a large cargo of furniture into storage at her farm.

The more precious items of the cargo travelled with Allah Ditta in my car.

We'd left Lahore early in the morning. The *azan*, the summoning of the faithful, had accompanied our waking and it was not beautiful: a discordant eerie chorus of wailing and nasal droning from half a dozen mosques, each voice probing high and low for an empty frequency in the sonically crowded airwaves.

Hearing that we intended to stop off at Multan, Zeenat had told us of the city's 'fake saints' who illegitimately claimed descent from the old *pirs* and used the reverence and homage they attracted for collecting votes.

'The poor and uneducated flock to touch their feet,' she said. 'But those close to these frauds know their feet are not those of saints. Your own faith is the healer, not the wrong feet.'

Her words had stoked my desire to meet one of the city's fabled holy men, even one of dubious lineage, who wielded extraordinary influence inherited from ancient forebears. Happily the Begum had rustled up such a venerable for us – a distant relation of hers – and he had invited us to stay with him at Multan.

Another incarnation of power lay ahead on our route: a 'feudal' landowner had agreed to put us up and shepherd us among the disciples at a remote dervish fair on the south-western limits of Punjab. Further curiosities included relics of the Raj, the spot where Alexander the Great received an almost-fatal wound, and a close-up view of rural life.

Seated on the back of the jingle truck, we were exposed to the attentions of the drivers of similar vehicles. On encountering such entertainment, two *goras* positioned in chairs as if for interrogation, they drove perilously close in order to examine us.

Their steeds, highly ornate hand-painted transporters of anything ranging from melons and coal to oxen and opium, were fringed with jingling chains. The sound of their approach heralded less a beast of burden than a war elephant. The spikes of their scythed wheels span viciously like those on the axles of the Persian chariots that succumbed to Alexander the Great on his quest eastwards at the Battle of Guagamela. Their raised cockpits, or *howdahs*, encased in carved wood, were shrines to saints and film starlets. Lit at all times by red- or green-tinted light bulbs, their ghoulish gleam complemented the hashish-induced tint of the eyes of the drivers – pirates of the road, who survive on *lassi*, that ubiquitous yoghurty drink laced with cannabis juice. If a driver asks at a roadside stall for a Number One, he will be stoned sufficiently to cover one hour's driving, a Number Two will cover him for two hours, and so on.

As we flew along, these road-kings feted and harassed us for five hours without cease. Smiling, hooting horns, flashing lights, laughing and wildly gesticulating for us to take tea with them, they made us the toast of that perilous donkey- and buffalo-riddled road.

It was a great relief when we turned off into small lanes criss-crossing tranquil fields.

*

We spent the next couple of days wandering about on foot from village to village, drinking buffalo milk, smoking eye-watering *hookahs* and taking siestas on string beds on flat roofs. Labourers, straightening and relinquishing hoes, paused to hail us from fields; local teachers motioned for us to ride on the backs of motorcycles and ferried us to small whitewashed domed shrines at the interstices of fields, framed by plumes of vitreous green grass and palm trees.

At a lean-to stall by a canal a man ground sugar cane in a fly-spotted metal mangle and handed us glasses of its thinly sweet juice and pointed to where salt had risen with the water table and encrusted the soil.

The old ways were still visible in this grassroots world: strings of chillies draped across the doors of village huts, which, the Begum's relation explained later, were to ward off the Evil Eye; people burn them after rotating them around loved ones, he said, a mix of Hindu and Muslim cultures; and they conduct the same ritual using the remains of a sacrificed chicken or goat, and then throw the carcases on a rooftop for scavenging birds. Lentils, seeds, eggs or money are left at the crossroads to thank benevolent spirits.

We passed earringed children with shaved heads and the rims of their eyes blackened with kohl. The effect was like a cross between a Buddhist monk and a lemur. The hair of insane people was also closely cropped to prevent scabies and to alert people to their mental condition.

Women bedecked in vibrant colours trod with rolling hips along footpaths, bundles of kindling on their heads, brown feet chapped white around the edges, eyes lined with strain. Stubbly men sauntered into fields of wheat and sugar cane, hoes resting on their shoulders, dressed in vests and simple *lungi* (sarongs). Oxen harnessed to geared wheels circled wells and goats ambled by, driving small clouds of dust into the upper leaves of plane trees. The earth was as grey as out-of-date cocoa powder.

We submitted to the nodding pace, our idle days in the fields coloured by the vague 'facts' with which one condemns or romanticises a place. Punjab (*panj* = five, *ab* = river) at heart: a wheat basket divided by the bloodiest events of Partition; home to beefy backslapping ploughmen and the supplier of soldiers to armies for centuries. In spirit, it is earthy, humorous, with a firm grasp of realpolitik. 'Don't eat shit with a spoon, eat it with a spade,' Punjabis say.

The country's most affluent province, due to its agriculture and textile industry, is in many places as backward as any part of the country. On a journalistic visit to another Punjabi village, I'd met a council of elders that decreed that five young women should be abducted, raped and killed for refusing to honour childhood 'marriages'. Here the writ of the state had petered out and justice was in the hands of a feudal elite that violently suppressed its serfs. From the rotten hierarchy's abuse of power flowed the country's problems. The widespread mistreatment of women was a symptom of this sickness. At another village I'd met a group of unshaven minor feudals in jail accused of raping a nurse who had refused to perform illegal abortions on their mistresses. Their victim, in a tearful and fatigued state had said with more hope than certainty that 'this is not the past when we can get pushed around'. By the end of that day the suspects had been released.

One evening, months before, I'd sat in the shade of a copse of mulberry trees with a circle of Punjabi village elders, surrounded by mud walls covered in cow pats and iridescent flies, in earshot of munching, shifting buffaloes. We discussed an abuse of power – the case of a local cleric who had just been arrested for running a drug rehabilitation clinic in which he had chained and imprisoned his patients. As shadows fell and the damp air thickened like mulch, the villagers, apart from an old man who had fallen asleep with his turban over his eyes, spoke in loud unrestrained voices.

'He wasn't that bad,' said one.

'At least he brought jobs,' chimed another.

There was silence. Then a saner voice spoke.

'God has flushed evil from this village. He heard the poor people's prayer.'

Now, as we bedded down under mosquito nets, the excitable beating of drums and the muted popping of distant gunfire, probably in honour of a wedding, prompted Chev to say: 'It's at night that the dark side comes out.'

Chapter 8
A Close Shave

W E APPROACHED MULTAN as the evening sky faded in a wash of nectarine above mango trees crested with gold-white blossom and cotton trees whose red flower-bombs thudded to earth. Sugar cane and cotton were being harvested; stalks lay discarded like fizzled matchsticks used to try to keep alive the setting sun.

Multan had achieved recent fame in the press: a local musical show had attracted puritanical wrath when buxom female performers, egged on by jeering spectators, had bared their breasts. There was no burlesque show during our visit and Multan remained for us truer to its old reputation: a city of heat, dust, beggars and graves.

Our host, a descendant of one of the saints whose tombs cast such a spell over the city, and a distant cousin of the Begum, was a constrained soul. Genial and without the appearance of a divine, he was bald with a regulation salt-and-pepper moustache and managed to turn the most exotic topics to dust.

Over a dinner of lamb cutlets, or 'Officer's Chops', a mainstay of Anglo-India, probably served out of respect for visiting *goras'* potentially fragile stomachs, he politely killed off any talk of Sufi saints.

'You see, it's just religious devotion,' he said, dabbing at a blob of gravy on his moustache with a napkin.

'Yes, but the old saints still command an extraordinary power over people and you embody that power, wouldn't you say?' I asked.

'The people respect the old saints. We do what we can to facilitate them. And that really is all there is to it,' he concluded with the wary breviloquence of an Anglican bishop who has been asked if he believes in God.

*

Our first morning in Multan, we set off on foot to see the city's two main saints' shrines. We soon came across a rickshaw *wallah* who refused to take us to the mausoleum of Rukn-i-Alam. 'I'm going to take you to Bahawal Haq first. He's the grandfather and you should pay respects to him first,' he said with a reproachful shake of the head. We gave way, squeezed into his death trap and pootled towards the grandfather's shrine.

The tomb of Bahawal Haq (also known as Bahauddin Zakariya) is an immense bastion of fired brick. The base is box-like and the second tier is an octagon upon which rests a dome, set like a pearl in a honeycomb cell. Multan's distinctive faience blue glazed tiles, Persian in origin but now an intrinsic part of the city, are represented in a panel decorating the eastern façade, the earliest known example in Pakistan. All the corners of the building are mounted with miniature minarets, like candles on a birthday cake.

We made our way inside. Whitewashed walls were moulded with unadorned alcoves. On a dais in a low-sided wooden pavilion, a *chador*-draped tomb rested under a heap of fragrant petals and garlands. In silence, as if leaning on the altar rails of an English country church, a man and a woman were bowed in prayer, their open-palmed hands raised in supplication. For once, there was no crowd. Without being jostled or eyeballed, we sat on the floor, admiring the inner sanctum of the city's spiritual heart.

Haq's tomb was erected near an ancient fire temple built by Hindus. It had once been home to a golden statue of a sun god, which had been smashed by various invaders, several times repaired, and finally destroyed by the Emperor Aurangzeb in the 17th century. The fire temple itself was destroyed again and again over successive centuries. Its last remains were finally extirpated in revenge for the destruction by a Hindu mob of the Babri Mosque in India in 1992.

The tomb was ancient, but represented something of Pakistan's present. Even 800 years after his death in 1262, Haq's direct descendants own thousands of acres and wield extensive political power locally and nationally, his sainthood having been handed down from father to eldest son. Our host was one of hundreds of Haq's descendants, whose disciples are numbered in millions. Some of them make the journey here from the interior of Sindh, often barefoot, looking at the ground all the way so that the only face they see from the moment they leave home until they arrive is the face of their *pir*. The ample buttocks of such holy men from this and the country's other saintly dynasties filled a large number of the national assembly's seats.

Like Data *sahib* in Lahore, Haq helped grow Islam's roots on the Indian Subcontinent.

Haq was descended from Arabs who came with Mohammed Bin Qasim, the first Muslim conqueror to reach India. In the 8th century, Bin Qasim executed or enslaved most of Multan's population and set up his headquarters in the city. 'The house of gold', the Arabs called it. He built a mosque, of which nothing remains, but his legacy to the city is Islam and Haq.

However venal his descendants might be, Haq was benevolent as well as powerful. 'If you give something to somebody,' he once said, 'you should give it with a flourish.' It's that flourish that you see all about you in Pakistan. It is in the salute to a stranger from a man working in a field; the hand that offers a stranger a seat or some food on a bus or train … or in the thwack that a minion gives to a fellow underdog to impress a new master.

We dusted ourselves off and walked towards the tomb of Haq's grandson. Before we got there, a middle-aged man in a checked tank-top sweater and grey *shalwar kameez* greeted me with a smile and an embrace, which I reciprocated before stepping back to fathom his identity.

'Mister Peter! How are you? How is your son?!' he said, joyous at a God-fated meeting in such an auspicious place.

'I'm not sure we've met…'

'You are not remembering me? From Islamabad…' His face clouded with pain.

'No, my name is not Peter. And I have no son.'

'But you are working at the British High Commission! Mister Peter!'

It was not the first time I'd been mistaken in Pakistan for Mister Peter, who was, it seemed, an affable man working as a diplomat, or the BBC, depending on the speaker, some time in the last twenty years.

'No. I work for a newspaper. I'm not Mister Peter'.

Disappointment then bitterness crossed his face. 'You are not remembering me Mister Peter.' He smiled in a sickly way and wandered off, leaving me asking myself if I couldn't have handled the encounter more deftly, perhaps by masquerading as Peter. Manners, charade, theatre, acting our roles with due aplomb; in Pakistan these things are as important as water, or more prized than the truth.

The magnificent dome covering the tomb of Rukn-ud-Din Abul Fath, known as Rukn-i-Alam, 'pillar of the world', gleamed like a white prayer skullcap. Supported by a brown brick octagonal drum that rests on a colossal, wider octagonal bastion, all ringed with strata of blue tiles, it is perhaps the fourth largest dome in the pre-modern world after Hagia Sophia, St Peter's and Gol Gumbaz. Reinforced at its corners by towering semi-circular buttresses, it is crowned with meringue-shaped miniature domes, which stoop protectively inwards over the mausoleum like relatives round a deathbed. We were about to go inside when a caretaker ushered us away. It was women's visiting time.

We hung about outside to admire the building. This tomb was a thrilling emblem of the whole country, a beacon of the Old Pakistan. Embodying the *genius loci* of a borderland where Persia, Central Asia and India meet, it is elegantly raw and feral, a totem to a hierarchy built on a feudal and tribal foundation, permeated with the mysticism of the desert.

But I wondered how much longer these tombs would remain sacrosanct. On the surrounding buildings, rooftops bristled with satellite dishes relaying images from television news channels, whose cameramen were poking their lenses into every corner of the country not prohibited to them by military intelligence. Militant Islam was not the only challenge to the old ways; modernity was threatening to break the spell that the living saints had for so long cast over their disciples.

*

The next day, we killed two birds with one stone. There was a barber in action among the rubbish and telephone wires beneath Multan's city walls. It was here that Alexander the Great had almost met his end. We settled into two neighbouring chairs facing the hallowed wall.

In Pakistan the local name for Alexander, Sikander, is never far from people's lips. Many Pakistanis claim descent from him. They also dig up coins engraved with his image. His colossal army thronged over the high passes from Afghanistan, battling its way down to the Indian plains before it turned home after his fatigued men refused to go further and handed him what the 2nd-century Greek historian Arrian described as 'Alexander's only defeat' – the lost opportunity of the conquest of India.

Before the shave began I asked the barber, a gangling, spare man, if he had heard of Sikander. Immediately, a small crowd of passers-by – manual labourers and shopkeepers – gathered to see the *goras* and listen to the chat.

'Sikander *sahib* very great man,' he said. He motioned to the wall and made violent gestures, an oversized thick silver watchstrap rattling up and down his forearm, as he described in a language incomprehensible to me, what I presumed was Alexander's scrape.

Silence ensued and I changed the subject by canvassing his views on politics. 'Benazir Bhutto [a former prime minister then in exile] is a *choor* [a thief],' he said, pulling a sickly face and flicking a hand backwards and forwards. Some of the raggedly dressed crowd laughed and joined in.

It was a game I often played in cities, asking for opinions about politicians, partly because I was always surprised by the forthrightness of the replies, and partly for the pleasure in seeing that the urban masses were under no illusions about their leader. In the countryside, where feudals exerted influence on every aspect of life, people were more circumspect, but television satellite dishes had now arrived in villages too.

'Nawaz Sharif [another former prime minister, also in exile]?' I asked.

'He is a *bohut burra choor* [a very big thief],' said a bystander, even more dramatic dismissive gestures of hands and even sicklier grimaces.

'President Musharraf?'

One of the group, a boy in a grubby *shalwar kameez*, stood to attention and saluted with pantomime mimicry.

'He is not so corrupt, but he is *fauji* [a soldier]…' said the barber, gulping with displeasure as if he had swallowed one of the flies revolving about us.

'But Pakistan is a good country,' chipped in another, a poorly dressed, middle-aged man with lines of responsibility written on his face, his voice loaded with anguish so that we understood. 'We are a peace-loving and *good* people.'

In 325BC Alexander, on his way downstream during his departure from India, arrived to besiege Multan, ending up near the spot where we now sat. He had fought his way through a swathe of Malians, as the Multanis were then called. Pressing ahead far in advance of the main body of his men, Alexander had scaled a ladder and breached the city walls. Leaping down on the other side of the wall he had found himself alone and encircled. A bowman struck him with an arrow, piercing his lung.

After the shave, the barber anointed my head with a slick of linseed so that it smelt like an oiled cricket bat. Then he played my scalp like a *tabla*, drumming his dense fingertips in a staccato, with a bass accompaniment provided by rhythmically thudding the heel of his hand on my skull.

I now experienced some of Alexander's pain as the barber gripped my arms and pulled them back in a torturous brace and then, his tongue clenched between his teeth, cracked and popped every joint in my upper body down to my knuckles with the ease of snapping a roasted chicken's wishbone. Alexander barely survived his wounds, which were nursed over weeks on a boat moored nearby. As soon as he had recovered, he put the city's inhabitants to the sword.

But the barber bore him no great malice. 'Sikander very *great* man,' he repeated as we walked away, slightly dazed, cheeks tingling with cheap aftershave.

Chapter 9
Sparrow Brains and Ketchup

WE HAD TO LEAVE MULTAN earlier than expected to make it to the dervish festival on time.

Typically for such a rural event it was going to be held two days earlier than widely believed – because like the agricultural seasons and many other saints' festivals, it took place according to the old Sanskrit calendar. Again typically, we only found out the real date by chance: a man whom we met at a *samosa* stall, an advocate of buffalo dung as a source of biogas, told us.

*

With Allah Ditta trailing behind us in my car, we drove westward on a dazzlingly bright morning towards the Indus in a Landcruiser loaned to us by a feudal, Sardar Jaffar Khan Leghari, a chief of the Leghari tribe who'd invited us to stay with him in his desert fort.

Accompanied by one of Leghari's armed guards in the car, who invariably had the barrel of his Kalashnikov carelessly pointing at our crotches, Abbas, his driver, an old acquaintance of ours, twirled his moustache, grinned beneath his Aviator sunglasses, turned up the volume of a Punjabi *bhangra* number and put his foot down. Carts and bullocks hastened into ditches, drivers swerved at the last second to avoid our cattle-bar and cyclists wobbled out of control in a struggle to leave the road.

We were on the edge of Punjab, where irrigated fields are bordered with acacia and eucalyptus and the province tapers into deserts and fragments into a jigsaw of castes and tribes and peoples. Poetic Seraiki-speakers and cotton-picking Hindus cluster round palm-groved shrines; and nomads materialise from the haze with brass pots, nose-rings, arm-bangles and secret verses. Then they disappear along invisible paths traversing deserts from Afghanistan to India.

We crossed the broad slate-grey waters of the Indus on a low bridge. Soon rolling desert took over and ran away across a torrent-riven plain to the spine of the Suleiman Mountains and Baluchistan. We drove on into Leghari country, peopled mainly by Baluch tribes that centuries ago had settled on this side of the provincial border.

On arrival at the village of Choti, Leghari's manager, a short white-bearded man dressed in a white *shalwar* that covered a significant pot belly, greeted us with formality as several servants scurried to pull back the palace's heavy wooden gates. The manager, whose disproportionately large white turban proclaimed his high status, marched us into the house, making up for his short height by walking gravely with his chin tucked in, his back as straight as a bookend.

The front of the house was a swirling, curving wave of concrete, a style that seems to have rippled through the Pakistani elite in the 1960s. But it was a façade for what was essentially a small 16th-century desert palace. As soon as we stepped through heavily studded carved wooden inner doors, we were again in that world: walls emblazoned with exquisite floral murals, marble mesh windows, painted wooden ceiling beams, recessed arched windows and passageways all revolving around a central hall.

Leghari was surrounded by a noisy crowd of his kinsmen. He was simultaneously operating six or seven telephones and a batch of mobile phones, arguing, berating, pleading and occasionally roaring. Now in his seventies, he was still black-bearded and youthful with pale skin and striking blue eyes inherited from his English mother. His audience consisted of Baluch tribesmen with narrow faces under huge black turbans, civil servants in crimplene blazers and old women huddling together, their backs to the assembly, clutching veils about their faces.

Vociferous supplicants waved papers in his face: one wanted electricity, another's daughter had been abducted, and someone had stolen someone else's land. Occasionally his anger boiled over and the crowd recoiled and fell silent, before slowly encroaching and again breaking out into a din.

Leghari had experienced the perks and infamy of Pakistani politics: a bachelor playboy until late in life, he had ridden high while his cousin was president but did a short stint in jail after his clan's inevitable fall. He was now in the middle ground, a parliamentarian

109

again, married, and like other feudals, working to keep his lands, mills and electorate afloat.

Noticing us, his face lit up and he beckoned us.

'Boys! There you are. Sweethearts. Darlings, come and tell me how you are!'

But his attention quickly shot off in other directions, a telephone pressed to his mouth, a servant on either side holding yet more telephones to his ears. 'Sir how kind of you to see me, yes the inspector general ... ah my dear old friend how was the match, *aitcha* listen I have a case here where the judge ... listen here you bastard I told you six months ago to transport that fertiliser...' Then suddenly he broke off, '... yes, you see I'm still the best-looking man in Pakistan, I do not have one white hair in my beard...' and with his briefly free hand he began to sign petitions asking officials to 'Please help the under-mentioned etc etc'.

We sat down on the edge of this *durbar*. It was only at this level you saw what oiled Pakistan's wheels: *safarish*, networking and nepotism, used to expedite the merry-go-round of bureaucrats, police officers and local officials, whom local feudals attempted to move about to suit their tastes, and who did one's 'work'.

A man came up and told us proudly how he had murdered the son of a neighbouring chieftain as part of an on-going feud. He had a particularly large turban on which I complimented him.

'The Baluch turban is so big,' he said, 'that we carry our coffin on our heads.' Noticing my confusion, he explained that they use the turban as a funeral shroud.

That evening we managed to have dinner with Leghari at a table crowded with local businessmen and politicians. He was the master of the Pakistani florid introduction: if your father was an army colonel, you would be introduced as the son of a field marshal; if you had exported some clothes from Peru to England you would be called one of London's greatest couturiers. I swiftly became a newspaper editor.

When he'd finished eating, he stood up to leave for some midnight appointment – here people work at all hours except the morning. Everybody instantly dropped their bowls, plates and forks or whatever they were doing and followed with the swiftness of a shoal of fish changing direction to avoid the jaws of a predator. A scene that could have played out at Louis XIV's court, it revolved around the Punjabi worship of power – nobody wanted to appear less than the most loyal of fawning disciples, nor to miss out on a morsel of favour that might fall from their lord's hand. People around him asked each other, 'Is he going to go or isn't he?' and then there was a mad scramble aboard vehicles as their patron, still talking on a mobile phone, moved off.

Leghari had had to hasten back to Lahore on some errand, leaving us the run of his palace. And we were in luck. The Sufi festival would, according to the latest reports, indeed be held the day after next.

*

Our bedroom was on the other side of the *shish mahal* ('mirrored palace', of which the most famous Mughal example is in Lahore's fort), a room whose ceiling had been covered with inlaid mirrors and whose walls had some of the house's finest and most intricate murals. Since our last visit a fire had ravaged large parts of the house: the *shish mahal* was now being restored, and the great hall was no longer great. Its upper storey, the *zenana*, from which the women used to look down from carved mesh windows, had been cut off by a new floor built to support the building's weakened structure.

But other important things hadn't changed. That first morning our bedroom door clicked open to reveal a file of servants bearing trays that rattled with plates of chilli omelette and toast wrapped in napkins, tea-cosied pots of *chai* and bowls of porridge.

After breakfast, we took our tea up on to the roof where there was a King David–Bathsheba view of daily village existence. With the elephant-hide grey spine of the Suleiman Mountains suffused in a sparkling haze in the background, we gazed (cautiously, because years ago we had been told off for ogling young maidens) at intimate scenes of family life in tiny brick courtyards. Doting mothers combed their daughters' thick black locks and old men reclined on *charpoys* smoking *hookahs*. Women covered head to foot in *burqahs* – which in the area have a pointed tip unlike the usual shuttlecock variety – darted along narrow alleys below the palace's walls.

We spent the day idling about the village. It was the usual Punjabi contrast of immaculate interiors and exterior squalor: dogs gnawing on buffalo carcasses, dozing goats and sewage channels. Above it all wheeled flocks of pigeons. They banked and rolled, breasts aflame with sunshine, coming to rest at the orders of pigeon fanciers whooping and waving staves at them from rooftops.

During our walkabout, people took us on unsolicited tours. They showed us black flags flying over Shia households, proudly defiant

111

markers of Islam's oldest schism; and the tombs of the Talpurs, a Leghari clan who went on to become the rulers of Sindh. Hindu women with bejewelled noses were pointed out as if apparitions from another world, and giggling mothers pulled us into their courtyards to sip tea and meet their children. Chev was taken to a side street and told in a low whisper that it was the domain of low-caste villagers. Here a barber must marry a barber, a *dhobi* a *dhobi*: pure Hindu traditions existing in the land of the Islamic Republic of Pakistan, layers of a palimpsest. We remembered an earlier visit when we'd been invited for lunch with a family, after which the men had danced to 'I am a Disco Dancer', a 1980s Bollywood *filmi* song.

Sparrow-brain nuggets and chips were served for supper at the fort. We thought it was chicken but when we asked the lovely old cook, Khardhim, he mimed first a small bird and then pointed to his head. These birds are often picked off with shotguns while they warble on electricity lines. They are good with ketchup.

*

The next morning we set off westwards to the dervish festival on the very edge of Punjab. We passed fields where lines of colourfully robed women plucked wisps of cotton, tossing them into linen sacks, and men slashed at fields of sugar cane with hand-axes. Children chased trailer-loads of cane, pilfering as much of it as they could.

Wherever we went when the sugar-cane crop was tall, we heard tales of men and women wandering off into the cover of these fields for illicit trysts. The pages of the local newspapers were full of *karo-kari* (the feminine and masculine of 'black') tales where a couple was killed after being accused of adultery. Often these cases were no more than a ploy by covetous relations who wanted to wrest land from their adversaries by levelling allegations and then accepting land as part of the settlement enforced by the village council.

The Suleiman Mountains rose abruptly in front of us. Wiry acacia trees and nomads' low-lying pitch-black tents darkened the clean graphite line of the pan-flat land. A few camels crossed the road and padded onwards to an unseen destination. We overtook small groups of ragged barefoot pilgrims. They were walking to our destination, the shrine of Sakhi Sarwar, a 12th-century mystic. Some of them, we found out later, were *fakirs*, wandering holy men who, having undertaken to spend a life paying their respects at the shrines of the saints, had been walking for years.

We arrived at the makeshift town that had sprung up about the shrine and discovered it was a camel-market-cum-saint's-festival. A tawny mass of foul-tempered, four-legged odour invested the shrine, with every dusty street crowded with groaning, masticating beasts and mounds of their green fodder.

We entered the crowded bazaar, a maze of dirty, fly-infested alleys covered with a canopy of old cloth, its stalls stocked with plastic trinkets and toys. Allah Ditta, so chivalrous in clearing a path for us through the crush and guarding our flanks from pickpockets, was himself pickpocketed within seconds.

We became enmeshed in a human stream that swept us towards the shrine. Resisting, momentarily, the heaving pressure from the mass of people behind us, we managed to take off our shoes and leave them on a pile at the entrance before being swept into the courtyard.

We'd become part of an orgy of lights, green arches and floral murals, blaring loudspeakers, drumbeats, bunting and dancers spiralling with arms raised. Above us, portraits of the *pir*'s living descendants, a roguish-looking lot, hung from a side of the shrine's cupola, seedy eyes leering over the jubilation.

Women danced in a section of the courtyard, one of them falling into a trance, flailing her arms and legs before dropping, head lolling, on to the floor. Her companions gathered about her as plump mothers, babies clamped to their hips, watched from the edges. This was it – the ecstatic dance, *dhammal*, of which we'd read years before, and here were women, usually sequestered and subdued, breaking out, flouting norms, throwing off their chains in the only public way they were permitted.

A group of prostitutes – one pockmarked, another with a lazy eye – took a rest from dancing, leaning sweating against a wall, covering their heads with *dupattas* to deter men's out-of-hours interest.

The perfume from scarlet petals, which were thrown in handfuls, bursting in the air like fireworks, competed with the spicy odour of mutton stew that simmered in brass pots over fires. Eunuchs with bright red gloss lipstick and twelve o'clock shadow taunted pilgrims, demanding alms. The scene enveloped us in its noxiously heady magic, the soles of our feet sticky with sweets that had been thrown over the crowd.

White plaster pillars, supporting a high wooden ceiling from which drop-down *punkahs* whirred, divided the interior of the shrine. The whole chamber was crisscrossed with festive lights like Harrods at Christmas. A mad press of people circled the head of the tomb, pulling and touching its green-and-yellow quilt now layered with petals.

All was confusion in my mind as I tried to decipher the meanings of chants, symbols, ex votos of oil candles, bracelets and coins placed here and there. Then Allah Ditta tugged at my sleeve, pulling me into a small darkened side chamber, whispering 'Shia, Shia'. In the middle of the gloom was a concrete bench on which lay a vicious-looking cat-o'-nine-tails spattered with blood. We left for the courtyard, me struggling to make sense of what we were seeing.

Chev and I soon became another facet of the fair, a subsidiary freak show. A kindly old man got up unsteadily on his rheumatic limbs, approached, shooed away a crowd gathered about us and warned that militants had threatened to blow up the shrine because it was, in their view, un-Islamic.

'It is no longer safe for foreigners here,' he said.

I looked about. The popularity of the festival showed that despite such threats folkloric Sufism was in robust health; but the old man's words chilled me and, combining with the memory of that bomb attack on the Sufi-minded clerics, deepened my doubts about the future.

Someone tapped me on the shoulder. 'Pakistan is a good country,' shouted the man, as if to contradict the warning about a militant attack. He stepped back to rejoin a posse of people, wanting us to watch them, throwing dance moves with wide eyes and a grin, to the racing drums.

I still didn't know much about the saint, apart from that he was a proficient healer of eye ailments and his good deeds had resulted in his death: he was murdered in AD1181 by men jealous of his reputation. In 1834, John Wood, a British naval officer, visited on his pioneer journey up the Indus to the source of the Oxus. He thought the camel fair could be transformed into an excellent showcase for British goods.

Local newspaper reports suggested that Sakhi Sarwar was indeed a market, not for imperial goods, but for 'ghost brides', women who spend a few months with a 'groom'. Some of these women appeared to be willing to be 'married' for a short time in return for remuneration; others were unwillingly sold as brides, or temporary sex slaves. Recently two sisters who had gone to say prayers at Data Sahib's shrine in Lahore had been kidnapped and brought to this shrine for sale or rent.

In the evening the festivities moved to the flat land below the shrine and Pathans, Baluch, Seraiki-speakers and Punjabis danced, recited poetry and gambolled about. Framed by an old padlocked wooden doorway, two Baluch shepherds sat crosslegged, their long faces half covered by the shadow of large black turbans, each holding the other's beard in their fists and each other's steady gaze, the old way of striking a deal.

All of life was here, a place where people from every province, Muslims of every hue – apart from the orthodox – and Hindus, Sikhs and Christians prayed shoulder-to-shoulder. Stepping among clusters of holidaying pilgrims it seemed to me the shrine was a rabbit hole through which to drop into a wonderland of curiosities, where nomad and city-dweller came together, singing, bartering, playing and stealing, transcending the usual proprieties and borders, and a fixation with these places began to take hold of me. Shrines were prisms, looking glasses through which to view the country, to step into the mysterious world that I was so eager to capture before it disappeared.

As we watched the last scenes of the day unfold, a police officer of some rank bore down on us. He asked us the purpose of our visit and explained politely that foreigners were no longer allowed into the region without permission. We discovered later that uranium had been found in the hills and the military were building a secretive base nearby. He said we must cross back over the Indus, but did not insist on enforcing the order when we told him we were Leghari's guests.

The sky had turned into an advancing battleship, full of dust and rain. A man was staring, as if he could not believe his eyes, into his inside pocket. He had been robbed.

*

At a loose end on the morning of our last day at Choti, we decided to drive westward to a colonial hill station on the Punjab/Baluchistan border.

With each mile the government's control became weaker as the voluminous turbans, black beards and Kalashnikovs of the Baluch became more prevalent. A marine sky enhanced the shining reds of the passing trucks. Women day-labourers, perhaps Hindu, dressed in flimsy caftans and saris, carried wicker baskets of rocks on their heads to a building site. Above us rose tall vertical cliffs of sandstone bristling with wild olive trees and jagged ridges.

We pulled over on the roadside so that Chev could photograph a man who had climbed into the branches of an acacia tree to lop off branches for his goats below. Jingle trucks stuffed with Baluchistan's apples and citrus fruit thundered past. There was a steady stream of traffic; it was a notorious smuggling route for stolen cars, vodka and drugs. For millennia it had been one of the principal thoroughfares connecting the plains of India with Persia and Central Asia.

The landscape around us was a treasure map of mounds, forgotten forts and still inhabited caves where relics of the past occasionally came to the surface. Leghari had a small museum room in his palace that housed a hoard of such artefacts, including statuettes of women dancing – one sprawled on her belly leaning on her arms, her legs folded up behind her, ankles in the air – remnants of a bygone Hindu age. Also among his collection were coins bearing images of Alexander's head.

Soon we reached the hill station. At 6000 feet, Fort Munro, an outpost built by the British to control the tribes, was a juniper- and pine-shaded refuge from the scorching plain in summer.

We walked over to the Christian Cemetery. Since our last visit, it had been vandalised and the graves smashed up. Shattered crosses and tombstones lay about. We looked in vain for the tomb of a Reverend Smith who 'Sank While Bathing' which we had seen before on our previous visit. A great crack gaped across a grave in the shade of a large three-trunked tree. It was inscribed: 'In Loving Memory of Maud Evelyn, wife of Captain ML Ferrar, Indian Army Punjab Commission, only daughter of WB Oldham esq, ICSCIE who died at Khar on 13th October 1906 aged 26 years'.

Looking at that broken grave, I thought how recently the tide of British conquest had surged into these mountains; how on my first visit, with its puttees, ruined officers' bungalows and macaroni served for tea, Pakistan had felt a little like a room recently vacated by people of my grandmother's type. But how quickly the Raj had ebbed, leaving its debris high and dry.

We walked over a hill to the nearby lake where Reverend Smith must have sunk. Shepherds scrambled down to its edge with their sheep and filled water tins. On the other side a group of women pounded clothes with rocks and drank from water skins. They greeted each other with an intricate kissing of hands and then placed their hands on each other's faces.

As we watched this scene, a local bureaucrat, whom we'd met near the cemetery, rumbled up to us in a 4X4. 'You have been invite to a wedding ceremony. Please join me.'

We sat in the place of honour in a circle on reed mats in a stubbly field with about one hundred and fifty tribesmen, their guns laid out in front of them. A goat's shoulder bone was produced and a sage divined the future from scratches on it. A man with a shaven head, who showed signs of mental illness, pranced into the middle, stopped, pointed at us, and cried something at which everybody fell about laughing.

'What did he say?' we asked.

The bureaucrat replied: 'He said you have such big heads that you cannot be human.'

A dish of the most putrid brain rolled in stomach intestine was placed with great ceremony before me, and then a dagger with which to eat it. The entire party looked on, licking their lips in anticipation of digging into lesser fare.

'I'm sorry,' I explained to our host, 'I am a vegetarian. But my brother ... he is very hungry.'

In keeping with his staunch character, Chev sighed and picked up the knife, saying, 'No man who has eaten British school food can be appalled by the fodder of another nation.'

Occasionally pausing to prevent himself from gagging or to mutter 'fucker' at me under his breath, he ate the delicacy with as much outward sign of appreciation as he could muster.

When Chev had recovered from his ordeal and was on speaking terms with me again, we drove down from the mountains in a mellow mood, happy to have visited an old and familiar spring.

*

We decided that we couldn't face Allah Ditta falling asleep at the wheel all the way back to Lahore, so we took the even more precarious twin-prop Fokker flight from Multan.

We joined the fray in front of the ticket office and the clerk took our money ahead of the others. A couple of mustachioed thugs, minor feudals dressed in Western clothes, came up to us and, apparently angry we had jumped the queue, started shouting at us:

'You are foreigner, how dare you behave like this. I will cut your balls off and shave your head, motherfucker.'

'We will take our weapons from the car and kill you,' rejoined his friend. We were shocked; their faces registered both anger and fear, but they did not seem to know what to do while we remained silent.

A humble old man intervened bodily, risking a blow from them.

'This is no way to treat our guests, *bas bas* enough enough,' he said gently. The thugs stood down, cursing, and the old man led us away. He apologised. The angry incident was forgotten. Even now Pakistan was one of those places: the sour taste of frustration and disappointment quickly erased by acts of kindness.

We returned to the capital, from where Chev left for home and I faced Pakistan's increasingly turbulent present. For, nationally, a sea change came suddenly.

SINDH:
LAND OF SAINTS AND SLAVES

Chapter 10
Heath Robinson Country

1 ST MAY, 2007. The onset of the hot season. Basil, the tubercular cook, had brought Allah Ditta for his lunch a chilled steel beaker of *lassi* and a bag of *samosas* wrapped in grease-stained newspaper. After he had eaten, I found him dozing on the cool bare floor of the kitchen, one arm behind his head, bearded chin pointing upwards. He had grown fatter on the rewards of his executive position in the household, and he was a man of property. He had purchased a parcel of land in his hometown and built a low, territorial wall round it. He was saving money to construct a modest house.

I ate lunch and then, cudgelled by the heat, stretched out on a string bed upstairs next to a floor-to-ceiling window overlooking the terrace. The pine-covered ridges of the Margalla Hills, lush green in the spring, had receded into a sack-brown dusty haze. The view's charm had also been blurred by a story told by a Pakistani friend who walked the hills several times a week: a man had recently sprung at her from behind a tree, masturbating furiously. A febrile tension was building with the heat.

Geckos were all about; some splayed on walls, others pitter-pattered across ceilings and floors, rattling into defunct air-conditioning units. Basil floated about the house in the still, baking air, a bunch of keys jangling officiously from his belt, his ratty eyes glistening with schemes.

Later that day he trudged in carrying two large, plastic bags straining at the seams, dripping a pink liquid. I asked him about it.

'Shhsssshhhhhh!' he said, looking around as if fearing the presence of a Muslim Inquisition. 'It's peeeeeeeg.'

'Pig? From where?'

'From mountainside.'

'Did you kill it?'

'Yes. Killed on the road. Muslim man no like but very good. *Just like bacon.*'

Allah Ditta, too, had surprised me recently. Driving near Hasan Abdal, not far from Islamabad, he pointed at a rocky triangular hill that rose from surrounding scrub with pilgrimage flags and painted rocks marking its pathways. He said that on its peak stood a shrine to a saint venerated by both Muslims and Sikhs.

'I once took my wife to a spring there,' he said, his hands balanced lightly either side of the steering wheel. 'We saw a woman swimming in the pond. She was...' he cocked an eyebrow and turned two fingers one way, then the other, 'half woman, and half fish.'

'Ah,' I said, mistrusting my grasp of Urdu. 'You say,' I twisted two fingers one way, then the other, 'half woman, half fish?'

'Yes sir.'

'She had a tail?'

'Yes sir.'

'And yet you say she had the head of woman?'

'Yes sir.'

'What did she do?'

'She swam about.'

'What did you do?'

'We kept very quiet.'

'And then?'

'She disappeared.'

'Are you sure you saw this?'

'Absolutely *bulkul* [absolutely] sir.'

He looked sidelong at me with reproach at my incapacity for insight into local affairs. I marvelled that one who had seen a mermaid so far inland was permitted to be in charge of a mechanised vehicle. I'd come across other Pakistanis who were susceptible to this kind of belief. Millions of Pakistanis were living in a state of medieval superstition, ripe for manipulation by *mullahs*, politicians and bogus holy men. But were they more gullible, I wondered, than us in the West, with our historic belief in a trinitarian god and a bipolar ideological world of left and right? There didn't seem much in it to me.

For months afterwards, as we sped past camel trains and jingling trucks in battering heat, I often marvelled at Allah Ditta's fishy revelation.

*

Militants had entrenched themselves in the capital's Red Mosque, which had become increasingly notorious for its anti-government, pro-*jihadi* rhetoric. Girls from a sister seminary, armed with staves, had staged violent protests against Danish cartoons that had lampooned the Prophet, and against brothels and the demolition of illegal mosques. 'Chicks with Sticks' local newspapers called them. In the north, in Swat, 'Pakistan's Switzerland', an area for decades famed for its tourism, a local militant nicknamed 'Radio Mullah' was parading about on a white horse sowing the seeds of an insurgency.

Most worryingly for Musharraf, he was also running into serious trouble with the country's lawyers. Two months previously he had tried to sack the Chief Justice, Iftikhar Chaudhry. But he, refusing to go, had instead taken to the road preaching the rule of law. Thousands of suited and booted lawyers were staging chaotic mass rallies across the country.

After seizing power years before, by rigging elections and mangling the constitution to suit his needs, Musharraf – still a serving general in charge of the military – had made himself president of a quasi-democracy. James Astill, a friend and fellow foreign correspondent, described this incongruous hybrid of democracy and dictatorship as resembling the cartoons of Heath Robinson, who drew preposterous assemblages of levers, cranks and pulleys, kept running by the tinkering of small bald men in spectacles.

The US and Britain, eager to maintain this haphazard machinery, began to push harder for Musharraf to share power with the exiled former prime minister Benazir Bhutto. Washington and London feared renewed political instability would thwart their attempts to tackle militant Islam in the region. They wanted to see politicians and the military reach an accommodation, a move that would involve another tinker with the apparatus.

With its overlapping allegiances to clan, Islam and state; its competing spheres of Sharia, colonial-era common law, tribal and feudal justice; its insecure borders, secessionist rebels and tussling civilian and military powers, Pakistan was entirely a Heath Robinson contraption. Its washers worn away, nuts and bolts rattling, pistons seizing, pressure gauges straining, alarm bells ringing, leaking oil and smoke, it was threatening to blow.

*

A couple of weeks after my return from Punjab, I stood in my office staring at the wall, gusts from the ceiling fan rippling the edges of files and papers strewn on the grey terrazzo floor. Allah Ditta was at my shoulder, gouging one of his ears with a car key, as many Pakistani drivers like to do.

He had sidled up after spotting me looking at a map that I'd hung on the wall. 'Pakistan!' he said, his eyes shiny with pleasure. 'Pakistan!' He shook his head with disbelief at the beauty of such a map, which was cheap, undetailed, showing the country's provinces in bold colours, with blue and red pins marking where I'd been in Punjab and Baluchistan.

He stood on tiptoes and placed one hand at the top of the map, one at the bottom, laughing that he could hold it all in his arms. I shared his wonder. Then I asked him to point on the map where we were. He tugged his beard, tilted his head and placed a finger some 400 miles from our current geographical position, which I showed him to his great indifference.

He sauntered off to lie down in the kitchen, leaving me surrounded by the Sargasso Sea of files and papers.

Since Chev's departure, I'd felt more keenly the stultification of the capital. A yearning to be back on the road, even in the intensifying heat, was building inside me.

This impulse to travel had been with me almost as long as I can remember, at least since the age of seven when I was sent from a loving, chaotic home to board at a repressively Victorian school. I often looked out beyond its bounds, across a no-man's-land of fields to a railway track, nursing a trapped animal's desire for freedom.

The peripatetic urge had also been fostered by my grandmother's stories of India and my naval father's tales of his journeys to the Antarctic and our ancestors' adventures as botanists, artists, sailors and soldiers in China, Africa, India and Albania.

To some minds, my restlessness was a disease. A bourgeoise French lady, an acquaintance of my mother, described my 20-year-old self as living '*une vie de baton de chaise*', a life of nomadic dissipation. A psychotherapist suggested that a fixation with travel and other countries was an artificial compensation for some essential ingredient missing from myself. All of which may be true, but I preferred the deduction reached in my final school report, which said simply that I was 'internationally curious'.

With the old impulse gnawing at me, I'd taken out all my files to try to work out what would be the next step on my travels, sifting through newspaper clippings and notebooks, looking for clues, leads, arrows to point me in the right direction.

At first, I leafed through clippings headlined variously 'Eunuchs pelt alleged kidnapper with rotten eggs'; 'Man pulls F-16 aircraft with twenty-seven-inch-long moustache', 'Mob attacks donkey funeral rites'; and on a literary note, 'Trite special editions have taken roots'. There were also numerous one-paragraph stories about women being hacked to death with axes in honour killings.

At last I found the file I'd been hunting for, on which I'd scrawled in biro 'Sindh'.

A more austere form of Islam was threatening the old, folkloric, mystical beliefs. Sufi shrines, which I increasingly viewed as epicentres, pulses of the Old Pakistan, were under threat. And Sindh was the region's bulwark of Sufi mysticism, a land in thrall to powerful holy men, where it was scarcely possible to tread without tripping over a shrine or a saint's disciple.

As I picked up the file, several articles pinned together by a paperclip fell to the floor. They concerned a great living saint from Sindh, Pir Pagara, whom I'd long craved to meet.

Recently, Pir Pagara had made the front pages of the local newspapers by prophesying 'the imposition of martial law' on the day the former Chief Justice was due to arrive in the city, adding that the detail of future events was 'known only to God and the hidden hand'. The latter phrase was a local euphemism for military intelligence, to which the *pir* was reportedly linked.

A think-tank academic in Islamabad had told me, the saint was politically effective because 'you will die if you don't vote for him'. I'd also heard that during a visit to the *pir*, the then President Ayub Khan (1907–1974), had been warned not to walk in front of him lest his followers perceived this as a slight and slay him. His disciples, the Hurs, were fanatical in their loyalty to the *pir*, believing him to be 'the shadow of God on earth'.

To meet him in his Sindhi shrine-citadel would be, I thought, to understand the heart of the province, even that of the country. It would also be a great coup because the saint was famously elusive. But if I didn't manage to corner him, at least I might see in Sindh whether the core of Pakistan's mystic faith was being eroded by the onslaught of militancy and religious conservatism.

The news also pointed to the province. The following week in Sindh's capital city, Karachi, the deposed Chief Justice was scheduled to hold a rally over which loomed a threat of violence.

I stood squinting at Sindh on the map, as yet unblemished by my red and blue pins, trying to imagine what lay ahead. Pakistan's southernmost province, it is bordered by the Thar Desert and India to the east, the swamps of the Rann of Kutch to the south east, the Kirthar mountains to the west, the Arabian Sea to the south and Punjab to the north.

Clustered along the banks of the Indus, it houses a multi-layered and ancient culture.

Here there are 'heretical Muslims', Hindus, Buddhists and Sheedis descended from slaves whose ceremonies preserve old African rites. Sindhi folklore contains tales of people eating saints to absorb their good qualities; landowners marry off their womenfolk to the Koran to keep wealth from being frittered away in marriage; and farm labourers fare little better than slaves.

Chapter 11
The Real Pakistan

DISEMBARKING FROM AN AIRCRAFT on to the tarmac at Karachi airport, I stepped into thick soupy air, which, spiced with a fishy, sulphurous tang, conjured up the sea and industrial pollution.

Karachi, a mega-city of roughly twenty million souls, sits in a perpetual fug of humidity. It's a fervid, jostling port-city; Pakistan's commercial hub. It lost its status as the country's capital in the 1960s when a military ruler, Ayub Khan, transferred the title to cooler, safer Islamabad, nearer to the centre of Punjabi feudal hegemony and army headquarters.

In Karachi riots followed frequent 'load shedding' or power cuts; traffic accidents led to outbreaks of ethnic violence; people were electrocuted when monsoon rains flooded poorly drained streets; few paid utility bills; the rich pulled strings to take delivery of water. Street crime was so rife that carrying two wallets and two mobiles, one to hand over to robbers, another to keep hidden, was the norm.

The international hotel where I was staying had long been corralled behind concrete fortifications because of the threat of Islamist terrorist attacks. I ran the gauntlet of x-ray machines, security pat-downs and barriers and made it up to my room. Checking my phone, I found a contact had texted me a dinner invitation for that evening.

*

My newspaper wanted an article on the 'real Pakistan', one that didn't involve terrorist attacks, but fashion parades, middle-class life and entertainment. But before worrying about that I wanted to set in motion my search for that powerful Sufi saint.

I'd first heard of Pir Pagara, a hereditary title meaning 'the turbaned saint', in my childhood. My grandmother had told a story about how in the Second World War my grandfather, then a very young army officer, had hunted the current *pir*'s father through deserts and jungles as other forebears had hunted the tigers and bears whose moth-eaten skins and gaping jaws festooned the floors of the old tower in Ireland.

My grandfather had been part of operations to track down Sibghatullah Shah II after he instigated a large-scale but now mostly forgotten insurgency against British rule in India.

A 200-year-old prophecy had said a pockmarked son of Sindh, a saintly keeper of a shrine, would rise up against enemies whose 'faces will be red like monkeys' and rule India. Inspired by this, the pockmarked Pir Pagara had risen against the British in the 1930s. Tens of thousands of his fanatical Hur followers went on a violent spree, assassinating political rivals, looting and taxing. In retaliation, the British raided the *pir*'s stronghold, seizing arms, ammunition and 'a young Mohammedan boy wrongfully confined in a box', his catamite. They claimed that there 'was evidence too of orgies of debauch and sadist practices to which this creature was addicted'. He was sent to trial (at which he was unsuccessfully defended by Jinnah), convicted and imprisoned in Bengal for seven years.

After his release from jail, where he'd met other anti-British agitators and become further radicalised, he and the Hur began again to agitate and in early 1942 the disturbances reached the 'proportions of a terrorist rebellion'. Martial law was declared after they derailed the Lahore Mail Train and slaughtered twenty-four passengers and staff with axes.

Both sides were ruthless. An air of desperation possessed the British administration and military, which carried out dozens of hangings, air raids and a parachute drop (the first by Indian troops) in order to quash the Hur.

In the desert, the Hur outjockeyed British forces on camels and in jungly swamps infested with malaria, snakes and crocodiles and humid temperatures of 120 degrees, they outwitted them with their knowledge of local paths. But eventually Pir Pagara was captured, convicted by a military court and hanged in 1943. The place of his burial was kept secret so that his grave would not inspire further insurrection among his followers.

The saint's life and the Hur Rebellion captivated me. The current Pir Pagara, the hanged man's son, was no less beguiling. He was a burly plump figure with a grey beard fanning out across his chest. In local press photographs he was often shown draped in a flowing velvet robe, encrusted with gems and wearing a tall conical hat of

Previous page: Joyous ritual at a Lahore society
wedding

This page
Top: Nawab Bugti's bodyguards at his fort
in 1996
Left: Nawab Bugti in his cave hideout in 2006
Right: Bugti tribesmen on watch

Opposite: Baluch wedding party at which
Chev ate the foul, guest-of-honour dish

Top: Revellers on Karachi's
Clifton beach

Right: The faithful at Lahore's
wonderful Mughal-era Badshahi
Mosque

Below: Pupils line the walls of a
madrassa to watch a political
rally in Lahore

Top: A Pathan bride is blessed by having a Koran passed over her head at a Peshawar wedding

Left: A wrestler, or *pehlwan*, greases up before a training bout of *kushti*, a traditional Indo-Pakistani form of mud wrestling

Right: Each *kushti* bout requires intense preparation, including hoeing and flattening the mud court where the fight takes place

Top: A boy parades a bear before the animal is set upon by dogs in a horrifically cruel bout of bear-baiting in Punjab

Bottom: Women, wearing pointed shuttlecock burqas common to the western Punjab, walk beneath Jaffar Leghari's fort walls at Choti

Top: A Punjabi village council ordered these women be abducted, raped or killed for refusing to honour childhood 'marriages' arranged to resolve a blood feud

Bottom: Jaffar Leghari surrounded by tribesmen in his council hall at Choti

This page: Villagers harvesting sugar cane in the Punjab for a feudal lord

Overleaf, top: Women dance to a mystical Sufi drumbeat at Sakhi Sarwar's festival in western Punjab

Bottom: Feverish devotion at the shrine of Sakhi Sarwar.

Above: This pilgrim appears to be channelling the saint's *baraka*, mystic force

Below: Beating *dolki* drums faster and faster, musicians whipped pilgrims at Sakhi Sarwar into frenzied dance

Opposite, top: Benazir Bhutto greeting crowds from a train in the Punjab in 1997

Bottom: *Jia* Bhutto! 1997 Bhutto rally in Lahore.

This page, top: Bhutto rally 1997. The drama of Pakistan's political dynasties, perpetually mired in corruption and abuse-of-power scandals, has held the public in its thrall for decades

Bottom: Educated at Oxford University and Harvard, the daughter of the charismatic leader Zulfiqar Ali Bhutto was famously haughty and entitled, but won plaudits in the West as a champion of democracy

Opposite, top: Chitral in the Hindu Kush in Pakistan's mountainous north, an oasis of peace

Bottom: Chitrali boy showing off his prowess with a catapult

This page, top: Boy sits in a food cauldron at Sakhi Sarwar shrine. Free food is doled out to the poor and pilgrims at shrines

Bottom: A Punjabi Christian holds up a cross charred and desecrated by a Muslim mob in a Sangla Hill church

Overleaf: A teacher instructs pupils in Kashmir in 2005 after their school was demolished by an earthquake that killed 85,000 people

the sort favoured by the Talpurs, the 19th-century rulers of Sindh. In attendance were usually his pet parrots, and a servant holding an overflowing ashtray.

A mystique hung about him. In the 1965 and 1971 wars against India, the Hurs, under his command, fought alongside the Pakistan army and in 2002 when the two countries almost went to war again over Kashmir, Pakistan activated the Hur Mujahid Battalions under Pir Pagara, reportedly mobilising six thousand men. His prognostications about Pakistan's future were given great credence.

There was also a darker side. His family's thugs were accused of shooting at crowds of supporters of other political parties, burning down the houses of tenants disloyal to the saint and murdering rivals over land disputes in Karachi, where the clan were known as a wild lot, a law unto themselves.

I had many questions for him, not least whether he knew what the British had done with his father's body. A local journalist had given me the telephone number of his Karachi residence. I dialled it.

'Who is there?'

I gave my name and trade.

A muffled noise. I heard 'English journalist' muttered in Urdu. Feet walking down a corridor. Feet returning. The line went dead.

*

Rebuffed, I headed by taxi to the tomb of an eighth-century mystic, Abdullah Shah al-Ashtar Ghazi – 'the most capable among the warriors'. He was Karachi's patron saint and was believed to have saved the city many times by warding off cyclones. I reckoned his shrine was a good place to get my bearings.

The city was emptier than usual. Old tribal signs had appeared: flags of several political parties fluttered above roads and on tenement blocks and graffiti were splashed on walls. These symbols were a foretokening of the bloody ethnic clashes that sporadically brought Karachi to a standstill. The city's *mohajir* – as the Urdu-speaking people who migrated from India at the time of Partition are known – and Sindhi and Pathan ethnic groups were staking out their turf ahead of a visit by the deposed Chief Justice. The *mohajir's* political party, the Muttahida Qaumi Movement (MQM), which ran the provincial and city governments, was allied to Musharraf, and had pledged to quash any challenge to its authority.

The shrine stood out starkly in the affluent chrysanthemum-potted neighbourhood of Clifton. Bedraggled junkies lay crumpled on the broken pavement either side of its gateway; helixes of flies swirled above a flight of steps rising to the top of a mound in which the saint's bones had been interred.

The shrine, encased in a large ugly modern block fronted with huge chevrons of blue-and-white tiles, was surmounted by a shallow gilt dome, which was ribbed like a whale's underbelly. Above it, pennants flapped above the seafront, giving it a piratical air. The saint offers particular succour to prostitutes, transvestites and members of the working class, who were all in evidence at the shrine, saying their prayers amid clouds of incense.

I looked out from a crowded platform in the direction of the sea. For millennia this port had traded in lapis lazuli from Afghanistan, turquoise from Iran, agates, chalcedonies, gold and timber from India and local carnelian, all goods bound for Mesopotamia and the Persian Gulf. After the arrival of Muslim Arabs in the 8th century, African slaves, whose largely destitute descendants are still scattered along this coast, were added to the list of goods. Two centuries ago, the East India Company set up a trading factory at Karachi, establishing a permanent British presence in Sindh for the first time.

The saint had helped me a decade or so before, his shrine acting as a gateway to a hidden side of Karachi when I'd been covering a story that had a bearing on the tensions now building in the city. The tomb brought back memories of learning how politics and crime elide here, and how love and ordinary lives are easily snared in deadly conspiracy.

A young Pathan woman, Riffat, had run off to marry a young man, Ahsan, a *mohajir*. The elopement had stirred longstanding enmity in Karachi between the Pathans and *mohajirs*, prompting days of rioting that claimed the lives of nearly fifty people. A Pathan tribal council had sentenced the couple to death. Policemen had tracked the lovers down and arrested them, charging Ahsan with having sex outside marriage; and then, as he was leaving a court building, still manacled to a policeman, Ahsan was gunned down. He was badly wounded but survived. The gunmen, Pathans, some of them Riffat's relations, were arrested and then released.

Riffat was freed and went into hiding, but I'd caught up with Ahsan two weeks after he was shot, lying on a hospital bed, his skin pocked with several dark bullet wounds. All he remembered of the shooting was that as he lay bleeding on the floor, his father-in-law's bearded face had appeared, and, laughing, had crowed, 'You are shot, you are going to die. Say your *qalma* [prayers].'

I'd spent days trying to track down Riffat. Finally, one of Ahsan's brothers had hinted that if I met him at the shrine, there might be a way. As today, stray dogs had prowled and scavenged among rubbish strewn by its entrance, and heroin addicts sprawled in its shadows. He told me that Riffat was in Lahore and I flew there to meet her in a safe house.

At first she kept her face veiled, but soon she revealed lips glossed with red lipstick and kohl-rimmed eyes twinkling above a strong nose. She had chatted animatedly about her romance. The young lovers had exchanged gifts of perfume and classical Indian music, and then they had given each other rings. Ahsan had begun to behave like a Pathan, walking straight-backed and chewing *naswr* (tobacco), and all the girls thought he was like an Indian film hero. Then her father said he would kill both of them if she continued the romance. But the couple had ignored the warnings. Riffat had loved all the Romeo and Juliet-type stories that abound in India and Pakistan, particularly the Pathan one about Yusuf Khan and Sherbani, both of whom end up being murdered.

But a Pakistani story is seldom so simple. The brother arranged for me to meet again with Ahsan, who had moved from hospital to a bare-walled safe house in a slum controlled by Karachi's big don, Altaf Hussain, the leader of the MQM. The brother told me that their first cousin was one of Hussain's parliamentarians and that the Pathan tribal council had had some enmity with him. The Pathans, he said, had stoked up the murderous riot and egged on the father to shoot Ahsan to settle a score and stir up trouble before local elections. Ahsan had previously been sucked into this underworld, serving as one of the big don's goons.

*

I had dinner that evening with a rich friend, a Memon businessman, who, over plates of oysters (his brother had dishes delivered to his house by air from Le Gavroche in London), told tales of corruption. The dissolute wealthy, he said, had Swiss accountants who travelled to Pakistan with paper shredders in case they were caught in a *coup d'état* with incriminating documents. He said that in Lahore it was fine to drive a Porsche, but if you flaunted your wealth that way in Karachi you might be carjacked. Lahore was still feudal, while in Karachi your servants might get uppity and murder you. Then there was the friend of his whose dining-room was ornamented with a large glass case displaying a complete pride of stuffed lions; and another who held drinks parties on a private platform he had built miles out into the Arabian Sea.

I left him after dinner and met a younger crowd at the stag-antlered, colonial-era Sindh Club, a source of gins-and-tonics and billiards, where it was 'Fez Night'. I was the guest of a young hereditary saint with slow, large, watery eyes, dressed in a Bugsy Malone pin-stripe suit. We drove to the club in his armour-plated Mercedes, accompanied by a bodyguard of hardened, heavily armed country boys. Among our company was a tall feudal with a Harold Macmillan moustache, who introduced himself as 'an agriculturalist who grows mangoes'. He had one of his two mistresses with him: a wan, troubled Frenchwoman and a luscious-lipped model from Lahore. We sat in a private booth, drinking heavily, supercilious above the dancing throng. After a while, the model, who had had her nose put out of joint by her master's recent attachment to the Frenchwoman, sought revenge by casting *oeillades* at me. As the evening and her attentions matured, the feudal became increasingly irritable. I passed the gents and overheard English voices. I looked in to find a British Pakistani vomiting in a sink, his friends laughing. Shades of the homeland.

*

My attempt to doorstep Pir Pagara was not successful. I got as far as the gates of his house in a large compound in a wealthy district of the city. A short, wiry gunman wearing a sequined cap blocked my entrance with an emphatic hand gesture. He radioed my name to the main house; a few minutes later a crackle came back, and I was told that the saint was not at home. I said that I was prepared to wait in the house – as is Pakistani custom – and made to move forward but stopped abruptly when the guard lowered his sawn-off shotgun towards my belly and shook his head. I wondered if he was a Hur. I passed my business card to him, which he took without interest, crumpling it into his top pocket.

*

Adnan Qadeer's bondage-wear factory on the outskirts of the city provided some 'colour' for my article on the 'other' Pakistan. There, women manufactured an assortment of S&M dog-masks, clothes with hatches and flaps and morbid-looking body bags. Qadeer said that his staff believed they were making sports equipment. As I delicately examined 'floggers' (with or without fur) and a patent-leather codpiece, a muffled giggle from one of the workers told another story.

The *mullahs* had stopped objecting to his business, Qadeer said, once assured that the goods were only for export. To whom did he export? I asked. 'Mistress Cordelia,' he replied. 'She has a dungeon in Britain.'

A couple of days later I went to a 'rave'. Its organisers had screened off a small section of a beach outside Karachi. About a dozen young couples in Western clothes trance-danced self-consciously; and a few burly mustachioed men sat in a circle drinking. They were from the Anti-Narcotics Force. Apparently they had provided the drugs for the evening.

Daylight broke and my young host (a documentary film maker), his girlfriend and I sat on the beach. He and I then mounted some scraggy beach horses. Brandishing a whisky bottle in one hand and reins in the other, he immediately rode into a knot of people with the disregard with which well-educated Pakistanis so often treat their poorer compatriots. Our conversation grew slightly bizarre as we gazed with addled eyes across a stony wasteland behind the beach and the heat became prickly. His accent became more fey, clipped and upper-class as he spoke of his social set's decadence.

Pakistan's hedonism, practised by the ruling class and opposed by the conservative middle class, is well known. The author Hanif Kureishi described a party where a Karachiite, high on heroin, paraded himself naked referring to his aroused manhood as his 'Imran Khan', a reference to the virile former cricketer who later rose to political prominence.

My friend on the beach told me of an evening he had recently spent in the company of a cross-dressing television comedian. 'It was totally wild. He was getting sacked awf by a good chum of his, not a gay in his day-job. He has the most *collawssal knawb.*' A year or so later I read that one of the circle's members had drugged and sodomised a young man of lower social standing, who returned later that night with his brother and murdered him; another had shot himself dead by accident when, during a cocaine-fuelled binge, his Rottweiler attacked him and he had tried unsuccessfully to defend himself.

*

All that week, with Hosnain, a tough, streetwise journalist I'd hired as a fixer, I met representatives of Altaf Hussain. They bent over backwards to hypnotise us with civility. Hussain micro-managed his party from London, which he had moved to over a decade before, following an attempt on his life in his native Karachi. His political harangues, conducted by telephone and relayed by loudspeaker, were known to last up to four hours. Addressing thousands of his disciples, he contorted his voice in a purposefully high-pitched, quasi-religious nasal drone, like that of the Shia clergy during *mohurram*. His supporters' adulation of him was the most vivid example of the country's cultish veneration of power. His followers called him *pir sahib*, or 'Saintly Sir' and his heavies extorted a *goonda*, or thug tax, from Karachi businesses. His slogans included: 'Don't be a leader, be a worker.' The movement ran on Greenwich Mean Time. His terrified ministers said they fielded his telephone calls through the night.

I asked the don's lickspittle mayor what would happen if the city's other political groups tried to stage rallies of support when the deposed Chief Justice came to town. Offering me another biscuit, he replied with a monstrous giggle: 'If they misbehave, we will slap them.'

*

On the morning of the deposed Chief Justice's visit, I was lying on my bed reading the newspapers after breakfast when, barely audible above the hum of the air-conditioning, I heard the dull crack and spatter of gunfire in the streets below.

Wearily I flopped off the bed, shambled to the window and saw smoke billowing above nearby buildings. I grabbed my notebook and camera and headed for the door.

As I walked along deserted streets from the hotel to the High Court, where the deposed Chief Justice and various political parties planned to meet, armed bandana-wearing gunmen zipped past on motorcycles. The city's subterranean powers had broken cover. I came to a junction where a black-suited lawyer crouched, waiting for a break in the gunfire clattering across the street in front of him. We decided to turn back, to try a different route. The empty windows above us, parked cars, heaps of rubbish, all potentially hid enemies. We couldn't find a way through and soon were trapped.

I called my fixer, Hosnain. Unflappable, he was with us in minutes, guiding us through backstreets, his eyes darting about, feeling his way forward. We passed scenes of strange calm amid the chaos: platoons of national security forces standing by doing nothing; and a squad of the don's armed men waiting in the shade of a line of trees for the order to go into action. We made it through a cordon to the sanctuary of the Court, where we met some less fortunate lawyers, with jaws and heads smashed by the don's men. Hundreds of lawyers milled about chanting slogans, receiving news on their mobile phones about the engulfing violence. Activists, wearing black suits, ties and white shirts, talked passionately about the pros and cons of *suo moto* legal powers. Violence didn't stop the serving of lunch, flirtation, and laughter.

By the end of the day, the shooting had stopped. The toll was forty-two dead, including an ambulance driver from a charity, and hundreds of people wounded. Bloodstained corpses lay where they had fallen: bowing over the ledges of motorway bridges, hanging out of cars, blood dripping from sleeves and heads. Bodies were piled up on morgue trolleys.

Where was the man orchestrating the bloodshed? More than 5000 miles away, speaking to his followers by telephone from London. I went back to the hotel, and lay down on my bed, queasy with the ease, nearness and narrowness of death, waiting for sleep to come, tinged with self-disgust for being part of it all. The former Chief Justice had not got beyond the airport.

Chapter 12
Season Change

Towards the end of July the temperature had soared to 52 degrees C in parts of the country. The earth was baked, cracked and parched. I'd returned to Islamabad to cover the news of the lawyers' push against Musharraf.

After my failed attempt to run Pir Pagara to ground in Karachi, I'd asked third parties to try to arrange for me to meet him. I was waiting for my quarry like a hunter who has set a trap.

My house was overrun with geckos. They often landed on the floor or the bed with a thud, bloated by the abundance of flies and midges on which to feast. Mosquitoes, cockroaches and rats were never far away. Mini-vans equipped with DDT cylinders sprayed clouds of white gas over public roads and parks as part of anti-dengue-fever drives.

Terrible events had just taken place. After weeks of provocation, Pakistani Special Forces had stormed Islamabad's Red Mosque. More than a hundred people had been killed. I joined a group of journalists on a tour of the mosque after the eight-day assault. It had been reduced to a bullet-riddled, fly-infested pit, smeared with charred human remains and littered with bricks and crushed ammunition cartridges. There were always more questions than answers. How had the situation been allowed to fester for so long, to enable militants to create such a heavily armed hub under the ISI's nose? Had the cock-up factor played a key role or was it orchestrated to play up the militant threat?

The siege had provoked further revenge attacks. In Swat, Radio Mullah had finally launched his insurgency. The angle of the country's decline had steepened.

*

There had been minor sadnesses and joys in my household. Basil the cook, a wily Christian survivor from the toughest gutter of Pakistani life, was inured to the season's travails; but Allah Ditta suffered sleepless nights because his own *mohalla*, or district, was permanently without electricity, and so without fans to fight the heat.

Our conversations inevitably returned to the question of the broken municipal transformer that was at the root of the problem. The nights were full of crying children, Allah Ditta said. Young sons and daughters fanned elderly people to try to help them survive heat. No rich or influential people lived nearby so nothing was going to happen about the transformer. I telephoned a minister whose constituency was Rawalpindi. He made all the right noises but nothing happened.

Allah Ditta's young son contracted a fever. One evening before he went home he asked for a small shot of brandy, which might have been for the child or for his own peace of mind. I gave it to him and advised him to consult a proper doctor, not the ones who charged Rs 100 for an injection that was most probably water. The next morning Allah Ditta came in full of bounce, joyfully reporting that a lorry had crawled into his district late at night carrying a shiny mechanical phoenix: a new transformer. Once again electrical fans were whirring and television sets blaring. He said that it had been done at the behest of the minister with whom I'd spoken, and Allah Ditta was the toast of his neighbourhood. As at every worthy celebration, 'sweets were distributed'.

The summer was not without pleasure. Nothing quite defines the season (*mausam-e-garma'or* – hot season) like a mango. The intense heat does wonders for the mango tree. The fruit ripens in its skin, plumping out to fat, green paisley shapes. The first crop is taken off at this unripe stage, while still called *ambi*. Chutneys and juleps are made and the *ambi* is cut, dried on rooftops and steeped in mustard-seed oil for *achaar* to last for the year. Mango bugs, chalk-white, appear everywhere, leaving entire driveways and gardens stained with yellow paste wherever they are crushed. Soon the last *ambis* turn to *aam*, a mango in all its glory. Truckloads arrived from southern Punjab and Sindh. In the countryside mango festivals were held. Landowners dispatched mangoes in wooden crates stuffed with straw to friends and family. I usually received a crate from a relation of the Begum. Allah Ditta and Basil gave me one or two out of thirty and ate the rest themselves. For days they lounged about in a sticky stupor.

We frequently had to top up our water tank. Mafias ruled in these urban areas and charged exorbitant amounts for a tanker full of brackish liquid. People secretly installed pumps on water mains to siphon off enough for their use. Kinder people in affluent neighbourhoods left earthenware pots outside their gates for poor passers-by to drink from. As a result of the heat, my garden had dried up and crows and mynahs could be seen fighting in angry hops around shrinking puddles after the gardener had watered the plants. Smells abounded. Watermelon vendors injected fruit to make it heavier, and dysentery, malaria, hepatitis and typhoid spread through the slums at alarming rates.

The dry spell invites *andheris*, stupendous thunderstorms with veins of lightning and powerful winds that carry tonnes of dust and fell trees. We were caught in such a storm in the car one day and, as in a cartoon, a hundred yards of wall and trees collapsed behind us as we sped away. Allah Ditta was delighted to see my open-eyed fear. '*Koi bat nahin*, don't worry', he said. '*Mausam* change.' It's just a change in the season.

*

Allah Ditta arrived at work one morning badly shaken with a black eye and bruised ribs. He was listless, with haunted eyes; the spring had gone out of his step. After much digging (and help from the Begum in support of my shaky Urdu and my even shakier grasp of Pakistani domestic realpolitik) it became clear that some of his cousins, jealous of his newfound 'wealth', had beaten him up in the course of trying to wring money out of him. The police were entirely useless in such matters, and so a friend of mine, a colonel in the all-powerful army, paid a visit to his cousins to instil a healthy measure of fear in them. For the time being it seemed to have worked.

*

Then a brief reprieve: the monsoon. The rain was greeted with wild celebration. It fell in grey sheets, drops so fat and heavy it hurt. The first few downpours were swallowed up in greedy gulps by cracks in the soil. Every time the rain stopped, earthworms – long, brown and mysterious – appeared, squirming and wriggling in the puddles only to shrivel and die before the next spell. Whiffs of fragrant *raat ki rani* ('Queen of the Night'), night-blooming jasmine, ambushed you as you brushed by its branches. Early-morning walkers spread the ends of their *kameezes*, making baskets to collect small jasmine flowers. Strings of them were sold at every traffic light. Husbands and lovers bought bracelets of them on their way home. Magnolias, pink plumeria, claws of red and pink flame of the forest burst from previously dead-looking tangles of branches. In between showers young men spent the long hot nights playing cricket, barricading public roads to use as pitches.

But what scented the north drowned the south. Areas of Sindh were declared disaster-struck as the land flooded. Dozens of people died. Millions set up camp on higher ground, often on the highways. Cattle wandered astray, causing major accidents. And this was a relatively mild year. At this time snakebites kill hundreds as vipers and cobras are flushed out of their underground pits by the waters. The Thar desert comes alive. Verdant green grass springs from its depths, turning huge swathes into meadows where the villagers' livestock feed, making up for the rest of the year's slim pickings. Gypsy women gather wet clay and plaster it on floors and walls.

*

After Islamabad's Red Mosque massacre in July, Musharraf continued to play bridge and made weekly avuncular, cigar-smoking appearances on state television to reassure the citizenry.

But by the end of August, his power was oozing away. The Supreme Court had reinstated the Chief Justice. His American benefactors had warned him not to impose martial law.

Musharraf had become jittery as the return of Benazir Bhutto, and another exiled former prime minister, Nawaz Sharif, seemed imminent. In keeping with the country's ethnic politics, the latter's support was drawn from his own Punjab heartland, the former's mainly from her native Sindh. Musharraf feared they would oust him from power in elections due in two months.

My colleagues and I spent our time glued to the capital, trudging, notebook in hand, among the burnt and bloody remains of suicide bombers and their victims. Concrete barriers and walls had turned Islamabad into a bunker. With heightened political tension and ever increasing violence, conversation narrowed. We endlessly discussed the constitution, judicial process and electoral reform (we had all become, in an ad hoc way, masters of legal Latin); we sucked our teeth and said, 'It's getting pretty serious' and in the guise of praising each other's work, pumped one another for information.

The capital felt more restrictive than ever. The British legation had blacklisted me over a lightly satirical article I'd written about the British Club, which was run by the High Commission in Islamabad, after it had turned down my application for membership, stating that 'journalists cannot be members as they would bring other journalists as guests'. In truth, I didn't want to join the club, a grim place, where Pakistanis were not made welcome; but after hearing of the ban on journalists, I wanted to goad its officers. Though what really did for me with the Brits, it seemed, was that my article had also made gentle fun of the then High Commissioner, Mark Lyall Grant. I had mentioned that the British taxpayer was funding a million-pound pilot scheme to deepen democracy's roots in Faisalabad, a city formerly known as Lyallpur, having been founded by one of his Victorian ancestors.

On the day of the column's publication, I received a telephone call from the High Commission. 'You've made us look like a right bunch of wankers,' said a strained voice.

There were to be no more lunches 'on the Queen', as the press officer described beanos paid for by the taxpayer, nor briefings from the Viceroy. The British legation dropped me as fast as a frisbee covered in dog turd.

Shortly afterwards, the sozzled wife of a diplomat accosted me at a party. 'You've ruined a special relationship and your life here,' she spat. 'You'll never get on.' Calmly, though drunkenly, I told her that I had subcontinental blood and wasn't going to worry about not hearing from a bunch of jumped-up *gora*.

The army had also blacklisted me over an article I'd written about its massive business empire. Apparently the generals were particularly piqued that I'd mentioned a report stating that they owned beauty parlours.

*

After the rains, at the beginning of September, I read in the papers that a massive saint's festival was due to begin in Sindh the next day. That would be reason enough to visit the province, but also I was keen to renew my quest to track down Pir Pagara. And again the province was in the news. Benazir Bhutto had just signalled that her arrival *was* imminent. She would land in her native province and visit her ancestral lands and the tomb of her father.

Benazir, who had been living in Dubai and London, said that she was negotiating the conditions of her return with Musharraf: he must drop corruption charges against her and her husband and give guarantees for her security.

Educated at Harvard and Oxford, she had inherited the political mantle of her late father, Zulfiqar Ali Bhutto, a charismatic, complex feudal who had become Pakistan's most powerful and tyrannical prime minister. He had spotted his daughter's talent and groomed her above her brothers for power. After suffering long stints in jail for opposing the dictatorship of General Zia-ul-Haq, who had toppled and executed her father, she restored democracy to her country after eleven years of military rule. A figurehead for the masses – a legacy of her father's populist socialism – she was also deemed by the West to be a pillar of secularism, moderation and democracy in a region of instability.

However, her two terms as prime minister had been hamstrung by a hostile establishment and sullied by her family's Borgia-like intrigues, corruption and misrule.

We had met a decade before in Sindh. During our recent telephone interviews it appeared she had changed little since then, being by turns imperious and excessively charming.

She said that she could not rule out giving her husband a position in any future government. Asif Ali Zardari – a smalltime Sindhi feudal, playboy and cinema owner with an exaggerated CV and a reputation for corruption – was blamed for many of the ills of her governments.

I asked her if she had learned any lessons since her last stint in power. 'I hope I am more humble,' she said.

Chapter 13
A Rigid Celibatarian

O N THE LONG ROAD from Karachi to the saint's festival at Sehwan Sharif, flamingo-pink and white lotus flowers spangled flooded paddy fields like buttons on a quilt.

In a mist of heat, by the roadside, boy vendors held up bundles of lotus stalks with petal-less heads. An expensive luxury in Sindhi cuisine, they are usually eaten with potatoes. Turbaned herders, submerged up to their necks in the paddy fields, wallowed face-to-face with water buffaloes, like dancers at a fantastical ball.

Accompanied by Declan Walsh, a newspaper correspondent and friend, and driven by a Pathan, Nasrullah, who had the habit of thrusting the palm of a hand towards the faces of other drivers – a signal that means literally 'I blacken your face' and figuratively something coarser, we gunned along at breakneck speed. To the west was a spine of grey barren mountains marking Sindh's boundary with Baluchistan, and to the east the broad, twinkling, grimy, crocodile- and dolphin-bearing Indus.

As we neared the outskirts of Sehwan Sharif, the festival of Lal Shahbaz Qalandar made itself known: roads jammed with overloaded coaches; broken-down cars rolled along by their passengers; packed rickshaws and oversubscribed bullock carts.

Hundreds of thousands of hooting and chanting pilgrims were gathering from across the country: middle-class urbanites with wobbling paunches; tribal women with large nose-rings; Pathans with grey tartan cloaks thrown over a shoulder; Baluch with voluminous turbans; Sindhi landlords in sequined skullcaps. Above all, there were the toothless faces of the impoverished majority.

Nasrullah moaned that the celebration was un-Islamic – he adhered to an Islamic strain that regarded worshipping at shrines as heresy. 'I do not believe in this,' he whinged. Ignoring him, we bailed out of the car and into a heat Declan described as a 'five-knuckle wallop'.

We became part of the wild and odorous human torrent. Some pilgrims danced along barefoot, others crawled on their bellies in the dirt, and some heaved themselves along in wheelchairs. The closer we got to the shrine the narrower the streets became. Soon we were covered in petals and rosewater, our clothes suffused with an aroma of sweat, hashish and animal dung.

Men blowing on spiralling goats' horns, assisted by the contagious beat of a *dolki* drum, led fraternities holding aloft red-and-black lengths of cloth fringed with tinsel and embroidered with Koranic verses. People grabbed at the cloth as they passed, kissing and touching it, hoping to absorb its blessings.

A rolling, exultant wave of noise signalled that we had entered the shrine's courtyard. The main area in front of the mausoleum was lit up like a wedding hall. A crowd of worshippers had gathered in front of the shrine. As if summoned by the tomb in a *danse macabre*, en masse they were reaching a feverish pitch of head whirling and body shaking, obeying the thwacking tempo of the drums.

Men and women danced, hands pumping the air. Every inch of available roof space abutting the courtyard pulsated with revellers. 'It's a fucking rave!' shouted Declan. Eyeballs rolled and pilgrims collapsed, their friends fanning them or splashing water over their faces and then dragging them off to the sides. As the cycle of music reached its climax people slumped to the floor, some beseeching the heavens with open arms, others dropping to their knees to kiss the earth.

We stayed in the courtyard for several hours, admiring legions of matted-haired *fakirs*, wandering mendicant holy men, dressed in red robes and bead necklaces; a group of Hindus with foreheads stamped with *bindi*; and men stripped to the waist and armed with heavy staves. A *fakir* had passed out on the floor, but still clutched a teak truncheon. Troops of dancing transvestites and transsexuals hopped about, their shins greaved and ajingle with clusters of bells. Merry eunuchs cavorted with holidaying prostitutes. Goats were everywhere on sale for sacrifice. People beckoned us to drink tea, smoke hashish and sit with them in comradely communion. As usual at such events, there were said to be hordes of pickpockets at work.

By nightfall everything – hair, clothes and skin – was glistening in an oily slick of sweat and dust. A circle was formed in the centre of the courtyard so that women could dance without being molested. Some of the women rolled their *dupattas* into long scarves; others had abandoned this symbol of their *izzat* (honour). Some wore skin-tight *shalwar kameez*, whirling their long black hair in arcs of sinful abandon. Dancers waved colossal sparklers billowing trails of smoke.

All about was a sensation of massive release, of forgetting troubles and casting off shackles. People ushered and pampered us, welcoming us with smiles wherever we went. There is a common political slogan, *Dama dam mast Qalandar*, which roughly translates as 'endless inspired intoxication for Qalandar'. It stems from this saint and denotes unrestrained agitation either in support of an ally or against an enemy – but here it meant pure exultation.

Suddenly, called by some of the dancers to join them, I leapt into the mosh pit. I am what P. G. Wodehouse would have called 'a three-collar man', and was soon drenched, sending tracer rounds of sweat into the night air. Declan, full of latent mischief, abandoned his usual journalistic propriety and launched himself after me with a beam of delight on his face, a jolly giant hopping about at a fairy tea party.

We sat out the next dance. An alluring young, full-bodied Punjabi woman was casting fruity glances at me. After exchanging smiles, she asked, 'Are you married?' and tapped the side of her nose, the place of the *nath*, the nose-stud of a married woman.

'No.'

'Do you want to come to my house?' she said, cutting the small talk.

I looked at Declan, who frowned. I shrugged pathetically. She looked down her nose scornfully and turned on her heel.

We broke away to find some of the living saints associated with the shrine. But we were sidetracked when we accepted an offer from an old man who motioned us to sit and smoke some hashish from a clay pipe with other goggle-eyed elders. As we lay there in a stupor, even no-nonsense Declan's eyes betraying a faint sheen of whimsy, I wrote in my notebook: 'It feels as if we are all breathing the same sea, becoming a hieroglyphic of a lost language.' I had tapped into the mystic notion of union with the divine and all its creation.

On a balcony above us some local noblewomen with long thin pale Modigliani faces, dressed from head to foot in shimmering silks of cardinal red, looked down on the scene with the self-conscious expressions of penguins sitting in an opera box. We chatted briefly with a lustrous-skinned transvestite called Cheeky.

In a small whitewashed office, part of a honeycomb of sacristies, we found a man who described himself as a secretary to a *pir*. We sat with him on a carpeted floor in a fog of incense. The secretary said the *pir* would be along shortly. He had a small beard and was nondescript except for his endlessly insinuating remarks. He made some slurred and salacious remarks about 'drums helping marriage ... women ... making sex ... faster and faster ... like a bomb...' but he was unable to finish as he was overcome by a laughing fit. He then grew serious and conspiratorial.

'We are the anti-Taliban force. We stand for love, tolerance and the great infinity,' he said. We entered into a theological discussion so heretical and abstruse that even the nimblest of Cairo's professors of divinity would have struggled to grasp: 'Ali, the son-in-law of the Prophet, has 500 names, God has only 99 or 100 names,' said the secretary in between bursts of giggles. 'We are not Shia. We are not Sunni. We are not Barelvi, we are Qalandari and Nowseri. This is a secret word. I am the voice between them. Qalandar is there when Prophet talks to God in the mirage. When Abraham sacrificed his son, Qalandar said I am that goat.'

More giggles.

'Qalandar is the Imamzada. He is the person who makes us to talk to God. We are Momin – *the* people,' he whispered, repressing another mirthful outburst. His eyes bulging, he looked furtively around for eavesdroppers. 'There is too much difference between Momin and Muslim.'

He saw Declan and I exchange confused glances. 'Would you like some whisky and hashish? The laws of the universe are not from any book – you must find other routes...'

Shortly afterwards there was a bustle at the door suggesting the arrival of the saint. Before he entered, a minion sprayed perfumed water in the air and plumped up the cushions on a chair.

Syed Baryal Shah, a burly figure wearing a cream *shalwar kameez* and a red skullcap, had the stubbly chin and moustache of a well-fed bandit. A hazy, rather decadent look in his eye suggested he had planned some great debauch for the evening. At first he spread himself out with some majesty on a tiger-skin rug. Then he moved to the chair from where he could better attend to the troublesome demands of a few of his disciples who filed in, kissed the rings on his fingers, and sat attentively at his feet. Several of them massaged his podgy toes while another held up a silver goblet for him to spit in. Fuelled with Qalandari spirit and other intoxicants, he roamed far from strict interpretations of Islam. 'Qalandar is our god!' he yelled to his disciples. It was not that far in spirit from the case of Hallaj al Mansur, a 9th-century revolutionary Persian mystic, who was beheaded for heresy after exclaiming in a state of ecstasy, 'I am the Truth!'.

The *pir* gave his followers sweets, oils for bone ache and bottles of soda. He waved two fat turquoise-ringed hands over them to conduct some of his power into their marrow. A shaven-headed simple-looking man was hustled on to the floor in front of him. 'He is spiritually sick,' explained the saint's secretary. 'His brain suffers from shadows.' The saint was handed a bowl in which he mixed oil from some tree and a pinch of herbs. He then sprinkled it over the man's head, pulling it violently into his lap and then snapped it back and forth with the palm of his hand. To end the treatment he banged a hand down on the man's head with a loud slap and exclaimed 'Mast Qalandar!'

The saint did not give straight answers to any of our questions, and we got the impression we were cramping his style. He soon got up to leave and scuttled towards his inner sanctum. The secretary invited us upstairs to share a bottle of what he called 'secret green whisky' that 'will help you reach the infinity'. We passed the *pir*'s bedroom, outside which, as Declan noted, were a pair of slippers certainly too dainty and feminine for the saint's big feet.

We left and entered the mausoleum itself. All around the shrine lamps of burning ghee glimmered and pilgrims placed bowls of dark muddy henna with candles in them as offerings. 'This is where Qalandar lives,' a man whispered in my ear. Obeying instructions from the Begum, I offered a prayer to him on her behalf.

On his arrival at Sehwan from his homeland of Central Asia in the 13th century, Lal Shahbaz ('Red Falcon') Qalandar found that the reigning raja was harsh and practised *droit de seigneur*. The saint took him on, often transforming himself into a falcon to perform miraculous feats against him. 'He died seven times and his body parts were cast to four corners but he was returned back to life each time,' a disciple explained. However, the 19th-century British adventurer Richard Burton, ignoring the Central Asian 13th-century saint's magical capabilities, judged his true worth to have been obscured by legend. Lal Shahbaz Qalandar's real name was Usman I Merwandi, and he was a 'great grammarian, philologist, traveller and saint ... a rigid celibatarian'.

The living saints, I thought, had grown fat and corrupt. But perhaps Lal Shahbaz's disciples revered him for his role as a '*Qalandar*', meaning uncut or unpolished, a fearless type of Sufi not bound by ritual or hierarchy. I thought again of *Dama dam mast Qalandar* and wondered whether the word *mast*, derived from Persian and meaning 'intoxicated', was related to the Hindi word *must*, the hormonal season in bull-elephants. The slogan seemed an expression of the region's volatility, the seismic restlessness of a subcontinental faultline. Pakistan's drum was beating ever faster; and this effusion of energy and prayer, an expression of the country's old self, seemed to reflect the gathering pace of events.

*

The next morning we watched glistening, bare-chested pilgrims diving into the earth-brown headwaters of the canal. After a few hours the town was deserted. The bloated carcase of a goat floated on the river. A dying donkey, abandoned in a salty wasteland, struggled to get up on to its forelegs, staggered, and collapsed in a halo of dust.

My notes from the festival, made partly illegible by the sweat of the dance, to this day smell of perfumed water and petals.

Chapter 14
Prophecies

WITH NASRULLAH DRIVING like a demon as usual, we blazed through the heat for several hours before reaching Larkana. The ancestral town of Benazir Bhutto was in the doldrums and had been since she was ousted from office a decade before, when the flow of her patronage, a local benefit of her holding national office, had dried up.

We stayed at the Sambara Hotel, a Bhutto-founded, single-storey block that had also fallen on hard times: there was no electricity, the swimming pool was in ruinous condition and we were ushered into the only habitable room.

In town, we found members of the Bhutto clan desperate for the *Mohtarma*, a reverential term for Benazir, to come home. Any penetrating questions about how lingering corruption allegations against her might undermine her suitability for re-election were batted away. 'We are her blind followers,' they assured us.

As Declan tapped away on his laptop in our dusty lodgings – he was always working, a worry for a fellow correspondent – I peered out of the grimy window to watch a peacock strutting in the garden, lulled by the heat and the pleasure of being away from the capital.

Sindh is a place of dreams, reverie. Recently, a little farther north at Sukkur, on an isolated outcrop of limestone rock, a man, having dreamt of a mosque on its heights, built one. Nearby is the leaning, coffee-brick, lantern-surmounted tower of Mir Masum, the artist, poet, historian, alchemist, calligrapher and architect who threw the philosopher's stone into the river to avoid handing it over to his master, the Emperor Akbar. Inspired by such a whimsical spirit, I slipped into a pleasant daydream.

I was increasingly sanguine about my job, my travels and my health: if after a year and a half of travelling and reporting in Afghanistan and Pakistan I hadn't come a cropper, then I must be a rare case. I simply took my pills as one would take vitamins and gave my condition no further thought.

This was to be as far as I would wander from the daily worries about my health – the farthest from that day in a Dublin hospital years before when I'd repeated to myself the word 'dialysis'. It was a malevolent, terrifying word, which in my boyhood I'd once overheard my mother use when describing some nightmarish, isolating and imprisoning illness that had befallen one of her friends, but would surely never trouble me.

In truth I had merely suppressed the fear of my illness returning. This latent concern, a fear of being imprisoned again, galvanised my urge to travel as much as possible, as if I were putting more miles between illness and myself.

All that was far, far away from the broiling surface of Sindh, where I was willingly enmeshed in Pakistan's woes and distanced from my own.

Turning from the window and the peacock, I saw Declan still tapping away and, passing him on the way to the bathroom, I tried, unsuccessfully, to catch sight of what he was writing.

*

The 130-feet-tall, domed, whitewashed *faux*-Mughal Bhutto mausoleum dominated a shimmering expanse of Benazir's farmland.

'Like Taj Mahal,' said a Bhutto minion, working at the mausoleum. Also a worshipper there – at the apex of the Bhutto cult – he wore a photograph of Benazir strung round his neck like a tag identifying an unaccompanied minor on a flight. Often the Begum's phrase, 'it's a tough country', came back to me. In an impoverished, corrupt, volatile land, revered leaders, imbued with imaginary sacred powers, offered a semblance of security and a promise of patronage.

Sections of the mausoleum were under bamboo scaffolding. Workmen were plastering and painting it as fast as they could ahead of Benazir's return. It was an immense marble testament to the Bhutto ego and tragic family history. Benazir's father, who had been hanged, and her two brothers – one mysteriously poisoned on the French Riviera, the other gunned down by police during his sister's tenure outside the family house in Karachi – lay interred under the dome. Colourfully patterned *chadors* or sheets covered the three tombs, which were engraved with Koranic verses.

Bhutto Snr, a '*shaheed*' or martyr, had initially offered hope. With his populist slogan of '*Roti kapra makan*', 'bread clothing and shelter', he had promised the downtrodden peasantry he would break the stranglehold of his own caste, the 'feudal' elite. Instead, he had focused on staying in power, locking up his opponents and crushing a Baluch insurgency.

But Benazir's troubled terms in office, however lacklustre, had kept the Bhutto flame alive. She had escaped further political vendettas after her last term ended amid allegations of corruption by going into self-imposed exile. Her husband, Zardari, who had been released after eight years in jail on corruption charges, was now living apart from her, in America, where he said he was receiving medical treatment.

What sort of welcome her followers would give her was uncertain, but if it were rapturous, her presence would rock the country's status quo and further weaken Musharraf's grip on power.

Staring at the tomb of her father, I recalled an earlier visit to it. My brother, Chev, and I had joined Benazir in her car during one of her election campaigns. As part of her cavalcade we travelled through northern Sindh on our way to the mausoleum to commemorate the anniversary of her father's death. We had passed from village to village, people waving petitions at her or trying to post them through the cracks at the top of the car's windows, faces pressed against the glass.

Such was the force of the persona she put on display, a blend of bizarre mysticism, evasion, charismatic power and awkwardly deployed feminine wiles, the memory made me feel faintly awkward.

Inside the car, Benazir had put a foot up on the dashboard to paint her toenails. 'I used to make a very nice date pudding,' she said as we passed a grove of date palms. It felt odd to be close to such an iconic face: pale, high cheekbones, dark eyes, straight, long nose and full lips, a look that catty high society ladies said had been created by a cosmetic surgeon's knife.

At one point, she rotated a string of prayer beads, muttering an incantation over and over. 'I can't tell you what the prayer is. A Sufi gave it to me. After all I've been through, prayer and meditation help still the mind. I have been born in the land of the mystics. My family has always gone to their shrines. I'd *love* to become one myself.'

'You have the potential to be a Sufi,' she followed up, smiling archly at me. 'I think you could be a little Sufi. I was in jail when I was your age. It made me more aware of these things, the hidden side of life.' She talked animatedly about voodoo and fatalism. She was representative of the old mixed culture of Pakistan, whose tolerance of heterodoxy was particularly strong in Sindh, a place suffused with Sufi spirit, where the lines between Sunni and Shia, Muslim and non-Muslim blurred. But she gave me the impression that her personal faith was primarily a tool to further her political gains.

Rivalries were all around her. Her brother, Murtaza, had died in a shoot-out with police in Karachi in 1996 when she was in government. Shortly before his death, she had made clear her displeasure at his attempts to share the family mantle of power. Her husband, Asif Ali Zardari, was also rumoured to have feuded with him and had been accused of complicity in his murder.

I asked her about this allegation, but instead she replied as if I'd criticised her husband's breeding. 'I am shocked when people say "cinema owner". Asif's father was a banker!' She ruffled her *dupatta* over her head, indignant at the thought. 'His great-grandfather was an inspector of prisons under the British.'

After she was ousted from office in 1996, rumours surfaced that Benazir had a Surrey mansion stocked with furniture and antiques sent from Karachi. Benazir and her husband denied owning it. But then it was discovered that Bhutto family heirlooms, hidden in crates labelled 'mangoes', had been dispatched to the house. 'These may or may not be ours, but...' she had said. 'Why don't people know I was already rich? I come from one of the oldest families from this area,' she spat. 'And now I have only what is left in my handbag.'

She changed tack again. 'I find that a lot of people are obsessed with me. They are so obsessed with me it becomes like a drama.'

'It's the Bhutto name,' I offered.

'No!' she boomed. 'It's not the name. It's not because of my *father*. It's because of *me*. People are interested in *me*.'

Later that day, in the sprawling home of a Sindhi landlord, Benazir's charm reserves ran low. Perhaps due to tiredness or the side-effects of medication (some close to her had later suggested she may have been on tranquillisers), she was wild-eyed and unsteady on her feet as we gathered in a big hall where men sat on chintz sofas deployed functionally around its edges. No sooner were we all seated than she launched into a tale that quickly became an angry harangue. She accused me of being part of a 'colonial conspiracy'. I had told her that my grandfather, as a young officer, had played a brief and unsuccessful role in scouting for the renegade Pir Pagara in the early 1940s. Perhaps her harangue was intended as an amusing conversation piece, devised purely in response to the pressure of being the one who always must command an audience. But she rambled strangely, confusing and conflating stories we had told each other during the day.

'Your grandfather killed Pir Pagara. Admiral Ahsan [a friend of my grandparents, a deceased Pakistani naval officer, whom I had mentioned also in passing – I later learned he was opposed to her father] threw his body into the sea. And so you kept us natives in our place!'

Chapter 15
Return of an Empress

IN MID-SEPTEMBER an aged assembly of *mullahs* announced the start of Ramazan, the local name for Ramadan, after sighting the new moon, which marks the start of the month-long Muslim fast.

I'd had to return to Islamabad and again abandon my hunt for Pir Pagara, as Musharraf, Britain and America stepped up horse-trading over Benazir's return.

There was a warm festive atmosphere in Islamabad. People filled the supermarkets to stock up on groceries, and there were frantic consultations over what quantities of dates, kilos of sugar, tons of *sooji* (semolina) would suffice for a household.

Beggars buzzed like flies outside stores. It was the season of giving and all manner of mendicants arrived at my doorstep, including transvestites whose special status confers upon them both privileges and ignominy. It was considered bad luck not to give them money for fear of one being born into one's own household. Fresh from an afternoon nap, it was a jolt to be greeted by false breasts, bouffant wigs and suggestive faces.

During the holy month, offices and businesses open an hour or two later and afternoon siestas are common. Old patriarchs retreat to rural sanctuaries to fast and meditate. Even those who didn't pray regularly strictly adhere to their prayers. Although I don't think Allah Ditta changed his religious habits much. No one thinks anything of blocking a busy road for the afternoon prayer by putting up a *shamiana* or tent in the middle of traffic.

The days themselves were turned on their heads. Before *iftaar*, the sunset 'breakfast' that signals the end of the day's fast, people started to slink home. Traffic swelled. Then as the sun disappeared vendors' voices became louder, as they pushed carts of freshly fried *samosas*, *pakora* and *jalebi* through the capital's markets. The first foods to be eaten to break the fast are dates. Fights broke out at intersections as drivers jostled to get home. Each year that I was in Pakistan the feast edged closer to the heat of mid-summer, and there was a great deal of thirst, hunger, foul breath and bad temper. Roads emptied five minutes before the *azan*, the call to prayer, and a lull descended. Perhaps at no other time do people eat quite so much as during this month of fasting. As soon as the *muezzin* cleared his throat, millions of hungry mouths reached for that first morsel, closed their eyes, and thanked God it was one day closer to its culmination at the feast of Eid.

*

A few days after the end of Ramazan, on October 18, 2007, Declan and I were back in Sindh for the arrival of Benazir at Karachi airport. Her plan was to travel into her family's heartland and offer prayers at her father's tomb. I planned to go along and then head east from Bhutto country to Pir Pagara's lair at Pir jo Goth.

Benazir's cavalcade was greeted by tens of thousands of ecstatic supporters, who hung from trees and clambered up buildings to catch a glimpse of her. They came despite death threats made against her by Islamic militants and opposition to her return from Musharraf's supporters. Political rallies in Pakistan were often spiced by the latent threat of violence. The atmosphere was charged with an apprehension of danger and excitement.

But the Bhutto name had lost none of its talismanic power.

As she stepped from the aircraft, a copy of the Koran was held above her head in the Pakistani tradition of blessing a journey's beginning. To tour Karachi's streets, she then boarded a converted shipping-container borne on a truck, bedecked in garlands. Wearing a green-and-white *shalwar kameez*, Pakistan's Muslim national colours, her right arm was bound with religious amulets. I watched the crowds of poor performing the *jelsa*, a political dance, to greet her, some smoking hashish and tippling on homebrew, all the while keeping my eyes open for signs of trouble. On foot, a group of several hundred unarmed young men, volunteers wearing T-shirts with the word *Janisaad*, 'Loyal until Death', formed a cordon around Bhutto's truck, a protective wall of human flesh.

At midnight, having failed to steal aboard her truck and tired from a day among the throng, I hitched a lift on a passing motorbike back to my hotel. I was sipping a gin and tonic, writing up the day's news and watching the remainder of the procession on television, when two massive bombs exploded near Benazir's vehicle. The streets were filled with screaming wounded people, smoke and charred flesh. Over one hundred and thirty people were killed. Benazir survived.

The next day I went to the morgue, where bodies were washed, swathed in shrouds and stacked on three-tiered metal bunks awaiting collection by relatives. Bits and pieces of human remains were filed in boxes filled with ice blocks: here an arm, there a torso or a head. I tried to focus on none of it. The bust of a man lay in perfect repose with a leg leaning over one of his shoulders. Some people had gone to the rally out of political belief, others in exchange for a bag of flour.

'The people who died belonged to the poor classes,' said the mortuary's director, Faisal Edhi. People streamed in and out holding their *shalwar kameez* or handkerchiefs over their noses. I was thankful that children's and women's bodies were stored in a separate room. To see them would have been too much for me. 'They do not see who they're blowing up...' somebody was saying, his voice dazed. 'It's just like the Americans with their bombs in Afghanistan.'

The silence of the mortuary was broken when an angry relative punched the air. 'We will sacrifice ten more brothers for the cause,' he cried. Another man identified the bodies of his uncles, two businessmen who were not party members but wanted to get a glimpse of Benazir. 'They died for nothing,' he said after loading the two corpses into an ambulance.

Afterwards, as I stood outside the morgue with Declan, waiting for a taxi, a man wearing an American baseball cap slowed his 4x4 vehicle as he passed. 'You want democracy?' he shouted, his face a spasm of anger. 'This is what you get, asshole!' He accelerated away.

*

Benazir emerged from the attack with bleeding ears and shock. Her closest acolytes, journalists and family members were all safe, if spattered with blood and gore. When it struck she had been resting her swollen feet in a bomb-proof compartment of the truck, re-writing a speech. But fifty of the young men who had been recruited to act as her human shield were killed.

I went to a press conference she held at her party headquarters in Karachi. Calm, at times buoyant and even jolly, Benazir said she knew who had tried to kill her: 'remnants' of the government of the late Islamist General Zia-al-Haq, who had hanged her father.

Rumours were abroad that Musharraf was linked to the attack, but Benazir was careful not to publicly accuse the man with whom she was negotiating a power-sharing deal. Musharraf's party accused her husband, Zardari, of being behind the bloodshed. It seems unlikely we will ever know the truth.

Chapter 16
Letting Go

T HE POLITICAL CIRCUS, or *bandarka tamasha*, 'monkey show', as
my Memon philanthropist friend called it, moved from Karachi
back to Islamabad and I followed it. Pir Pagara would have to wait. I
found my household in disarray: Basil and Allah Ditta had fallen out
over the use of the car in my absence and it took several days to cajole
the latter back into service.

The Professor alone appeared unaffected by national events. His
only concern was for his sons who had returned from American
universities and had found themselves working in low-paid jobs. There
was an open-mic comedy club, and, for the urban upper middle class,
fashion shows, ice-cream parlours and coffee shops. These were places
where students returning from America could flirt in expensively
acquired accents. Whereas many of their fathers spoke in clipped
British anachronisms ('This chap has gone wonky'), the new breed of
returnee graduate spoke the new international patois ('It's like just so
whatever, dude').

One day, returning home, I received some strange intelligence
from the guard about the Professor. It turned out that he was not
completely alienated from world affairs. The guard said that during my
absence he had twice caught the Professor's servant breaking in to my
house. I sent Allah Ditta to gather further intelligence and he returned
with precious facts. The servant had climbed on to my roof from the
Professor's house and slithered down and twisted through one of the
upper windows. On his first trip he had taken my copy of Musharraf's
unintentionally entertaining autobiography, *In the Line of Fire*. A week
or so later, he had replaced it. After digesting this news I bought a new
copy of the book and gave it to the Professor as a gift and he was very
pleased. From then on I took seriously his complaint about the British
Council closing its libraries in Pakistan.

*

Mausam-e-khazan, autumn, was in the air. Holed up in the capital, I could only imagine the season taking effect elsewhere. Nowhere are autumnal colours as resplendent as they are in Baluchistan and the Northern Areas. Towering oriental plane and walnut trees turn fiery red, then yellow, then bare. The rice plant ripens and servants at the Begum's house take leave to go home for the harvest. The long summer gives way to spells of cool breezes. Noisy air-conditioners are switched off and for the first few days thereafter the *azan* for morning prayers is audible once more.

In Islamabad, cricket pitches were being rolled in preparation for the cooler weather, and hours spent discussing and betting on the coming matches. Grapes, persimmons and pomegranates arrived in the market. With ideal weather, the wedding season arrived. Loud music filled the night.

*

This year, however, unease permeated the country. Musharraf had bowed to Western pressure by allowing Benazir to return, but he had effectively kept her under house arrest since her arrival.

Then in November Musharraf gave a television address that opened with the words '*Meray aziz humwatno* [My dear countrymen]...' an expression well known to Pakistanis as the standard salutation at the beginning of all previous announcements curtailing their freedoms. He imposed emergency rule and (again) sacked the Chief Justice, prompting yet more rambunctious protest by street-fighting lawyers, clutching moth-eaten copies of the much-abused Constitution.

One morning I telephoned Musharraf's office to see how my request for an interview with him was faring. 'Er actually, Bard', came back the voice of one of his generals, 'we are asking you to leave the country.'

Pause.

'I'm sorry?'

'We are expelling you from Pakistan. People are saying that a *poisonous* editorial carried by your newspaper was written by you.'

I vaguely remembered someone had called from the paper in London and read out an editorial, but I was busy, so without listening had said, 'Yes, excellent, absolutely, it sounds good to me,' to get him off the line.

'What did it say?' I asked the general.

'The opening sentence said: "Musharraf may be a son of a bitch, but he's our son of a bitch…"'

As he spoke, my eye caught the ticker tape flowing along the bottom of a local news channel broadcast on the television in the corner of the room. There was my name and those of two other journalists from the paper, saying we had been expelled.

Within minutes, there was a knock at the door. It was a Western reporter with an anguished look of sympathy on her face, asking if I was OK, her notebook and pen clutched behind her back.

There was some confusion at the newspaper. To meet the demands of the multimedia age, the management had recently sacked almost all of its veteran foreign correspondents. Older heads, hearing that the expulsion order was an effort by some senior officials to curry favour with Musharraf, suggested I ignore it. But the office in London thought it wise to deal with it as a 'diplomatic incident'. The new foreign editor called to say that I must 'withdraw' because of his concerns that the phrase 'son of a bitch', referring to a dog, might offend Muslim sensibilities, and therefore lead to me being beheaded. 'Do not mention this to anybody professionally or in your private life,' he added, mystifyingly. The newspaper had called on all British media to cast a blackout over the news of the expulsion, citing security reasons. I could not imagine why.

While I was in London, Musharraf resigned from the army in the hope that he might stay on as a civilian president. He gave a hesitant speech and had a few problems removing a ceremonial baton from its brass fittings.

The following month, in December 2007, Benazir Bhutto was assassinated during a political rally in Rawalpindi. I found out while walking in the hills in Ireland. The news filled me, as it did everybody else, with despair.

*

Gifts of strategically directed bottles of whisky and a grovelling letter of apology from the newspaper finally did the trick: I was permitted to return to Islamabad. In mid-January, Allah Ditta greeted me at the capital's airport with such a large bunch of hideous orange flowers that it took me a while to spot him hidden behind them.

Since Benazir's assassination, a veil of gloom had lain as heavily as the winter fog over Pakistan. Blobs of rain hung like buds from tree branches, giving Islamabad a thickly maudlin air. So many people had seen the assassination coming, and yet it had still happened. With the 'hidden hand' or 'dark forces', there was powerlessness. Conversations at dinner tables or with taxi-drivers all revolved round the same questions: Was her husband behind it? Was it Musharraf and the military establishment? Or was it the militants? Or was it India? The truth would probably remain alongside the country's other unsolved mysteries.

Benazir's controversial husband, Asif Ali Zardari, had taken charge of her party and there was a possibility it might gain power in the elections, which had been delayed by Benazir's assassination. The couple's gawky British-educated son occasionally appeared at his side to reassure followers concerned about dynastic continuity. On posters in the North-West Frontier Province, whose inhabitants set great store by virility, a moustache was photoshopped on to his face.

*

My expulsion had knocked me off course from my travels and it took a few weeks after arriving back in Pakistan to regain my bearings. I momentarily gave up all will to work and resorted to drinking gin and reading *Kidnapped, Treasure Island* and *Wind in the Willows*. There was a colour advertisement carried in the English-language Pakistani newspapers at the time advising alcoholics to seek help. It depicted a gent past his prime, wearing a cardigan, slumped in an armchair in front of the television, a glass of liquid gold catching the light at his elbow. Contrary to its intended message, it seemed to say, '*What to do?* You may as well drink anyway'. It captured Islamabad's low spirits.

Gas load-shedding was the latest sign of utility shortages. The queues at petrol pumps circled the block many times over and snaked down Islamabad's Blue Area.

But all was not gloomy. Handcarts were laden with roasted maize and braziers crackled with chestnuts. Garden parties were held and meticulously pruned roses shown off. Crowds made their way to Data *sahib*'s, Sehwan Sharif's and Abdullah Shah Ghazi's shrines in the cool weather. *Qawwalis* (sessions at which Sufi devotional music is played) and *milaads*, gatherings for the Prophet's birthday, were held while the good weather lasted. The well-heeled flaunted their brocade *jamavaars* (Kashmiri shawls) and Jimmy Choos.

*

Slowly, I picked up the thread of my travels. Once more I activated all my contacts, beseeching them to find a way for me to secure an audience with Pir Pagara, the Sindhi holy of holies. I was fully aware of how slippery he could be. In the 1960s, an English travel writer, Peter Mayne, inveigled his way into his inner sanctum, only to find the enigmatic seer had gone on a crocodile shoot.

At least, with the help of my naval father and the British Library's archives, I'd been able to confirm what had become of the Pir's father's remains after his execution by the British. His body was secretly transferred at night to a ship of the Royal Indian Navy. It was then ferried to a small, uninhabited islet off Baluchistan called Astola ('waterless but infested by poisonous snakes', according to a colonial account), where it was buried with full Muslim rites.

British officials noted that even two months after his burial, despite Pir Pagara's body having been shown to as many Hur leaders as could be brought to the jail, not all his followers believed that their saint was dead.

*

Aware that my search for Pir Pagara might not bear fruit, I began looking for other ways to encounter Pakistan's old roots. I wanted to trace those roots back further in time, to the bedrock of shamanism, which I hoped, in its remote groves, could still be found high in the mountains of the north.

Not long before, in Islamabad, I'd met Adam Nayyar, an academic and expert on Pakistan's Sufism, spirituality, music and dance. He described shamanistic practices that he said lingered among Muslim peoples in the northern mountains, saying that these rites and beliefs were in many cases prototypes of the devotions I had witnessed at Sufi shrines. Due to the encroaching tide of Islamist militancy, he added, people were reluctant to speak of them.

THE MOUNTAINS:
A LOST WORLD

Chapter 17
Corruptus in Extremis

A PRIL, 2008. The heat was again building and the mountains behind Islamabad once more retreated behind a haze and the sword-like leaves of potted plants in my garden were dulled with dust.

Maps and guidebooks on the mountains lay open on my dining table. Ice on the passes was now melting and it was the ideal time to go, but political uncertainty bound me to the capital.

The elections had been bloody, particularly in the North-West Frontier Province, where Pathans bravely turned out to vote despite a wave of bombs that killed scores at polling booths.

Musharraf's political party, which had run a rubber-stamp government at his beck and call, had received a drubbing – contrary to American and British predictions. Benazir's party did well in the wake of her assassination and, supremely dishearteningly for all save himself and his cronies, her husband, Zardari, had returned to Pakistan to take command of the civilian government. He controlled it through a prime minister appointed from the ranks of what was now his party. The opposition party of Nawaz Sharif joined his government as a coalition partner.

Though still president, Musharraf's grip on power was now feeble. Violence, in the form of suicide attacks, assassinations and bombs, was striking fear in cities across the country as militants, who loathed both him and Zardari, stepped up their campaign against the army and government.

Rumours began to circulate that Musharraf would resign to avoid being impeached.

*

The politics of my household took another turn for the worse. Basil the cook had recently attained domestic ascendancy. He had levelled allegations of theft against Allah Ditta and to separate them I banned the latter from the kitchen, which left Basil in sole charge of the purse strings and responsible for any future financial discrepancies. Since then there had been a period of uneasy calm. But Basil was bent on Allah Ditta's complete ouster from the household and had kept up a steady stream of insinuation against him, now cocking an eyebrow at a missing amount of money, now smiling slyly at a duty overlooked by his rival.

Things came to a head. At midday there was a crash of pots and pans and a storm of men's voices shouting Punjabi curses in the kitchen and then a woman's loud shriek. I raced in and saw Basil standing at the back door, beyond which several poorly dressed and unshaven men restrained Allah Ditta, his collar and hair awry, as though he had been in a scuffle.

'What's going on? Who are all your friends,' I asked, peering round the corner to where a group of women were huddled over plates of food.

'Allah Ditta he trying to take food sir,' Basil said calmly, with a patronising smile, as ever in control of himself.

'No, sir, Basil he taking *sahib*'s money and feeding his friends,' Allah Ditta broke in, freeing himself from his restrainers' clutches.

'No sir, I feeding peoples with *my* money – no *sahib*'s money,' countered Basil, slick with self-assurance.

I separated them and tried to fathom what was going on. Basil, brandishing his arsenal of receipts, invited me to examine columns of accounts, claiming he was feeding his friends on his salary – to which, as they were clearly poor, and because I could not penetrate his dubious accounting – I could not object. Allah Ditta claimed not only that I was being diddled more than usual but that he himself was being given next to nothing to eat, only the worst cuts of meat and leftovers.

Another compromise was reached. From then on I gave Allah Ditta money to buy his own food and Basil continued to feed his people at my expense, running a charitable food dispensary, a sort of Basilaid, in return for which his guests, I found out later, would give him goods in kind. He knew I couldn't face breaking in a new cook – most of whom were reputed to be up to the same sort of dodge; he knew I only wanted peace; and so he won a little more terrain.

*

Basil also sensed that I had lost some vital power, a thing that I'd not yet realised or admitted to myself. A year or so before, one of my journalistic assignments across the border had ended badly. British adventures in Afghanistan usually end in massacre, harrowing retreat and humiliation. I'd been desperately trying to get to the frontline, harbouring a secret urge to burnish my credentials as foreign correspondent by 'coming under fire', but instead I was 'cas-evaced' – or urgently evacuated – from Camp Bastion, the British desert base in Helmand in southern Afghanistan.

The last *Daily Telegraph* correspondent to be removed from the field in such a way was airlifted out of the Balkans after being peppered by a Claymore mine. I had a bad dose of the runs.

Not that I went without fuss. Delirious with heatstroke and gut disease, I invoked the spirit of Captain Souter, one of six soldiers taken prisoner after the 1842 massacre at Gandamak. He wrapped his regimental colours around his waist as he was assailed by tribesmen wielding long-barrelled *jezails*. I gripped my laptop as I sank, shaking feverishly, on to a camp bed, fearing that if my kidney transplant suddenly failed I would be kaput.

Military surgeons, surprised at the stupidity of someone with a kidney transplant entering such an environment, took me in and kindly and expertly patched me up. Luckily, I hadn't taken up a bed that could have been put to better use. The only serious casualty in the field hospital at the time was an Afghan Taliban fighter whom British surgeons had saved from dying, and who, when he became conscious, leapt out of bed with extraordinary strength and tried to kill the first person at hand.

After three days in Camp Bastion's tented hospital, I was escorted on to a Hercules and flown to Kandahar, where we picked up a wounded soldier before going on to Kabul. The young soldier's bandaged thumb looked as if it had been partially blown off. I sheepishly explained my difficulties and asked him about his injury. 'I fell over,' he replied with a grin.

Having stopped off in Cyprus, we finally disembarked at Brize Norton. A nurse had then accompanied me on a flight from London back home to Ireland. 'I find things go much smoother if we use a wheelchair,' she said by way of introduction. She was clad in a white uniform with a blue cardigan while I sported a de rigueur Afghan beard and a wild 'psychiatric' look. We had an entire corner of a busy Heathrow sub-terminal to ourselves. I cursed my bowels.

I thought I'd escaped without any long-term damage. But unknown to me the disease, dysentery or whatever Afghan lurgy it was, had weakened my immune system and now I was suffering increasingly from bouts of illness.

*

The mountains were beckoning ever louder, and I asked my brother, Chev, if he would fly out to see them with me.

On the morning of his arrival, we discussed whether or not, given the volatile political atmosphere, we should risk the longed-for trip into the Hindu Kush, at a time when Musharraf might suddenly resign as president.

A few days later, we scooped up maps and guidebooks, shovelled them into knapsacks, and headed for the hills.

Chapter 18
Land of Mirth and Murder

REPORTS OF 'A TOURIST'S SHANGRI-LA' had tempered my enthusiasm for visiting Chitral, a small town gathered around an old fort on a bend in a river high up in the Hindu Kush. I expected to dislike it. How wrong I was.

The exhilarating, at times stomach-churning, twin-prop flight from Peshawar heralded some of the wonders to come.

Flying over the northern mountain border of Swat, the tallest mountain in the Hindu Kush range, Chitral's white-topped mountain deity, Tirich Mir, came into view over the pilot's epaulettes, a belt of cloud around its waist. Before we dipped down on to the steep-sided green valley floor, we caught a glimpse, north towards China and east towards India, of a spectacle that perhaps only polar landscapes can rival: hundreds of snow-capped peaks lit by bronze sunlight, and above and beyond them, effortlessly remote and numinous, Karakoram and Himalayan giants.

Clambering down on to the tarmac of an airport that was similar in scale and languor to an Irish market town bus station, lungfuls of mountain air and the slow spacious movements of the local ground staff set a calm, dawdling pace.

Our little crowd of passengers – all Pakistani, perhaps here for business or to visit family – appeared suddenly drowsy after landing in this silent, upland world. Quietly they picked up their suitcases and dispersed into the cool thin air, leaving Chev and me sitting on our bags, pleasantly dumbfounded by our sudden arrival in a place aloof from the apoplexy of the plains.

Above us were the mountains of the Hindu Kush, which runs west into Afghanistan and east towards the edge of the Himalayas and the Karakoram, separating Central Asia from South Asia, part of an ethereal world of glaciers, meadows, valley kingdoms and high passes over which pilgrims and merchants have trudged for thousands of years.

'Is it really *this* good to be here?' asked Chev. 'Or just relief that we survived the flight.'

An hour later, we were trundling in a jeep away from the town, past stone walls and farms, mountains all around us, towards the Hindu Kush Heights Hotel, built into a ridge overlooking the valley.

Its owner, Siraj ul Mulk, a scion of the family that had until recently ruled Chitral, welcomed us into a low-key sanctuary of cleanliness, Persian rugs and carved wooden pillars. The antithesis of princely pomposity, he was dressed in an old tweed jacket, corduroys, trainers and a Chitrali *pakol* (an itchy, woollen flat hat with a rolled rim all the way round, sometimes worn with a feather). In his sixties and of medium height and build with thick greying hair, his brilliant eyes seemed to hold much back. An amused smile was never far away. His craggy profile spoke of a life lived with pleasure. His unhurried passion for his family's old kingdom quickly became infectious.

Later that morning, we sat out on a verandah colonnaded with slender carved wooden pillars, soaking up the panorama of the hazy valley and its shallow fast-flowing river, breakfasting on perfectly cooked, unspiced omelettes and succulent sticks of asparagus.

Apart from us, the hotel was empty. Cut off for four months of the year by snow, Chitral is accessible by land only by hazardous jeep journeys over the tops of two passes, or through war-torn Afghanistan. Flights do not operate during the winter and even in other seasons are often delayed due to poor visibility. Although the troubles besetting Pakistan had not yet reached here, Siraj told us wearily, their proximity put off many potential visitors.

In the spring warmth of April, it was impossible to imagine snow as deep as a horse's belly, despite the presence of a small fireplace in the corner of our room and a powdering of snow on some of the higher ridges.

Siraj described some of the people who stayed with him in more peaceful times: a flock of pilots had flown here in a squadron of single-seater aircraft from Britain; the son of a London billionaire had arrived on the back of a local bus to sample the famed local hashish; mountaineers; hang-gliding enthusiasts; British people with a penchant for battlefield tours and a bearded Robert De Niro, whom Siraj said he had not recognised until the actor had identified himself.

'I wish I could say Osama bin Laden had stayed here too,' he added wistfully, in his dry, husky voice. 'It would be excellent for business.'

Recently there had indeed been rumours that the Arabian fugitive had sought sanctuary in the mountains of Chitral.

Siraj said that he and his family, although dethroned when their princely state was merged into Pakistan in 1969, worked hard by whatever legitimate means to preserve their former kingdom's peace and culture. He expressed concern about the fate of the country as a whole, adding that many of his generation were already 'yearning for a country that was disappearing, one which the younger generation, teenagers, would never know'.

Chitral falls within the Pathan-dominated North-West Frontier Province (since my travels the province's name has been changed to Khyber-Pukhtunkhwa: 'Khyber – land of the Pathans', the name is an affront to its many non-Pathans). But it is culturally and ethnically distinct from it. Its people are peaceful.

Siraj spoke of the threat posed by the troubled Pathan-dominated parts of the province to his area's peace. He explained that the locals, ethnically, were Kho, speakers of Khowari. Known as Agha Khanis, they belonged to the Aga Khan's Nizari Ishmaeli Shia Muslim sect, which here had adopted some of the ancient shamanism and ritual of the Hindu Kush and become a faith apart. Locals viewed both Shia and Sunni with some ambivalence. They believed in the transmigration of souls and they had their own mystical, ethical and metaphysical books (mostly written by their mystic, Khusro). Any elder could perform a marriage ceremony; people freely drank wine; and they were not fussed about the manner of slaughtering animals. At all this my ears pricked up, thinking that the traces of shamanism, for which I'd come looking, were within easy grasp.

But now, Siraj said, an increasing number of Pathans were migrating to Chitral, raising fears that they would bring their violence with them.

After breakfast Siraj and the cook walked us through the warm sunny garden. Fruit blossoms wafted a heady perfume about them, the strongest aroma coming from a *shinjoor*, which resembles an olive tree and bears an edible brown berry.

The cook, a burly, gentle man, perhaps recognising a kindred soul in Chev, was soon kneeling under bushes, lifting branches, and holding leaves in the tips of his fingers, showing him the secrets of the garden. He pointed to a scattering of purple wild tulips by some graves, a sign of life reborn after a winter under snow.

He talked excitedly of two of his favourite mountain products, *thikh* and *manghol*, grassy vegetables, which shepherds bring from the high pastures down to the bazaar at this time of year.

This prompted Siraj to tell the story of how, during a visit to Chitral in the 1990s, the then prime minister, Benazir Bhutto, had taken a liking to *manghol* and he had given her a box full of it to take back with her to Islamabad.

'I remember this incident,' he said, rubbing his chin with a suggestion of reticence, 'because of the huge trouble and interrogation I was subjected to before the airport and security agencies allowed the carton to be loaded on to the prime minister's aircraft.'

'Perhaps they feared another case like the exploding mangoes,' I replied, referring to one of the most notorious incidents in Pakistani history. A crate of mangoes, now suspected by some conspiracy theorists to have contained hidden explosives, was loaded on to the flight carrying the military ruler Zia-ul-Haq, which mysteriously crashed shortly after take-off, killing him and thirty others in 1988.

'By mentioning the case of the exploding mangoes,' he added, with a penetrating look at me, 'you have hit the nail on the head. That is precisely what the agencies had in their mind when I was being grilled. Even her aircraft was the same type, a Hercules C-130.'

There was something odd in his manner.

*

Chev and I sat for the rest of the day on our bedroom's carved wooden balcony, dozing, chatting and reading. The tensions of the past few months, which had crept into my limbs without my knowledge, seeped away. On the plains, we were all a little on our guard, suspicious of strange sounds and people; here there was nothing but air and freedom.

In the evening, we looked down on stone-walled fields bordered by the youthful Chitral river, and listened to cow bells clanking, the commands of women organising their cooking fires, and children's voices, as the sun flared, bowed and exited behind a bulge of mountain whose cold shadow drove us back inside for supper.

Over stewed goat's meat and potatoes, Siraj told us that he had once been a soldier and an airline pilot. But the crashed Pakistan International Airlines aircraft we had seen abandoned and rusting at the end of Chitral's airstrip, he had skidded to a halt a decade or so earlier and decided to stay at home, barricaded away in this refuge. We could spend a few days here, he said, and then go to meet his father, a legendary old man of the mountains.

*

That night I started on *The Making of a Frontier* by Algernon Durand, a copy of which I had picked up in Islamabad, thinking it was a description of how the Afghan–Pakistan border had been drawn. It was far more than that.

Written by one of the first British officers posted to the northern mountains in the 19th century, it described a trove of pre-Islamic customs still extant during the colonial era: a land of hidden butter vaults, slaves, winter solstice feasts and cellars of jars brimming with wine. In places people dressed in cloth woven from the great vulture and ibex skin, which gave the wearer a strong goaty smell; men competed to lop off the heads of a bullock with a single blow; infidelity was not regarded as a grave offence; dead bodies were burnt, dressed in all their finery, instead of buried; there remained relics of fire worship; rulers, protected by guardian fairies, possessed magic drums with which they could produce rain, and conducted trials in which the accused was obliged to walk seven paces holding a red-hot axe-head without dropping it, or be pronounced guilty.

The early British frontiersmen had loved Chitral and its people. They nicknamed it 'The Land of Mirth and Murder'.

Durand recorded that the ruler's great-grandfather – one of Siraj's forebears – had married a fairy and their offspring, a daughter, had still been alive during his visit, dwelling on the flanks of Tirich Mir, where fairies, our host had said at dinner, even now still meet by a large flat stone on Fridays.

I turned its pages briskly, wondering how much of that world still survived and how much of it we would see the next day when we visited a non-Muslim community, the Kalasha people or, as they are sometimes known, the Kalash Kafirs, the Kalash infidels.

*

Before turning off the light to sleep, I noticed Durand's book contained a translation of a Chitrali ditty: 'A bulbul has alighted on the turf for shade/I am ready to be cooked like an onion for you ... Your cuckolding husband touching your milk-white neck/Is like a fly defiling cream'.

Chapter 19
Infidels

IN THE MORNING, on the way to the Kalasha pagans, we stopped off in Chitral town at the bachelor bungalow of a well-known relic of the British Raj.

Geoffrey Langlands, the 91-year-old headmaster of a local school, had 'stayed on' in the newly created Pakistan, after colonial rule had ended. He was seated in an armchair, hunched up in a duffel coat, surrounded by piles of dusty books and pots of pens, reading a *Spectator* from the previous year with a magnifying glass.

'You are the first person to sit there,' he observed. I'd found a seat under a heap of books. Chev remained standing for lack of a chair.

The Major, as he was known, fought in the Second World War as a commando, was later kidnapped by Waziri tribesmen, and survived his adopted country's turbulent early history, including three Indo-Pakistani wars. During one of these he formed a defence militia in Lahore recruited from among Aitcheson College's cooks and gardeners.

Before meeting him, I'd expected that he would be a hearty, minor-public-school type or an irascible colonial like Tusker in *Staying On*. He was neither. He was a sticklerish schoolmaster to the bone.

Speaking in slow, crisply enunciated English, which he occasionally punctuated with '*Aitcha, aitcha*' ('OK, OK') – his only cultural concession from his ironclad Britishness – he described the routine of his life. It was a parsimonious one. He woke at 5am to the BBC World Service news; and an hour later his bearer served him a breakfast of Quaker's Oats porridge, two poached eggs and two cups of Lipton's tea. He enjoyed a single tot of whisky on Saturday evenings (he deemed the local brew of the Kalasha people to be 'very ordinary table wine'); and his salary was £40 a week.

He said he would be delighted to have dinner with us at the hotel that evening.

＊

We bumped southwards out of town and on towards one of the three valleys that are home to the Kalasha, passing foaming streams and woods of oak, walnut, deodar and holly, and countrymen in fields who greeted our driver with a casual wave of a hand.

I was fired by tales of the Kalasha people being as fair as ghosts, of their animist religion, with its Vedic and pre-Zoroastrian borrowings, wife-elopements, clan shrines, wine, dance, rituals of obscene song-singing and exogamous lineages; but also nervous the experience would fall a long way short of this fantasy.

On entering the Kalasha valley, we were met by one of the area's community leaders, Lakhshan Bibi, who invited us to sit on the verandah of a broad-eaved, red-roofed concrete house.

An attractively confident 30-year-old with lustrous dark eyes, fair skin and black hair, Lakhshan did her best to satisfy my illusions.

She wore ordinary grey baggy trousers but also a long Kalasha frock of woven black goat hair, with red edging, worn girdled, and embroidered with cowrie shells. She showed us the rest of her full ceremonial attire: a cap, normally worn over hair braided in five plaits with huge pom-poms like hackles, and a train at the back studded with cowrie shells, buttons, beads, and coin-like metal discs. It was not unlike headdresses across the border in Ladakh in India, where some of the Bacchanalian frivolity also lives on but behind closed doors. She also showed us numerous coils of aquamarine glass-bead necklaces.

Lakhshan was a little awkward about her folkloric garb. She had trained as a commercial pilot, she said, but that career hadn't taken off and now she was working for a non-governmental organisation to develop the area, acting as an ambassador for her people.

After giving us a few small glasses of the local insipid white wine and drams of mulberry and apricot spirit, she spoke enthusiastically of a journey she had made to Macedonia, since some claim the Kalasha are descended from stragglers of Alexander the Great's army.

We discussed the theories about her people's origin. The Kalasha are also thought variously to be: descendants of the Aryans of the Rig Veda who came to India over the northern passes; descended from people who once ruled over the region and whose wooden graves Alexander's troops used for kindling; or the offspring of a group of Greek colonists transported forcibly by Darius, a group that preceded Alexander's foray; or a slave-race once owned by the rulers of Chitral; or refugees who fled from the advent of Islam; or descendants of outlaws who took refuge in these mountains in the last century.

She mentioned some of the old traditions such as mulberry juice tattoos and faces blackened with burnt goat's horn, but like other people here with whom we spoke – with militant Islam on the march in neighbouring areas – she was less keen to talk about the Kalasha's polytheistic beliefs, insisting they had 'one creator god' and that all religions are the same.

Lulled into an alcoholic haze, I was not primed for a theological debate, and concurred that it was all much of a muchness. Chev, sensing that he was on an all-too-well-worn tourist path, had begun cleaning his cameras.

I asked Lakhshan about the Kalasha's future. She replied that her people wanted roads and progress, but also to retain their old customs. A Kalasha convert to Islam had set up a *madrassa* nearby, she complained; a sister and a brother had been converted; the young no longer wanted to sit with their elders.

I looked about us. A sludgy trail of missionaries, charities and tourism was visible across the valley in cheaply built concrete houses. She said Muslim men came to their festivals only to goose unveiled Kalasha women or trick them into dubious marriages. It was depressing.

She then told, in an unconcerned way, a confusing tale about a Pathan of her acquaintance who had recently kidnapped and then released her. Chev and I exchanged glances – and let what seemed a delicate subject drop.

We left Lakhshan and walked up the steep-sided valley overlooking flat, interlocking roofs of tightly huddled village houses with rustically fretted carved doors and lintels. The remains of old Kalasha graves, built above the ground, lay randomly among the trees.

In former times wooden effigies of male ancestors, some mounted on horses, *gandao*, stood over the coffins. But we saw none, apart from one in the reception area of our hotel. Collectors and museums have carted off most of them.

As we climbed a side of the valley, a lush, abundant country of stone water channels and bridges, small neat fields bordered thickly with trees and bushes, perhaps blackcurrant and rose, gave the impression of a land of milk and honey.

But for all its beauty, there was an emptiness in the valley, a feeling that what was left of the Kalasha way of life was being curated, museumified, a claustrophobic sense of the valley being squeezed up against the Afghan border by outside forces.

Evening began to fall and Chev and I turned back towards Lakhshan.

She greeted us with more drams of mulberry and apricot spirit, and I pressed her further about Kalasha lore. But she again raised concerns about the future. 'You must take notice that our valleys are being treated as a no-man's-land between Pakistan and Afghanistan,' she said as we hauled ourselves into the jeep to leave. There were rumours the valleys were being used as a conduit for smuggling *jihadis* over the border. 'This is becoming a land dominated by Muslims and is being sold to outsiders.'

As we drove away, I thought that we had at least caught a whiff of shamanistic ways, which I hoped we would soon find more of among the Muslim communities of these mountains. The Kalasha did still erect totem-pole-like planks of carved wood, sacrifice goats on altars of stone and wave sprigs of walnut trees about as they drank and danced. Siraj said that at a Kalasha festival he had seen lines of men, women and children descend snowy slopes at midnight holding aloft flaming juniper torches.

*

That evening, Major Langlands entered the dining-room exactly at the appointed hour, silver hair parted like a schoolboy, bright blue eyes taking it all in as he made his way to the table, walking stick probing ahead, oversized blazer and shirt and a large tie making him seem smaller and frailer than he was.

'Punctuality is very important,' he announced, as he sat down, grasping the menu. 'It's something that some Pakistanis are not so good at.'

It quickly became clear that he would transmit and we would listen, which was fine by us. He ate and talked prodigiously, far happier jawing about scholastic affairs than telling tales about the frontier.

'Benazir came here years ago when she was prime minister,' he said, blazered elbows up, brandishing knife and fork over a steak like a third former out on an exeat. 'I cut through the crowd and I said to her: "What I want from you is one million rupees for my school." And she gave it to me.'

About his school, which was his life, he was single-minded to the point of mania.

'I will teach until I am no longer able,' he said, pouring more gravy over his potatoes. 'But it would be nice to know things are taken care of in the future.'

He paused and looked up from his plate.

'Ah,' he said, in his wavering, slightly monotonous voice. 'And that's where you come in.'

He was very clear about the publicity a newspaper could give him: he was looking for money to complete school buildings and for an endowment fund 'to run things after I am gone'. An article on the subject would suit us both, we concurred.

After he had got his message across and had seen off a steak, he did speak a little about derring-do.

In the 1980s, when he had taught at a school in the Pathan tribal areas, a Waziri chief, who had taken part in a local by-election and lost, had kidnapped him in the hope that he might have the result overturned. His kidnappers had taken him to an outlaw village, where he met the ringleader's parents who had laid on 'a rather good dinner'.

'They insisted on taking a souvenir photograph with me and later invited me to join them for target practice.' Elders negotiated his release in return for a pledge that his kidnappers wouldn't face punishment.

Undoubtedly, he was brave. There was also something solitary about him, and as the pudding came round, I asked him about his childhood.

He explained, without any self-pity, that he had been born into an impoverished family in the depressed Britain of the 1920s, orphaned at the age of 12 and raised by 'a very ancient grandmother'. He had struggled through school and took evening classes so that he could become a teacher. Then came the Second World War and after serving as a commando sergeant in the disastrous amphibious raid on Dieppe in 1942, he was selected for officer training and dispatched on a three-week voyage in a troopship to the Indian Subcontinent where he had been ever since.

Later, I observed how Pakistanis dutifully looked after him, appreciating his doggedness, honesty and astute grasp of Pakistani affairs; and enduring his headmasterly overtures with forbearance.

To my mind, they saw something of a golden past in him, as well as something of their better selves. He represented not only the self-vaunted, often breached, values of the Raj – decency, honesty, loyalty, etc – but also their own aspirations to those qualities; he was of the Old Pakistan. And they rewarded his steadfast love for their country with their most outstanding gift: hospitality. They looked after him as they would a beloved but slightly querulous uncle.

As supper ended, I asked him whether he would ever go back to England.

'I am one hundred per cent British,' he replied. 'But I do not want to go back. It would be quite dull by comparison. And I could not afford to live there.' It was a sentiment to which I could wholly relate.

His England and the Raj had all gone; but Pakistan had given him an extended life of adventure, much as it had done for my grandmother, and indeed, as it was doing for me.

We ended our evening with Chev and me playing a parlour game of sorts, soliciting his views of his better-known former pupils at Aitcheson.

'Imran Khan [the former cricketer politician]?'

'Mmm, not so good.'

'Jaffar Leghari [our host at the Choti desert fort]?'

'The less said the better.'

After Langlands's departure, the cook, and another hotel worker, a Kalasha, cracked open a bottle of local spirits and soon we were singing and dancing round the otherwise empty dining-room. Hereabouts, at least at present, there was more mirth than murder.

Chapter 20
Fratricidal Tendency

ONE MORNING, Siraj offered to show us Chitral fort. He introduced the idea, saying that it was the site of 'an interesting bit of family history', a phrase that so often prefaces an episode of unremitting tedium.

But in this case it led to a tale of multiple fratricide, the intercession of an imperial power, a siege, two epic marches, several battles, a series of betrayals and the enthronement of his grandfather at the age of 12.

Chev was particularly delighted at the thought of visiting the fort. He was reading about Siraj's family 'incident', an episode in the 19th-century Great Game, when British and Russian officers vied for influence in these intractable mountains, the no-man's-land which then separated their two empires.

*

Hoiking a leg through a hatchway in the fort's solid, metal-plated gate, Siraj ushered us into a courtyard of grand crumbling buildings, *chinar* trees, dilapidated arched colonnades and old Indian lotus-leaf plasterwork embellishments.

At its corners stood rustic, square stone towers and beyond its walls, a backdrop of mountains.

He then detailed the beginnings of the story. The death of his great-grandfather, Aman ul Mulk, in 1892, had unleashed a war of succession. One of his sons, Afzul, happened to be in town and he murdered some of his numerous half-brothers before he set out to kill the real heir, his elder brother, Nizam, who was hunting in the north. But on hearing of his brother's approach, Nizam fled to neighbouring British-controlled Gilgit.

But before the British could help him secure his rightful inheritance, a third contender for Chitral's throne threw his *pakol* into the ring: the late ruler's brother, Sher, who returned from exile in Kabul and, having lured him into a trap, shot Afzal dead at the fort's gates. On hearing of his brother's death, Nizam set out for Chitral with British support and gathered such a following on the way that Sher fled back to Afghanistan.

From the courtyard, Siraj led us past moth-eaten and badly taxidermised heads of a snow leopard, an ibex and a markhor, into a baroquely gilded council hall.

Chev was now in transports of delight. This sort of historical intrigue had long pricked his imagination, but its attraction was compounded by an interest, perhaps natural to an elder brother, in the subject of fratricide.

The hall's whitewashed walls were neatly blazoned with floral murals and not very skilled portraits of turbaned and bearded Chitrali rulers who eyed one another suspiciously across a dining table, trying not to betray, Chev and I fancied, a local weakness for the brotherly kind of murder.

'You see, there was a race to bump off people around you,' Siraj said catching our gazes. 'Because they were trying to bump you off,' he added, as if explaining the rules of a childhood game.

He continued the story: Nizam claimed the throne and held on to power for less than a year when his teenaged half-brother, Amir, killed him while they were on a hunting trip. Nizam had not killed this brother only because the British had asked him not to – fools!

Rightly fearing British retribution, Amir forged an alliance with the ruler of neighbouring Swat, Umra Khan, who started off with 3000 men for Chitral. A British Political Officer based in Gilgit, Major George Robertson, fearing his counterpart in Chitral was in danger and that the Russians might have taken advantage of instability in the crucially strategic state, set out with 400 troops for Chitral, where he removed Amir from the throne, replacing him with the late Aman ul Mulk's second youngest son, the 12-year-old Shuja ul Mulk, Siraj's grandfather.

But, then, perhaps not totally unexpectedly, Sher returned from Kabul, allied himself with the Swat ruler, Umra Khan, and joined the march on Chitral. Robertson was forced to take up a defensive position inside the fortress, and so began the siege on March 3, 1895.

Siraj now led us back into the courtyard and showed us a row of cannon dating back to that year, the charred part of a tower which saboteurs had set on fire, and the place where attacking tribesmen had dug a tunnel in which they had hoped to detonate explosives under the fort's walls, a plan thwarted by a charge of Sikhs under British command. Before long, food, ammunition and morale had been running dangerously low, but unknown to those in the fort, help was on its way in the form of two British forces.

From the south, General Robert Low had set off with fifteen thousand men from Nowshera, defeating Pathan tribesmen in Swat before crossing the 10,000-foot Lowari Pass and entering Chitral.

More memorable still was the role of Colonel James Kelly and a force of 900 irregular mountain warriors from Hunza and Nagar and 400 Sikh Pioneers who were more used to road-building than fighting.

From Gilgit, in the north, they marched 200 miles across some of the world's most forbidding terrain, carrying heavy cannons over the snow-blocked 12,000-foot Shandur Pass and fighting their way down through Chitral. They arrived at the fort first, where they found 'walking skeletons'.

We returned to the council hall, where Siraj began the story's dénouement. Umra Khan of Swat fled, with eleven mule loads of treasure from his palace, into Afghanistan, and Sher was eventually captured and sent into exile in India.

The British had impressed their will on this remote corner of mountain fastness, locking the gates of India against the Russians.

Siraj picked up a framed black-and-white photograph of bearded turbaned tribal leaders, at the centre of whom was seated a slight 12-year-old boy on a throne, his grandfather, smartly booted feet dangling above the ground.

Chapter 21
Old Man of the Mountain

IT WAS LATE MORNING when we struck upcountry with Siraj on the track from Chitral to Mastuj to meet his father.

Soon the scale of the mountainous landscape was so great that at times I almost failed to see entire villages, set up like architect's model settlements on ledges, hidden among clouds of cream blossom. In the valley ahead, lines of poplar trees flashed brilliantly as their arrowhead leaves fluttered in the wind.

At the first village, we stopped to watch a chukka of the tough and scrappy local variety of polo taking place on a rough tract, possibly the equivalent of the municipal square. Villagers were gathered on earth banks and under trees, all seated on their haunches, ready to spring up should the dust-raising scrum of charging ponies career towards them.

For much of the journey, the fairy-abode mountain of Tirich Mir stood centre-stage, a reference point for all Chitral. It was the stunning tower of rock we had seen over the pilot's epaulettes. The British traveller Wilfred Thesiger, recalling a landscape visible from its peak, of grassland, brown patches of bog and glittering water, wrote not long before he died that it was 'probably the finest view I had ever seen in my life'.

It was easy to believe the local lore that fairies visited the mountain on Fridays and used its large flat stones as washboards for their clothes.

This was a country of nimble cragsmen and swaying rope bridges and, at a part of the valley where it narrowed to a bottle-neck, we got out of the jeep and crossed such a bridge to look at the foundations of an old stone *sangar* (a temporary fortified position, latterly usually made of sandbags).

There, Colonel Kelly's men, on their way to rescue Siraj's besieged grandfather, had fought off an ambush by tribesmen as the force made its 200-mile march south along the road we now travelled. Chev said he half expected to come across a fossilised trooper, still crumpled against a low defensive wall, where he had fallen after hearing the echoing crack of a matchlock fired from a ridge above.

We drove deeper into the heartland, Tirich Mir now at our backs. The track followed the course of the Chitral river, which rustled far below.

Shortly afterwards, outside another village, we came across a man up a ladder, replastering an unobtrusive local place of worship, a prayer house that looked no different from other flat-roofed, stone and mud dwellings we had passed. Siraj bantered with him for a while. As we drove off he said the man had joked that he wasn't building a mosque, as was becoming a fashion up here. 'Gulf sheikhs who come here to buy falcons are pumping money and their own ideology into the place and financing mosques with minarets and all,' Siraj said, adding with concern that locals were trying gently to curtail the practice, fearing that new, alien, markedly less dovish beliefs would bring conflict.

Now we were in the midst of a buttressed fortress of gleaming black granite. We left the jeep to climb up on to a flat crag overlooking a sheer drop of perhaps a thousand feet dangling our legs over the edge, and ate a picnic.

Above us on all sides were soaring triangles of sheer grey rock, with snow on their upper reaches. Running between them were upland valleys scooped out by the slow advance of glaciers from which streams poured into a sparsely cultivated strip of valley floor, where a sapphire river hurried below us.

I felt a light-headed disorientation, a weightless suspension. Large birds – golden eagles, bearded vultures, griffon vultures or lammermeier? – hung above chasms beyond which lay darkened valleys.

This echoing cocoon of ice, wind and stone felt like a place of beginnings older than the civilisation of the plains; a place high enough that one only had to extend a hand to reach God.

We walked for hours for much of the rest of the way to Mastuj, free from worries over the future, happily suspended in the remote present. Boys and men, grazing herds of goats among rocky scrubs, rushed to greet Siraj, who set a brisk pace. He had walked and ridden most of his family's old kingdom.

At a hamlet, a family welcomed us with smiles into the enclosed yard of a small mud farmhouse. Its roofs were stacked with drying hay and beyond its walls lay an apple orchard heavy with blossom and lanes where well-fed labradors, terriers and collies – breeds I hadn't seen elsewhere in rural Pakistan – dozed or scampered.

As we neared our destination, we travelled again by jeep but had to dismount several times where the road, cut into the mountainside far above the river, had disappeared beneath an avalanche of shale. We walked over this rubble on foot as the driver, abandoned by us to his fate, inched and lurched the vehicle over rocks, the edges of the wheels often having nothing between them and the valley floor a couple of hundred feet below.

We were near that point on the map where I had first put my finger at the beginning of these travels, on the glacial northern border, what Curzon called the 'southern eave of the Roof of the World'. It's a watershed in the Pamir Mountain Range, from where the rills of the Oxus trickle westward into Afghanistan, and streams, forded by fur-coated, yak-riding Mongols, race in icy streaks to join the Indus. And the freezing rivers are a milky turquoise.

Siraj chuckled as he told how Pakistani military intelligence had recently ordered that a yak-polo festival, played near the Baroghil Pass on the road ahead, be moved to a neighbouring district because it was too close to a CIA listening post. These hardy yak riders – poor, semi-nomadic Wakhi people – complained that the move would entail herding dozens of yaks over a glacier to more distant passes that opened on to lands alien to them.

Up here, Siraj said, it was unlikely you would meet Osama bin Laden, but you might meet a Kirghiz herdsman, an Uzbek émigré or a *mullah* en route to Kashgar, or one of those yak-polo-playing Wakhi.

*

Khushwaqt ul Mulk, the 95-year-old 'King of Upper Chitral', Siraj's father, was a radiantly delightful soul.

At rest, his face fell into a rosy, open-mouthed smile, his eyes half closed. His chin was limned with a short white Abraham Lincoln beard, and his ruddy and relatively unwrinkled face, bereft of worldly anxieties, exuded good health. He wore a neatly pressed oyster safari suit and dark brown tassel moccasins. His trim frame was a study in the benefits, he said later, of mountain air, the company of women, an active life and the moderate consumption of whisky.

After a welcoming glass in a sublime precinct of ancient walnut and mulberry trees, Khushwaqt, the ninth son of the ruler Shuja ul Mulk – the 12-year-old the British had put on the throne after the Siege of Chitral – took us for a stroll around his fort, now just a high-walled shell.

It sat among blossoming orchards and terraced fields bordered with trees yet to come into leaf. He explained why he had moved out of the fort and taken up residence in a small bungalow outside its walls in a beautiful garden: 'We couldn't keep up with the earthquakes.'

He held a dim view of democracy. Jabbing a walking stick at the imposing barren mountains above us, he said gently: 'If you British had not introduced it, these would still be covered with trees,' and then with a gleam in his eye, added, 'you stopped us from using the rod of iron'. The British had prohibited the ruling family from executing illegal loggers. Absolute monarchs, it seems, were ecologically sound.

There were still forests of cedar and pine in the west of Chitral, he said, which the government had designated as a national park, and where urial, ibex, markhor, and a few snow leopards sniffed the air from high crags. Its Marco Polo sheep, he said, which could be found here in the British period, now dwelt mostly beyond the Wakhan in Tajikistan.

We wandered back to the grove and, seated outside the guesthouse where we were to sleep, he chatted about his life. He was a soldier, campaigner for local issues, player of the rough local variety of polo (he had roped Wilfred Thesiger into a game), huntsman (whipper-in with the Peshawar Vale Hunt), and humanitarian; and he had had two wives, the first to whom he had been betrothed at the age of two. He described how even more remote the area had been in his boyhood. He would start off for boarding school on the plains of India with a ten-day journey by horse, crossing the Lowari Pass, to reach the nearest railway station, escorted through these dangerous Pathan lands by the British Political Agent.

Then, after prompting from me, he described how pre-Islamic beliefs in spirits and fairies still prevailed: Shawan is goddess of the high mountains; Shiri the goddess of the cattle shed; Khangi the god of the living-room; Pherothis the god of hearth and Jashtan the god of the watermill. Without the pleasure of these spirits one cannot be comfortable. Fire is used to wish safe travels and a happy marriage; and a handful of barley flour is thrown on relatives to welcome them back after a long journey, or to welcome a new bride or bridegroom to a house.

He said that in neighbouring areas the spirits of malevolent djinns inhabit the bodies of wild goats; shepherd and shepherdess seers, who enter into shamanic trances by inhaling juniper smoke, suck the blood from the necks of recently decapitated goats and are seized by wild fairy spirits; and even centuries after the advent of Islam, the most binding oaths are sworn not on the Koran, but over prehistoric stones.

Smiling at the beauty of so simple a scheme, Khushwaqt added that the Chitrali calendar is divided into periods whose names relate to natural events such as the arrival of wild duck; the time when black marks appear after the melting of snow; the arrival of sparrows; the waving of corn; and the falling of leaves.

There was something about this way of life and the uncomplicated local mindset that appealed to me. In the mountains, doctrines of social control and theology, so layered and wrought on the plains, were pared down to essentials in the same way that winds at high altitude strip back soil to bare bedrock. Paganism flourished beneath a veneer of Islam.

*

Chev and I had supper that evening with Khushwaqt in his bungalow. The walk there was short and glorious: Mastuj stands at the junction of three large valleys, and we stopped, momentarily awed. The mountains, buff and crayon-grey granite at their base, soared to blazing pink-apricot peaks.

After dinner Khushwaqt produced a bottle of whisky, and lying back in our chairs, about as far as it is possible without lying down, we chatted next to a crackling and hissing fire late into the night.

He talked about how he had fought during the Second World War against the Japanese in Malaya and Burma; served as a soldier in East Pakistan (now Bangladesh) and Baluchistan; and worked to shelter Afghan refugees and to develop health, roads and education in Chitral. But he saddened when he spoke of his soldiering in the North-West Frontier's tribal area of South Waziristan.

At the time, the Fakir of Ipi, a legendary tribal *mullah*, was leading an insurrection there. He compared the campaigns of his past with the Pakistani army's current operations in South Waziristan against the Taliban. 'Today's war is very sad. It's unnecessary. The Mehsud [a Pathan tribe from Waziristan] are *good* people,' he said gently, lifting a hand slightly off the armrest of his chair.

His eyes softened and in a voice that protested the present with a memory of a kindlier past, he spoke of an experience of frontier warfare. 'We were on patrol one day and we came under fire from Mehsud in a *nullah* [ravine] and so we took cover, lying on our bellies. We were pinned down for a long time and I noticed that bees had made hives among the rocks and so I ordered my men,' at this he laughed – 'to take out their ration of *chapatti* and to dip them in the honey'.

'My father was at the Siege of Chitral,' he told us later that evening as he rose on his way to bed. 'But that story you must already know...'

*

The next morning, we walked miles up the valley. It can have changed little since Durand visited in 1888. On the edge of a village, we saw young boys showing off with catapults, slinging rocks at small birds perched in the branches of far-off trees, and shepherds came out of bothies to greet us.

But things of course *had* changed. During Durand's visit, one of the Mehtar's younger brothers had showered him with gifts and showed him the best of local life: a white grape as tasty as the 'finest muscatel'; and shooting ibex and markhor over dogs. He took him on journeys into the farthest valleys where the Chitralis, to the horror of the Pathans among Durand's escort, forded freezing rivers stark naked. There was one other detail that stayed in Durand's mind about his host: a habit of blowing his nose on the end of his minions' turbans.

*

That night, we had a late dinner with Siraj and his brother, Sikander, a rugged 50-year-old polo-player and local politician. We crammed ourselves – two brothers facing two brothers – round a wooden table in one of the trekkers' cabins outside the fort.

We ate a dish of the wild mountain vegetable – *manghol* – the sort which had been boxed for Benazir Bhutto on her visit years ago, but which now was fried with tomato and garlic.

The vegetable again prompted mention of the story of the security concerns about putting the carton on Benazir's flight and the crate of mangoes suspected of causing the crash that ended President Zia's life.

A vague memory crossed my mind.

'This is perhaps insensitive, Siraj,' I said, groping clumsily for diplomatic phrases, 'but have you ever been caught up in such events, conspiracies, coups ... it seems few people have escaped the intrigues...' I tailed off like an aircraft engine petering in mid-air.

Siraj laughed gently to himself and put down his fork. 'Your query takes me back to 1971. I am a 26-year-old major in the army. We have lost half our country. East Pakistan has become Bangladesh. Morale in the army is low. Despondency is high.'

He looked up to check the faces of his audience and continued.

'There is anger towards both the army as well as the political leadership in the country who are being blamed for causing this. Junior officers are especially angry. They are calling [then president, later prime minister] Zulfikar Ali Bhutto a traitor and they are saying that the military leadership has no right to lead after the disaster of East Pakistan.'

So I was not going totally mad. My memory had been trying to tell me something.

In his tempered, dry voice, Siraj then described how he had met with a group of disgruntled air force officers who were 'talking about getting up and doing something'. They were a good lot and he joined them and their leader had given Siraj the task of contacting ex-president Field Marshal Ayub Khan – because his sister had married into the former military ruler's family – to tell him that if their coup succeeded they would like to reinstal him as head of state. And so he met Ayub Khan at his residence in Islamabad, along with his sister's husband, another army major who was part of the same group.

'He heard us out patiently, and,' Siraj said, his voice rising wearily, 'I cannot forget his clear and firm reply: "Such an action will certainly mean the end of what is left of Pakistan. I should actually be reporting you two for telling me all this. If you don't want me to then you must promise me that not only will you have nothing to do with this matter but you will also convey my message to the others to stop this right now."'

Siraj picked up his half-full tumbler of wine, and before sipping, said: 'That was almost the end of my part in this coup which is known as the "Attock Conspiracy Case". I conveyed Ayub Khan's message to everyone and said that as per my promise to him I was disassociating myself from the group.'

Almost a year had passed and Siraj was doing his normal duties when he was arrested and subjected to a series of interrogations and investigations by military authorities. Another 200 officers were also arrested. The army announced that a coup had been unearthed and the culprits had been apprehended.

'When the authorities were satisfied that my role had not been beyond what I have mentioned, they gave me a lenient dismissal with benefits of pension and medical facilities.' He smiled to himself. 'My marriage was around the corner so I wasted no time and went ahead and followed it with a very long honeymoon.'

Before we went off to bed, we returned to the subject of their family's old fratricidal intrigues and Chev said to the princely brothers, 'It's quite a thought that in the not-too-distant past you two would have been trying to kill each other.'

They laughed politely, but an awkward silence ensued before Siraj broke it.

'As I said before, you had to bump the other chap off, before he did it to you.'

*

Could it be, Chev insisted, as we got ready for bed, that even among this extraordinarily affable and loving family, there survived a glimmer of the old Chitrali impulse? Impossible, I said.

Yet after Khushwaqt's death a few years later I heard a tale claiming that in his youth he had tried to raise support for a palace coup to oust his nephew.

AFGHANIA:
BULLOCKS AND WASPS

Chapter 22
Bogeyman

THE EARLY-MORNING SKY above my terrace in Islamabad was the blue of a linnet's egg. I was lying on my back on a *charpoy*, a string bed, where I'd slept the night; earlier, the dawn call to prayer had woken me; and my sheet was fragrant with dust.

Basil edged open the door on to the terrace with a toe, grinning sycophantically, hair smarmed down in preparation for another day on the take. He bore a tray clattering with plates of omelette stuffed with tomato, *paratha* and a pot of strong milky tea. Allah Ditta, somnolent and carrying the newspapers, followed him.

The sun would soon lift this day, in early June 2008, a month or so after the journey to Chitral, on a bed of shimmering heat, raising donkeys' knees, bicycle tyres, civil servants' bellies, dust-girted trees, concrete buildings, hills and all into a spectacle of levitation that pained the eyes.

Chev had gone home, ending our travels together in Pakistan. He had left me bolstered, recharged with purpose, his presence restoring confidence in my mission to capture all the mad, bewitching, beloved parts of the country before they disappeared.

Musharraf was clinging on as an impotent figurehead; and the militants had grown ever stronger. A month before they had blown up several Sufi shrines in the North-West Frontier Province, strengthening my notion that these places of worship were repositories of the country's old identity, which was now under attack. I wanted to get to these damaged shrines to see for myself the signs of this deepening ideological fissure.

This leg of my quest, to reach those shrines, would turn out to be my last. But it was delayed for a short time by political events, which again forced me to remain in the capital.

The newspaper headlines that morning reported that Musharraf was about to face his old nemesis. Thousands of black-suited lawyers demanding his dismissal were gathering in the humidity of Karachi for a 'long march' to the capital.

The army had stepped back from the fray, leaving him to his fate, at least in political terms. While politicians wrangled over the manner of his departure, the country faltered under rocketing food prices, energy shortages and a rapidly devaluing currency.

After 'withdrawing' from politics, the military (still very much in charge of defence and foreign affairs) allowed Zardari's civilian government to experience for itself the ignominy of brokering a peace deal with Taliban militants on the frontier. The result was more chaos.

Islamabad's calm was rattled again: a car bomb exploded with deadly effect outside the Danish embassy – revenge for cartoons published in Denmark lampooning the Prophet. A couple of months before, a bomb had been tossed over a wall into the garden of an Italian restaurant popular with foreigners, killing a Turkish woman and wounding several American FBI employees. The city retreated further into itself.

*

It was my third summer in Pakistan and I greeted the season with mixed feelings. I was falling asleep everywhere and experiencing frequent bouts of sickness. I noticed a sallow darkness under my eyes that I hadn't seen since before my kidney transplant and wondered how many more hot seasons I could take. I was beginning to feel like the earth at this time of the year – baked, cracked and parched – and, like the earth, I couldn't escape the heat, only submit to it.

Once more my house was a furnace overrun by geckos; in the garden, crows and mynahs once more fought over dragon-fly-encircled pools of water; thunderstorms blasted dust through windows and felled trees; Islamabad's mountains disappeared behind a haze; and Allah Ditta shed his cardboard mattress to lie on the cool of the dining-room's stone floor.

Basil, undeterred by the soaring temperature, continued in his ferrety way. One morning, I spotted him clanking about in the kitchen, wearing a fur hat. I asked him the purpose of his headgear. It transpired that a friend from England, who gardened for the Aga Khan up in the mountains of Baltistan and had left trunks of notebooks and plant specimens in my house, had deposited a hare in the freezer so that I might have it jugged. We hadn't done so and I'd told Basil he could throw it away weeks before, but instead he had made it into a hat. He said he wore it when he opened the fridge so that he wouldn't catch a cold.

I wondered with awe at the resourcefulness of this wizened, small, tubercular man. What made Christians in Pakistan such survivors? In Islamabad they lived in shanty districts from which they emerged wearing immaculately ironed 'pant-shirt' to work in our houses. I'd come across their communities on the frontier where some had been cajoled into converting to Islam.

In a remote town of Punjab, I'd been mobbed by hundreds of Christians asking for help after their churches had been burned. Local Muslims had turned on them after they'd lost a bet on a game of cards to a Christian and instead of paying up had accused him of blasphemy.

The vast majority of the twelve million or so Christians in Pakistan traced their ancestry to the 'untouchable' Hindu Chuhra caste from Sialkot, Punjab, where mass conversions took place during the 19th century under British rule. The low-caste Hindus who had converted to Christianity to better their lot a century ago had not reckoned on the creation of Pakistan, 'the Land of the Pure'.

*

Waiting for the lawyers to reach Islamabad before I left for the frontier, I visited a local saint on the west of the city, at the large and lavishly decorated shrine of Golra Sharif.

Taciturn with a stubbly chin and a Nehru-style Kashmiri hat balancing high on his head, Pir Shah Abdul Haq was seated in a bamboo chair, hunched over his paunch. He gave a man kneeling before him a thwack on the left cheek then told him to move off. Next came eight women draped in their best clothes and jewellery, proffering donations of bundles of cash. The plump hobgoblin flicked the women with water and wafted a podgy little moist hand above them in benediction, while a minion bore off with their banknotes on a tray.

I tried to question him about the shrine and his role. 'There is no concept of speech, only in a private meeting,' he snapped, refusing to answer my questions.

One of his disciples, a man from Barking, Essex, embarrassed by his saint's curtness, showed me the shrine. Next to the tomb of the saint's ancestor was a basket full of small pieces of paper on which had been written Koranic verses. My guide explained these were 'holy medicine'. A piece of paper was put in water, dissolved, and then drunk 'for all diseases to be gone within eleven days'. There were also three small table tennis bats with which to beat out djinns from people's bodies. These were quickly removed when the custodians noticed they had caught my attention.

He explained that the saint's popularity rested on his knowledge 'of crops and the bureaucracy'.

The bureaucracy?

'Yes. If you are a civil servant and want to be promoted to bureaucrat 22 level you ask him. Then you go into a room while he makes the phone calls.'

I asked him to explain.

'The saint is friendly with politicians because he can tell his disciples how to vote during elections, and so politicians come to him from all over Punjab. In turn he can then ask politicians to support his followers or to help them. It is a holy *safarish* (network of patronage). This is how we operate.'

Thus the shrine performed a role as a cog in the Heath Robinson machine of state. Not for the first time it was obvious why with such unscrupulous representatives of Sufi Islam, more austere reformist forms of the faith might have a sort of Lutheran appeal.

But the shrine had more than one function.

Another disciple, seemingly an influential follower of the saint, took me off to a side room, to tell me that his spiritual leader's other purpose was to wage an ideological battle on behalf of Pakistan against the country's population of 'heretic' Qadiani (a Muslim sect who believed that Mohammed was not the last prophet).

He led me into a room where toy train engines and carriages were displayed on shelves. He pointed to a large copy of a Terence Cuneo painting of a steam engine billowing smoke across a British railway platform. I asked him the meaning of the trains. 'Our saint will go to paradise and take us all with him in the train, whether we are in the first or third bogie [railway carriage].'

I'd visited the Qadiani, or Ahmadiyya, at their colony at Rabwah, near a broken spine of russet rock in central Punjab close to a rickety train bridge over the Chenab river. The town, founded on a salty wasteland, was surrounded by conservative mosques from the minarets of which clerics routinely bellowed hateful slogans against the Qadiani.

Twenty years before, the entire population of Rabwah had been charged with 'impersonating Muslims'. Militants had long killed people for being Shia or Ahmadi but among the 'elite' I used to hear that so-and-so's aunt was a *Shia* or their grandfather was an *Ahmadi* and nobody ever really paid any attention. Now, even in those circles, one's religious identity had become a divisive factor and possibly a fatal one.

The concept of purity in the Land of the Pure was nonsense. Rivers crossed Pakistan, deserts stretched across it, and like the deserts and rivers, peoples extended across its borders, making a mess of the map: Pathans into Afghanistan; Baluch into Afghanistan and Iran; Punjabis into the frontier and Indian Punjab, Kashmiris into Indian-held Kashmir; Kirghiz and other northern peoples into Central Asia and China. Nomads from Afghanistan, following ancient migratory paths, traversed the country on their way to Indian Rajasthan, where Sindh's harassed Hindus now felt more at home. Many of the families that migrated at Partition to Pakistan from Bihar and Bangladesh stored part of their identity in their distant ancestral villages.

I only had to pick up a newspaper and turn to the classified pages: '41 years old with good health, government job in Rawalpindi, wheatish complexion, Rajput caste, Urdu speaker, migrated family, 3 wives divorced and need fourth marriage. Must be Urdu speaker.'

In a few words, a great chunk of the social map was laid out: concerns over race, caste and skin colour, differences of language, tribal affiliation, the country's internal borders, signposts on the way to the barriers that break us down from groups into individuals, dividing one ego from another.

Chapter 23
Rum, Bum and Rebab

B Y THE TIME Allah Ditta and I crossed the Indus into the North-West Frontier Province, we looked as dishevelled as Inspector Clouseau and Cato after one of their rumbles. Both of us had spent most of the day in a foul mood, due to heat, hunger and having got ourselves lost for hours.

We had forsaken the swiftness of the new Islamabad to Peshawar motorway, hoping to explore off the Grand Trunk Road and arrive at a river crossing farther south. For much of the journey we had bucked along rough tracks, rodeo-style, unsure of our whereabouts. Allah Ditta had driven much of the way striking a familiar pose: with the index finger of one hand touching his lower lip, a caricature of lostness. Clouds of dust kicked up by the traffic were so thick and acrid that my nostrils were bleeding. It was my fault for insisting on no air-conditioning and open windows – a policy I had also implemented at home to the detriment of my fast-deteriorating health, out of a mistaken notion that it would harden my body and allow me to acclimatise.

But there had been consolations: birds perching on buffalo horns, wheat and rice fields and mud farmhouses. And as soon as we reached the bridge over the Indus at Attock I sensed relief in both of us. Ahead, obscured by a dirty boudoir-pink sunset, was the frontier.

We had escaped Islamabad at last. The lawyers' march had come and gone, leaving Musharraf dangling by a thread (the marchers had called for him to be dangled from the end of a rope), and me free to roam.

The North-West Frontier Province was the last empty corner of my map. I had frequently visited the province to cover its troubles, but these butcher-and-bolt forays – reporting on a bomb explosion or snatching quotes from tribesmen or sitting crosslegged in mind-numbingly dull debate with *mullahs* – were unsatisfactory.

Now in front of us lay jagged khaki hills and silky green vales and orchards and passes, over which almost every conqueror of the Indian Subcontinent worth his salt had swept; the land of the Pathans, one of the world's largest and most bellicose tribal groupings, whose ancestors ruled Afghanistan and northern India for centuries and from whose ranks the Taliban were largely drawn.

Our destination, Peshawar, its capital, offered more panache than any other city in the country. As flourishing as the sweep of its name, it was a place of intrigue, its markets murmuring of ancient bedevilment: Storytellers' Bazaar – dubbed the 'Piccadilly Circus of Central Asia' – and Smugglers' Bazaar were two of the crowded, tattered-canopied hubs of commerce where carpets, heroin, precious stones and looted Gandhara statues were traded with furtive glances and wads of rupees plucked from undergarments. A recent spate of attacks across the city, targeting everywhere from its potted-and-painted military cantonment to its hotels, cinemas, police stations and mosques, had revived a whiff of the cordite that had burnished its name.

Allah Ditta and I had made the journey to Attock many times before (albeit by a straighter route) and we usually stopped here, as we did now, for a break, eating biscuits and slurping tea on the bridge overlooking the Indus. Below us, its turquoise, mountain-fresh waters merged with the purplish murk of the Kabul River. It was where the landscape transformed from bullock-ploughed plains into arid hills dotted with lonely Tardis-like paramilitary pickets; and the Indian Subcontinent drifted into Central Asia.

The bridge spanned the river in the shadow of the rambling Mughal crenellations of Emperor Akbar's Attock Fort, half castle against the Pathan, half jail into which the military slings politicians to cool their heels.

Near us now, a Pathan truck-driver jumped from his cab, unfurled his prayer mat and stood with his face towards a blood-orange sunset. He cupped his hands into seashell shapes and raised them behind his ears as if listening for the word of God, folded his arms in front of him, then knelt with his forehead touching the floor.

A peaceful, simple scene, it magnified the free and heady sensation I often felt when approaching the frontier, and which sharpened with every mile we came closer to the Afghan border.

As Allah Ditta and I sat there, a couple of Afghan workmen, with pickaxes slung over their shoulders and large callused hands, approached me. They were friendly and merely wanted to know what I was doing. As we left, one of them said with a laugh, 'Be careful. People here want to kill you.'

Long after nightfall, having crossed a fertile vale of wheat fields and poplar trees, we entered Peshawar. To the north and south rose the silhouette of the ridges of the tribal areas; to the east lay the Khyber Pass and Afghanistan.

*

Splendiferous in starched white robes, with a smoker's cough and a podgy gut threatening his waistcoat buttons, Yusuf Khan, a feudal-cum-saint, was amused by the idea that an ideological motive lay behind a recent attack on his ancestor's tomb, a locally revered shrine. 'No, no, no! My dear chap! The Taliban did not do this for religious reasons,' he wheezed, blue eyes watering with mirth. 'They are miscreants who went looting and took half a dozen vehicles.' He was probably half right – the militants' ideological mission was underwritten by plunder.

The *khan's* (or Pathan landowner's) house, built on the foundations of a four-centuries-old fort on the outskirts of the city at Shaikhan near the tribal area, looked out on to a yellow-pillared courtyard encircled by castellated brick walls. The main entrance had a panelled, wooden door carved with the Star of David and flowers. Inside was a sitting-room filled with dusty English books – including *Vanity Fair* – a stag's head and a glass-fronted dresser stacked with antique imperial Russian porcelain made by Gardner. A dog like a bald Alsatian was tied up in the courtyard where we sat sipping green tea.

The place had a seedy decadence about it, which appealed to me all the more as I had woken earlier that morning, my first in Peshawar, in a very different environment – an international hotel offering the usual glass-fronted carpet shops, marble floors and foyer music.

Sitting in the courtyard, I could almost feel the modern age clamouring at its walls, wanting to bash down its gates and slay its lord, who I imagined would have gone without a murmur, accepting his fate as the natural order of things. It was already hot and the courtyard offered some shade as well as a welcome respite from the outside world.

A few months before, five hundred militants led by their leader, Mangal Bagh ('Green Garden') – a former bus conductor turned self-styled reformist – had charged out of the adjacent tribal area and blown up my host's saintly forebear's shrine, killing over a dozen people and kidnapping the same number again.

A rugged inaccessible region between Pakistan and Afghanistan, home to fiercely independent Pathan tribes straddling the border, the province's seven, semi-autonomous tribal 'agencies' were a refuge for the Taliban fighting against an American-led coalition in Afghanistan. Leaders of the al-Qaeda terrorist group, including supposedly the Arabian fugitive Osama bin Laden, and other Islamists – both Pakistani and foreign – had also found sanctuary there. The tribal belt had become, in diplomatic parlance, an 'ungoverned space' that 'posed a threat to the rest of the world', the much-vaunted 'frontline of the war on terror'.

Pakistan inherited the tribal areas from the British who had created them as a buffer zone. In the words of one historian, the 'tribesmen were like tigers in a national park' and omnipotent political agents acted as 'gamekeepers', attempting to control them with draconian laws.

Then, as now, political agents struck peace deals with hostile tribesmen and, when they failed, the military conducted creaking campaigns in which 'bullocks endeavoured to tread down wasps'.

Yusuf Khan appeared indifferent to these events.

'The tribals have been marauding here for centuries. We know them. They are ruffians and criminals,' he said, tugging the whiskers on his upper lip. 'This is not just about what is happening here, it is what is happening across the country.'

He didn't want to show me the shrine himself as he was unsure of his popularity in the village, preferring to remain safe inside the walls of his fortress. 'There are many rivalries,' he sighed.

Local journalists told me that Mangal Bagh was waging a deadly turf war with a religious leader who followed a Sufi tradition. The religious rift merely veiled a gangsterish quarrel over smuggling routes. The Americans had used Bagh's militia as a proxy in an attempt to gain control of Khyber's troublesome Tirah valley, but the move had backfired and he had now turned his guns on Pakistani and American interests, and was on the rampage locally.

Getting up to show me out, Yusuf Khan added with a titter: 'To think this bearded Mangal Bagh has gone from bus conductor to international man overnight.' There was a hint of respect in his voice for the hairy parvenu. Doubtless his ancestors had started off their now decrepit dynasty with a similar entrepreneurial flourish.

Among the debris at the shrine, which stood among villagers' rough-hewn graves, I found a white-bearded custodian sitting on a reed mat. Rocket-propelled grenades had shattered thick plasterwork walls decorated with floral motifs.

'We respect the saints but the militants told us not to come here,' he said mournfully. 'They objected to the flags and to the *chadors* [cloth] of the tomb.' Perhaps, he added, they also thought *charas* (hashish) was sold here and were opposed to women visiting the shrine. He informed me in a surly voice that I wasn't welcome – a foreigner would bring more trouble.

I walked into the village and found shelter from the heat in a *hujra*, a courtyard where men chatted and smoked *hookahs*. They gave me the place of honour at the head of a string bed, and then their opinions on the attack. One man said Mangal Bagh had killed indiscriminately and that the tribal area's political agent and his militia covertly supported him; another complained that the anti-hashish drive was merely a pretext for looting. A man who spoke excellent English, who had been sitting silently in a corner, unleashed an angry tirade. 'This game is being played by your government and my government. It is a big game,' he fumed. 'If something has happened in my village it is because someone has willed it in Islamabad or Washington.'

Nobody seemed to know what was going on. Who was doing what to whom. Conspiracy ruled on the frontier. America accused the Pakistani army of not doing enough to take on the militants and its intelligence service of covertly supporting the Afghan Taliban. Washington had recently tripled its use of missile strikes from pilotless drone aircraft, killing scores of suspected militants and civilians in the tribal areas.

Pakistan's policy of quashing militants at home and striking deals with them, but employing them abroad in Afghanistan and India had resulted in blowback: groups of tribal militants, fighting under the banner of the 'Pakistani Taliban', had launched attacks beyond the tribal areas, turning their fire on the army, the government and the rest of the country. Pakistan accused India of backing the Pakistani Taliban. It was the new Great Game. But the actual fighting seemed to fall to men like Mangal Bagh.

A *mullah* with a black cap turned up to join us, but when I asked him what had happened at the shrine, said: 'No comment.' He too was a target of Mangal Bagh.

I thought that I had gleaned all I could from these polite but morose men, when another man piped up. 'The saints are here to listen to everyone,' he said. 'Even the prostitutes who we consider the dirt of society used to be welcome at their shrines, because if the saints reject these women then where will they go?'

*

That afternoon, with the help of the English-speaking man, I sneaked a small distance into Mangal Bagh's fief in the Khyber agency, an area forbidden to foreigners. There, I met a merry band of his bandoliered and armed followers. Wispy-bearded and long-haired young men, wearing baggy robes and Chitrali caps as large as dustbin lids, they were clear about their leader's attributes. 'Our leader is a very beautiful Muslim. He was a bus conductor and chosen by God,' said one. 'He is against alcohol, prostitution and opium.'

They demonstrated the freedom of the tribal areas by showing me an electricity bill – and laughed because nobody paid for amenities here. They were less sure about Mangal Bagh's other strictures. They took me to see the remains of a small roadside shrine that recently had been razed. 'It is against the *sharia* to have a tomb of such height,' said the leader among them, a burly, thickly-bearded man of about 30 who had tucked a rose behind his left ear. 'But we don't like to destroy them as they were revered by our grandfathers.'

Evening fell over the valley and with the dark came a rush of people going home, some behind handcarts slopping with curds and broth, others leaping on to the tailgates of fast-moving buses, and the mood among our company – the English-speaking man from the *hujra* and a small group of Mangal Bagh's men and me – became excited by the thought of some mischief.

They brought me to a shoddy compound where we sat on the floor in a small, darkened room. Giggles and whispers were followed by gestures to close shutters and bolt doors. The leader said they would show me some illicit goods. I wondered, with unease, if they were speaking in evil euphemisms and if perhaps I had badly misjudged the company. Their facial expressions showed a maniacal desire to share something with me, something which I hoped was not pain or death.

One of them tugged from under his shirt a packet filled with hashish-stuffed cigarettes, another produced a small glass flagon of spirits. These were passed about and soon I was swept up in the smoky exuberance. But then the leader leant back to retrieve a black cloth sack from under a string bed. Slightly stoned and open to paranoia, I hoped it didn't contain a severed head. With a big grin, he carefully unsheathed a bulbous-backed stringed instrument, a *rebab*. He said they had rescued some musical instruments from the destroyed shrines. If they were caught with them, he added with extra pleasure, they would be heftily fined. 'Honestly, we miss the music, but we are scared of Mangal Bagh.'

Straightening his back, instrument resting on crossed legs, hands clasped to his chest, he excused himself for being out of practice. Then he smiled, took up the *rebab*, plucking it as he sang a crisp and jaunty Pashto folk tune, hairy bare feet jigging to the beat. Soon we were dancing.

I stumbled out of the shebeen an hour or two later into a night illumined by a smuggler's moon, my hosts all bright eyes, smiles and embraces, and snuck back across the border.

*

The next morning, before the heat flayed the streets, Allah Ditta and I set off on a walk round the colossal walls of Bala Hissar fort towards the Old City.

We were killing time before a meeting with a local journalist, Haq Nawaz, whose help I would seek to visit other targeted shrines.

This was no longer the city of which the travel writer Paul Theroux wrote in the 1970s: 'I would gladly move there, settle down and grow old watching sunsets in the Khyber Pass.' Anglo-Muslim Gothic mansions still slept on broad roads under cool trees, but now there was a frisson about the city, which was heightened by reports of suicide-bomb attacks, kidnappings and assassinations. Local journalists had recently noted the appearance of unarmed Taliban in its markets, causing further concern that the militants' influence was spreading to its heart.

Imagining that some people here might leap at the chance to claim a *faranghi* scalp, Allah Ditta took on the role of bodyguard. At times he walked behind me, at others he stayed out on my flank scanning oncomers for signs of hostility, and then, to my surprise, he went ahead and joined people standing on the threshold of a shop and gawped at me with them, giving a running commentary on my business.

We passed carts heaped with grapes and melons, almonds and lemon grass. Fair-skinned, rosy-cheeked boys ran in between the baggy-trousered legs of wrinkled, tea-stained old tribesmen with hawkish and Mongol faces. Women mostly wore the sun-faded, blue all-enveloping *burqah* or veil, while others screened their faces with gilded *yashmaks* or *hijabs* – foreign fads that nodded piously to the Middle East. Stallholders fired up gas burners under giant skillets of grease in which they would soon be cooking the frontier's staple, *cabob*, a delicious spicy meat patty. At *qawah khanas* (tea shops) trays rattled with pots and cups of green tea spiced with cardamom.

Haq Nawaz, often my companion and guide on the frontier, was portly, gentle and cheerful. He had a benign moustache, often glistening with beef fat, and wore a conical white hat. Nothing was so urgent that lunch could not first be taken and any high-handed attempt by me to get things going with unnecessary haste was met by him coming to attention in a mock imitation of obedience and the words, 'Yes, of course, Sir Lord Mutton Singh Afridi'.

We soon found the small and unimpressive neighbourhood shrine of Pir Syed Qasim Ali Shah.

Builders were wielding sledgehammers on the roof, clearing away rubble created by a bomb blast a few days before. It was a humble place and its obscurity begged the question of why somebody would bother to blow it up. They had not aimed to kill or injure anyone here – they had merely attacked the pacific idea that these shrines represent. Its visibly sad caretaker said that the followers of the saint had 'worked for the unity of Islam' but that extremists had taken exception to the *pir*'s Friday sermons in which he spoke against the use of suicide bombers.

Haq Nawaz too was saddened by this little piece of violence and as we drove away he spoke of the old tradition on the frontier of vigils at saints' tombs and pilgrimages of spiritual exploration. He told the story of one of his brothers, a graduate, who had one day disappeared leaving a note saying that he was going to wander in search of God from shrine to shrine in the old manner, ignoring the boundaries of Afghanistan and India, along ancient sacred routes. His family hadn't seen him for several years, but had been able to keep track of him through a method I found surprisingly common among Pakistanis looking for lost relations: they had asked a friend working for a telecommunications company to locate the SIM card of his mobile phone, and had thus kept track of him remotely, reassured of his safety.

Later that afternoon, we witnessed a less tranquil Sufi response to militant aggression. At Peshawar's football stadium we joined a protest held by the disciples of a Sufi leader from the Khyber Pass who had been assassinated a few days before. Being Pathans from the tribal areas, these Sufis were not matted-haired, loin-clothed, horn-blowing *fakirs* but tribesmen wrapped in ammunition belts and carrying assault rifles. Whereas elsewhere Sufism was defenceless, apart from prayer, here it was armed to the teeth. They shouted Sufi slogans but leavened these obscure (to me) theological exclamations with calls for an uprising and death to Musharraf, America and the Jews. This non-pacific form of Sufi expression surprised me; hitherto I had associated mystical Islam with peace, love and unity (although, on reflection, of course Pir Pagara's Hur were also militant Sufis). Then they came forward, one by one, and bent down and kissed the hands of their newly anointed Sufi leader – a form of obeisance I had thought anathema to these supposedly egalitarian hillsmen.

Nobody I spoke to among the congregation seemed to know who had assassinated their leader or why, or what was going on in general along the frontier, and all were open to conspiracy theories. One held that the Jews were behind the conflict as part of plans to divide the Muslim people and that they were helped by the West, who had started polio vaccination programmes to sterilise this part of the Islamic world.

*

That night, I fell asleep watching a Pashto film on Khyber TV. At one point it depicted a Pathan luxuriating in a swirling rose-tinted hashish-induced cloud of pleasure. He sat on a sofa, plucking a *rebab*, while a woman with an epic backside danced provocatively before him. Judging by his heavy-lidded stupefaction, he was in heaven. It was a well-deserved break for him from a lot of gun battles. There were thunderclaps every time a goodie or a baddie – I couldn't tell which was which – appeared.

It's never long before a visitor to Pakistan is regaled with the following stanza, which is sometimes, probably erroneously, attributed to Khushal Khan, a great Mughal-era Pathan poet and warrior: *There is a boy across the river/whose arse cheeks are like the pomegranates of Kabul in spring/alas, the river is wide and I cannot swim.*

The poem may come from an old marching song.

This, I thought, is the land of rum, bum and *rebab*.

*

My trip to Peshawar was not entirely motivated by damaged shrines. A couple of weeks before, I'd met a Pathan woman, Kashmala, at an

Islamabad restaurant-art gallery. She'd suggested I look her up when next in Peshawar. Now I was here, I hesitated to do so. But solitude, curiosity, boredom and lust won the day.

Pathan colleagues, both here and in Kabul, had told me about the frustration and difficulty of meeting women in an area where such a thing is strictly forbidden, and women, particularly in this climate of militant oppression, are seldom seen. This restricted access to the opposite sex engendered potent powers of observation. In Kabul, one of my friends had been able to spot 'an available woman' among a group all wearing the enveloping blue 'shuttlecock' *burqah*s. He had explained how he could gauge a woman's figure through the garment's billowing cloth, and that he could judge a woman's desirability from the form of her ankle and her 'availability' by the style of the henna on her hands or the turn of her shoes. There is no barrier fearful enough, man-made or otherwise, to thwart youthful passions.

In his *The Lives of a Bengal Lancer* (1905), the British soldier-turned-yogi Francis Yeats-Brown (who unfortunately in later life became an enthusiastic fascist) noted while serving on the frontier in Waziristan, that 'Sex life is more necessary in a hot country. The hysteria which seems to hang in the air of India is aggravated by severe continence of any kind. At the end of Ramadan, for instance, my fasting squadron used to become as lively as a basket of rattlesnakes'.

I telephoned Kashmala and she agreed to meet in my hotel room. The next evening she knocked at my door and entered quickly before anyone in the corridor could see her. She sat down on a chair in front of the desk, putting her handbag next to her as if waiting in a surgery for a doctor's appointment. Voluptuous and in her early twenties, she had dark blue eyes, an aquiline nose and large lips. I sat at the foot of the bed, almost at the far end of the small room; we were two strangers anxious to bridge the divide. I'd brought a bottle of rough red wine with me from Islamabad and we drank the half that was left.

Soon, I realised that neither my small talk, nor my observations about local life, made the slightest impact on her; in fact she looked disturbed by my attempts at conversation. Her English was limited and the wine, drunk on an empty stomach, far from having a soothing effect, exaggerated the jangling nerves in the room. It dawned on me that the whole thing had been a mistake.

I sat back, determined to see out the evening as politely and painlessly as possible. Kashmala, perhaps sensing the decisive moment was on the turn, launched into a fast, at times incoherent, bullet-point exposition of her recent life: she had married; her husband had taken her to Dubai and prostituted her; she had left him; and now she had influential friends and was having fun. The revelation was disconcerting but before I could absorb it – was it true? a plea for sympathy? a blunt introduction to her sexuality? – she got up, pulled two pillows off the bed and asked me to sit on the floor opposite her. I did so hesitantly. She placed the empty bottle of wine between us and with a bravado that barely masked her awkwardness, she asked: 'Do you know how to play spin-the-bottle?'

Later that night, lit by a bedside-table lamp and reflected in a mirror, her limbs, youthful and sharply angled like those of a courtesan in a Mughal miniature, dominated the foreground; beyond them, sallow and shadowy, lay my own. The dizzying realisation that illness had returned to my body and that I was nearly 40 struck home; but before I'd even rolled on to my back, the thought had disappeared with reptilian stealth, submerged in the mudbanks of my mind.

I saw Kashmala again several times in Peshawar and in Islamabad. Before each meeting, she would send a text message out of the blue asking for a tryst. Then she would arrive and our time together would be brief. After leaving, she would send another message: 'Love you soooooo much baby'. We had no real concept of each other but we shared the light and perfunctory companionship of strangers on the road.

Chapter 24
Passing up the Khyber

MUSHARRAF'S FALL appeared to be close at hand, so postponing my journey to the frontier's troubled areas, I hotfooted it back to the capital.

The long hot month of July passed in a frenzy of protest, speculation and political intrigue. I spent it with phones pressed to my sweat-drenched ears, on occasion with buckets of my vomit being ferried from my office by Allah Ditta. I was becoming increasingly unwell. Yet I continued to try to decipher the horse-trading between political parties, the military and foreign diplomats, the high-wire, crisis-prone process that tried to corall the country into some sort of stability.

Musharraf finally resigned in August, but the country as a whole, and Islamabad in particular, reeled under a further series of misfortunes. On the same day as Zardari's inauguration as president in September (never make predictions on the frontier, Curzon had said), a suicide bomber drove a dump truck filled with explosives into Islamabad's Marriott Hotel, blasting a sixty-foot crater and killing over fifty people.

Shortly afterwards, in the last days of President George W. Bush's tenure in office, two helicopter-loads of American soldiers crossed on foot from Afghanistan into the Pakistani tribal area of South Waziristan, but were driven back by Pakistani border troops shooting over their heads. A week or so before, American airborne troops had assaulted a nearby village. American officials claimed the raid had killed a score of al-Qaeda militants, but Pakistani officials and journalists said only civilians, including women and children, had died. Tension on the border was at an all-time high.

In November, Barack Obama was elected President of the United States (days before his election he had pledged to work seriously on resolving the Kashmir dispute, a pledge that remained unfulfilled during his tenure) and Pakistani terrorists launched coordinated attacks in the Indian city of Mumbai. At a party on a Karachi beach shortly after the attacks, our revelling was interrupted by news that Indian fighter jets had breached Pakistani airspace. People around me, who until that moment I had thought moderate, shouted for war against India. Beneath the surface, even Pakistanis habitually cynical about their own country sometimes harboured prickly chauvinism and rage.

*

One night towards the end of November, I returned to Peshawar and found a wintry city. Men clad in thick shawls bent over roasted maize on carts lit by hissing gas lanterns, cyclists muffled their faces with scarves. All was normal except the place was under siege.

The Taliban had attacked paramilitary and police posts on the outskirts. Reports had begun to appear in the press suggesting it could fall. Girls' schools had been blown up, kidnaps and suicide-bomb attacks within the city had increased, critics of the Taliban had been assassinated and America's chief diplomat in the city had narrowly escaped assassination in an ambush on her way to work.

Militants or criminals – it was difficult to tell who was who – looted Western military supplies intended for coalition forces in Afghanistan.

It was now dangerous to move outside the city. Like other Pakistani cities, its colonial-era police force was ill-equipped to deal with heavily armed militants. Leaning on his desk, a burly police chief listed on his fingers his requirements – weapons, armoured cars, instructors and funds.

I'd come to Peshawar for two reasons. To try to enter the countryside near the province's insurgency-hit district of Swat, where, several locals had told me, lay a shrine of great enchantment perched on a hill, a sacred grove in which Pathans, Hindus and Sikhs rubbed shoulders, danced and meditated, the last bastion in the province of unbridled Sufi expression.

My attempt to do this had ended in failure. Halfway there, the man deputed by a local landowner to escort me had revealed he was too scared to go on, and explained – as we were driving over speed bumps in a notoriously militant village – that the clinking noise coming from the car's boot was made by bottles of alcohol he intended to distribute to his friends in the locale. We had ended our journey at a farmhouse where he promised I would savour locally produced wine – of which previously I'd never heard and that transpired to be pure alcohol mixed with a carton of Nestlé grape juice. I would try to reach that place, the final shrine of my travels, another time.

My other aim, for journalistic purposes, was to find a way to enter the tribal areas without getting arrested or scalped.

I spent a few mornings sitting in the office of the Khyber Tribal Agency in Peshawar, trying to curry favour with the political agent in the hope that he might grant me permission to enter his area.

He explained that it would be difficult because militants had obliterated the traditional power structure of tribal leaders, elders and councils with whom he normally worked. And recent Pakistani military campaigns had been piecemeal and much of his fiefdom was now lawless.

Knowing that he was a brave and bombastic official who prided himself on being the most fearless and active of his peers, I goaded him by saying that surely he could take me up the Khyber Pass, where until only recently, before a spate of ambushes, skirmishes, feuds and assassinations, tourists had gone for jollies on an old steam train up the pass's remarkable railway and foreign dignitaries were herded along a well-worn path to the Afghan border.

He told me to come back in a few days and he would see what he could do.

*

I didn't hold out much hope that the political agent would deliver the goods, so I also preyed on my host, asking for his help. The city's hotels were now likely targets for bomb attacks (indeed the one at which I had last stayed in the city was soon blown up) and so I'd put up at the home of an acquaintance, the head of the Pathan Marwat tribe, Anwar Kamal. His house was thick with pile carpets, chintz curtains and doilies. Its 1970s cosiness was jeopardised by an anti-aircraft gun installed on the roof and by a sitting-room that seemed more like an arsenal.

His lands, in the district of Lakki, some distance south of Peshawar, abutted the tribal area of Waziristan, which had largely fallen to the encroaching tide of militancy. 'Talibanisation' had seeped from the tribal belt into these 'settled areas' in the form of violence and edicts targeting barbers, shrines, music and women out in public.

Anwar had just returned from his lands, but he was not dispirited. Indeed, he crackled with energy and derring-do. An astute and gentlemanly man, his moustache, whiskered like coconut fibre, was permanently set to 'action stations'; his nose was as large and ebullient as a port drinker's, his eyes pearly flames. A couple of years before he had taken a posse of heavily armed men up into the hills of Waziristan to avenge the abduction of two of his women by a neighbouring tribe. They had killed eighty people and razed a village. 'I'm not proud of it,' he said, stiffening with pride. 'But justice was not just *seen* to be done. It *was* done.'

Anwar had seen off various gangs of Taliban and showed me pictures on his mobile phone of the corpses of those who had strayed on to his land. He had travelled into the heart of Waziristan to speak to the Taliban leadership. 'I told them that the next time I see a Taliban on my land I am going to screw him as hard as I can – I spoke to them in traditional language.'

He had shown me some of his own arsenal of weaponry. 'I have a *lakh* [100,000] of bullets for my personal use only.'

I made impressed noises.

'I also have a 30mm gun,' he said, and then showed me where it was stored in his kitchen, leaning against a shelf of painted porcelain chickens.

'Remarkable.'

'It takes half an hour to assemble. My servants can do it. I am waiting for the enemy any time, any place.'

As he chatted animatedly, he swiped a rocket head about like an old gent practising sword strokes. 'Very effective, very effective,' he said, seeing my eye following its arc.

But he refused to take me into the tribal areas, saying it would get us both into trouble or killed.

*

One evening, we visited a mutual friend, a senior Pakistani military intelligence official. Our host's brain worked at a rapid rate and he smoked incessantly, jigging a leg up and down, rattling off future scenarios for the government and country.

I had to restrain my amazement when, revealing another mechanism in the Heath Robinson contraption, he explained how military intelligence, which often used Islamist political parties to further its own ends – for example by organising protests against things it disapproved of such as the government talking too enthusiastically about peace with India – then found it difficult to control them. He personally had had to travel hundreds of miles across the country, he said with indignation, to pay off the head of a religious group to stop him from mounting a riot at an airbase used by American aircraft.

He said that military intelligence's senior echelons had limited control over its mid-ranking officers – *jihadis*, who had been arrested in the tribal areas, had sometimes been mysteriously released by his rogue underlings.

He went on to narrate another tale from the murky intelligence world. Not long before, a retired two-star general, Faisal Alvi, who had commanded Special Forces operations against militants in the tribal area, had been assassinated on the road from Rawalpindi to Islamabad. Elements of British intelligence put it about that he had been forcibly retired and then assassinated on the orders of senior generals whom he had accused of going soft on the Taliban. To counter that, Pakistani intelligence put out a rumour that he had had an affair with a British intelligence stooge. My friend said that there *had* been an altercation between him and two senior officers who, after he had openly insulted them, mounted a smear campaign against him, which included a reference to an indiscreet affair he had had with a fellow officer's daughter.

But the real cause of his death, according to our friend, was otherwise: a Special Forces officer who had served under him in Waziristan had grown disillusioned with fighting against his co-religionist Muslims and had resigned his commission to join militants waging war against coalition forces in Afghanistan. Before he had gone on *jihad*, he had told his brother, another officer, that if he died in battle he was to avenge his death by killing Alvi. He was killed in battle and his brother, joining forces with a handful of militants, carried out the assassination. Encouraged by their success, the band turned to kidnap and extortion. They were caught when they ran into a routine checkpoint, where police officers found one of their kidnappees in the boot of their car.

*

One morning, a few days later, Haq Nawaz, my local journalist fixer, and I went to the office of Tariq Hayat Khan, the Political Agent of the Khyber Tribal Agency.

On entering, a file flew past my nose and on across the room, bursting in an explosion of papers on the head of a man.

'Get out you rascal!' Hayat Khan shouted, his face mottled with rage. At first I thought he was talking to me. But he jabbed a finger towards a clerk who had clearly fallen into disfavour and now cowered among sheets of paper in a corner of the office. The Political Agent shouted through the open door in Pashto and two uniformed tribal levies ran in clutching rifles, looking about the room for signs of trouble. 'Throw him in the guard room,' bellowed Hayat Khan, pointing at the hangdog clerk. The guards appeared reluctant to manhandle a *babu*, but one of them gave him a light-fingered tug on the sleeve and they escorted him from the room.

Haq Nawaz whispered to me, 'He wants a role in Hollywood'. Pleased that I had seen this fit of passion, Hayat Khan smoothed his hair and motioned for Haq Nawaz and me to sit opposite him at his desk.

A tallish mustachioed Pathan with nostrils that flared frequently with belligerence, he was dressed in a white *shalwar kameez*, over which he wore a grey jacket. He lit the first of many cigarettes he smoked during our stay in his office, as minions came and went, one placing a file in front of him, another emptying his ashtray.

'Now, what can I do for you?'

'You mentioned that we might go up the Khyber Pass and I wondered if you could arrange that please?' I hoped my directness would appeal to his man-of-action idiom.

'Of course, why not?'

He then turned his attention to other matters, speaking on telephones, issuing orders. Half an hour later I shot Haq Nawaz a glance that asked, 'Is this man for real or are we hanging about for nothing?'

Haq Nawaz laughed and, cupping a hand over one side of his mouth so that Hayat Khan, who was talking on a phone, should not hear, said loudly: 'He is enjoying the show. Let us see. I think he is mad enough to do this thing.'

After a further hour of waiting, Hayat Khan turned his attention once more to our petition. He explained that the Khyber Pass was now closed to foreigners, that it had been overrun by a patchwork of militants, some of them backed by America, others by Pakistani military intelligence, and others pursuing other agendas. Mangal Bagh, the former bus conductor turned reformist who had been used by Americans and Pakistanis as a proxy, was up to his usual tricks. Not for the first time, nor the last, the use of proxies in the tribal areas, he said, had 'become a bullshit fuck-up'.

He sprang to his feet, marched across the office to a wall-map and pointed to the whereabouts of the 'troublemakers'. He said that 'a confederacy of crooks and brigands constitute the Taliban' and that he had no time for peace deals and ceasefires that in his view had stymied efforts to bring these people to heel.

'You name it. They do it!' he explained, his voice rising, a cigarette-wielding hand slicing the air.

'What can be done about them?' I asked.

'Hit them! Hit them! And hit them hard!' he shouted, cigarette ash flying over the map.

Haq Nawaz could suppress his laughter no longer, and his shoulders shook as he guffawed into his lap.

Hayat Khan, who hadn't noticed Haq Nawaz's lapse in etiquette, walked back and sat at his desk and asked him in a low voice, 'What was that Clint Eastwood film where he is in the bath and the bandit hesitates to kill him and so Eastwood pulls his pistols from the water and finishes him off, saying, "If you are going to shoot, shoot"?'

With great effort and tears of laughter at the corner of his eyes, Haq Nawaz muttered, 'I do not know sir.'

'Well, no matter,' he replied, his voice once more gaining volume. 'What I say is if you are going to shoot, shoot!'

At that moment a helicopter passed overhead. 'Ah,' said Hayat Khan, beaming and spreading his hands across his desk. 'My beloved gunships.'

He leapt to his feet again, shouted some orders and immediately we were caught up in a flurry of activity as militiamen scrambled for weapons, clerks brandished papers in front of their master's face and we loaded ourselves into pick-up trucks mounted with large machine guns.

The morning's sky was faded cobalt and we were heading for the Khyber Pass, which sparkled ahead of us.

Our cavalcade of four pick-up trucks – from whose sides hung a guard of immaculately turned out tribal levies armed with rocket-launchers and Kalashnikovs – roared along at high speed to avoid the attentions of suicide bombers, but also out of respect for the spirit of panache that ruled the frontier.

I was nervous that we might be attacked but drew strength from our escort's impassive faces. At the same time I was delighted that Hayat Khan, doughty man, and true to his word, had ignored commands from his superiors and was taking a foreigner into the pass. Seated next to me, he explained with puff-chested pride that at this time he was the only Political Agent of the seven tribal agencies to venture into his territory.

On the outskirts of Peshawar, we passed the Smugglers Market, a place where I had been before and seen stalls stacked with Korean and

Chinese electrical goods, skin-whitening cream and sex products such as delay sprays, breast-enhancing cream, replica Viagra and hardcore pornography, and *jihadi* DVDs.

We barged our way to the front of queues at checkpoints, climbing up into the narrow, arid, twisting thirty-mile-long pass under forts perched on hillocks and regimental badges painted on rocks.

By the roadside, camels and donkeys stumbled along, their panniers filled with contraband. We passed a mansion owned by a drug baron, a crumbling Buddhist *stupa*, and a line of veiled women descending sinuously on foot to the valley floor to draw water from an emerald stream.

Of the mountains beyond I knew only the little I had gleaned while on media jaunts with the Pakistan army: a landscape of rocks and goat trails, forests of pine and meadows, and orchards of apples and apricots that now included among its inhabitants not only formidable, double-dealing tribesmen but also foreign *jihadis*, spies, agents provocateurs and embattled soldiers, a place which the locals themselves spoke of proudly as being in 'purdah'.

For these trips we were ferried in by helicopter and only allowed to see what the military wanted, bar a few mishaps. A favourite Pakistani English phrase was 'There's many a slip between cup and lip'. An officer had disclosed that a fellow soldier's head, which had been cut off by militants, was put back on so that his family would not be too distressed at the sight of his dead body. On another occasion we were scheduled to meet a Taliban commander allied to the Pakistani government, but the meeting was cancelled at the last minute when it was realised this would not play well with Pakistan's American allies against whom the militant commander was waging war. Then there was the time when we almost tripped over militants giving their wounded brethren piggy-back rides through a town supposedly under the army's control. And once we had to hide in some buildings when we got mixed up in a firefight between the army and the militants.

Often, the army paraded before us suspected Taliban militants, blindfolded and handcuffed. 'Were you tortured?' the press pack would bray in unison. 'No, I was not tortured,' the correct answer inevitably came. The questioning over, a journalist or two would then ask if this parade had not been in breach of the Geneva Convention, but such quibbles were quickly forgotten amid a clatter of porcelain as military mess servants clad in green and yellow striped cricket sweaters laid out tea and *samosas*. It was a scene that discomfited me, this display of cruelty, but one to which I had partially hardened myself, wearing as a shield the scaly carapace of my trade's cynicism.

We continued up through the pass, whose topography begged a thousand ambushes, towards the border, the men's eyes scanning the landscape with more vigilance, holding their rifles tighter.

The desire to come under fire, which had a couple of years before propelled me into ill-fated places, had greatly subsided in recent months. Earlier, I had suppressed my fears of coming to harm in hostile zones with grand thoughts about how life's disappointments, stifling conventions, boredoms, the onset of middle age and a thousand petty compromises were worse than bullets, but now I admitted to more honest views about self-preservation.

At Jamrud, some miles from the border, Hayat Khan beckoned me to join him in a government office. As he spoke with one of his officers, I looked up the pass towards Afghanistan as I had done on my first trip up the pass aged 18 with my grandmother in an old Mercedes.

For a young man just out of school, the arid hills, pickets, regimental shields and tales of conquering Muslim warriors and tribal lore had been exhilarating. On assignments since then, I'd seen Afghanistan beneath the pall of the ongoing war; it had been too fraught a time to relish the sight of tribesmen clutching nasturtiums between their teeth, meadows of asphodel and the Minaret of Jam. Mainly, I'd sensed the foreigner's alienation, which was written all over whiteboards in bold felt-tip pen in the tents of the West's military camps, alongside prints of mug shots of villainous-looking Afghans described as 'known drug smuggler', 'corrupt' and 'illiterate' – the coalition forces' local allies.

Afghan scenes flickered through my mind: the Taliban commander sitting on a bank of the Helmand River eating watermelon, who had warned foreigners not to upset his opium-smuggling business or he would give them war; the quiet, soft-spoken driver who had been beheaded after being kidnapped with an Italian journalist (who had been ransomed); the good and bad soldiers on both sides, the stoned ones and the corrupt ones; the Kabul cant about 'ink-spots of security', 'kinetic warfare', democracy and development; the heavily armed and bearded military contractors with ray-bans and their personal armouries of Glock pistols and sniper rifles; and the furry handcuffs and coffee and burger bars of the coalition camps; the artifice that sustained the theatre of war.

It was now dusk. I watched the trundling progress of the last of the day's NATO supply convoys, which had become prey to militants, head up to the border. Hayat Khan said his local commanders advised us not to go farther up the pass. Beyond Jamrud his writ was even shakier. We emerged from the office and amid a hail of commands our cavalcade raced back into the darkening mouth of the pass, towards Peshawar.

The pass had once held something of a storybook quality for me, but now tales of beheadings, and of brainwashed young men blowing themselves up, shaded the surrounding cliffs of shale and limestone with malefic shadows.

Suddenly, not far from Jamrud, a convoy of pick-up trucks with black Islamic pennants fluttering on their bonnets ferrying heavily armed militants approached us. A sharp intake of breath. Soldiers cocked their rifles. Repressing a surge of fear in the pit of my stomach, I asked who they were. Nobody knew. A stand-off: we looking at them, them at us. Hayat Khan barked at a subordinate. He barked into a walkie-talkie. A crackle of static and a voice from the other end. The junior man looked carefully at the cars and answered something rather uncertainly.

'It's OK. They're on our side,' Hayat Khan confirmed at last. 'At least for now.' Some minutes passed and then he added reflectively, 'Mangal Bagh is a crackpot, a nut, but he has his plus and minus points. He is a commercially minded person.'

Looking sideways at him, I admired his *sang froid*. But I saw a hint of fear in the whiteness of his compressed lips.

Chapter 25
We Have Come to Correct Things

BESOTTED BY THE IDEA of visiting the mountain shrine on the edge of Swat popular with Pathans, the one I'd tried but failed to reach, I was frustrated again in my plans. The area had by now fallen completely under militants commanded by Mullah Fazlullah, the former ski-lift operator.

Within six months of my trip up the Khyber Pass, life had become even more alarming. Gunmen had attacked a bus carrying the Sri Lankan cricket team in Lahore; and in the same city militants had run amok at a police academy, before blowing themselves up. I saw one of their decapitated heads resting on a windowsill wearing the gaping, burnt-out expression that Caravaggio captured in his *David with the Head of Goliath*.

The government had ended a ham-fisted four-month operation in Swat with a ceasefire agreement that had led to the introduction of Islamic law there. But instead of laying down their arms, the Taliban had expanded their rule, taking control of Buner, and the shrine, sixty miles from Islamabad.

Whippings, executions and bombings of schools were now commonplace in Swat. A video emerged showing a young woman being flogged. People – suspected criminals, those who opposed the Taliban and prostitutes – had been executed in the main square of Swat's capital, Saidu Sharif, but this beating prompted international outrage.

Then, at the beginning of June 2009, the military launched an effective operation in Swat. Hundreds of thousands of people had fled from the area, leaving golden and titian crops of peach, apricot, persimmon and maize to rot. As a sign of Washington's approval for the operation, a special envoy arrived at Peshawar airport and, clasping his hands in prayer in front of his chest, bowed his head and performed a *namaste*, a common salutation across the border in Pakistan's rival, India.

Militants had not taken long to exact their revenge: a suicide squad attacked a headquarters of the Inter-services Intelligence agency in Lahore. The attack – not the first on the ISI – hinted at the complexity of the war the intelligence agencies were waging, with former proxies turning on their puppet-masters.

The attacks on shrines had continued.

*

In May 2009, my consultant nephrologist in Dublin had recalled me to Ireland on the basis of bad blood test results ('Your creatinine has shot up by 33 per cent...'). He had carried out a biopsy to determine whether the original disease that I had mysteriously contracted in my twenties had returned to invade the transplanted kidney. It had. He advised me to come home on a permanent basis and put me on a massive dose of steroids and an increased daily dosage of immuno-suppressives in the hope of reversing the kidney's decline.

Instead, I had returned to Pakistan, blind with fear that my travels were coming to an enforced end, labouring under the illusion that if I could keep going, then all was well.

I hoped that by some miracle, I could adapt and find some way to continue. I could give up my job as a correspondent, I thought, and, in a secular fashion, follow the dervishes, like the English Sufi saint, John Gilbert Lennard. Born to a wealthy family of paper manufacturers, he had quit his studies at Oxford in the 1930s, and along with his elder brother, renounced his inheritance, converted to Islam in an East End mosque, and after a spiritual quest across the Muslim world, had come to live, under the patronage of the Nawab of Bahawalpur, in southern Punjab. He died in 1978, revered as a healer and seer, and as a competent importer of quality paper, his tomb in Karachi revered as a Sufi shrine. His brother had died in 1945 and was buried within Data Sahib's compound in Lahore, the grave marked 'Brother Devotee Farooq Ahmad Landlord Englistani'. That sort of thing would do me nicely I thought.

The Begum, my grandmother (who had come out on her annual visit in the spring) and I had driven out to Jhelum in Punjab to consult a mystic healer who intoned prayers over my deteriorating transplanted organ. He blew on the top of a bottle of water and suggested that I take a glass daily.

'I want to see results,' the Begum had cautioned him. 'And then we'll know if there's any truth in this or whether you are a charlatan!'

He had turned a little pale.

With illness, the usual tenor of my life changed; I had pushed off to a place of drowned senses, unwholesome sleep and poisoned days. I became impatient with the mummery, the tiresome emphasis on religion, the petulant talk of *our* book, and *our* prophet, the blue-chinned thugs eyeing the main chance, the narrowing nature of the news, and, what I had never admitted to myself before, or needed to, loneliness.

Quietly at the back of my mind I stored a list of bugbears. New puritanical mores dictated that Pakistani ladies were no longer allowed to wear the sari, the elegant, midriff-exposing length of unstitched cloth, draped over a petticoat and a cropped blouse. More often now one heard such disapproving questions as: 'Do they wear saris?' 'Do they speak Urdu?' 'Do they dance at weddings?' 'Do their women attend funerals?' The good ladies of Salem would have been proud.

There were other causes for my black mood: I had met women whose faces had been melted in acid attacks, victims of gang rape and fugitives from false accusations of blasphemy. I felt that the balance of good versus evil had tilted irretrievably towards the latter.

Pakistani novelists of a certain vintage remember a golden era in Pakistan's first decades when Anglo-Indians danced at Karachi's Metropole, hippies spun vinyl at discotheques, Pakistan was advertised as an exotic holiday location and Dizzy Gillespie beguiled a Sindhi snake charmer's serpent with his trumpet. That innocent age, if it ever existed, was now dead.

*

Things had also worsened on the home front. A few months before, Allah Ditta had fallen in with a very tall and dubious 'transporter' from Peshawar, Mahbub Ali, and our relations had become frayed.

The Pathan (or so he called himself, but I suspect the Pathans would not have owned him as he didn't speak Pashto, but Hindko, the language of Peshawar's old city) had used Allah Ditta as an intermediary to rent me a car at an inflated rate, for which Allah Ditta perhaps received some commission. Then he'd tried to foist a weak and over-priced generator on me.

Mahbub Ali claimed to be a Sufi mystic, which was why he needed to drink my whisky straight from the bottle, he told me when I caught him at it red-handed, to give him 'double Sufi power'. He kept a small, mouse-like French wife in Islamabad who followed behind him with her head bowed when they walked the streets; but unbeknownst to her, Allah Ditta told me, he had a first wife and family back in Peshawar. It emerged later that he beat his European wife. He exercised a Svengali-like influence over Allah Ditta too, apparently grooming him for some role in his transport empire, filling his head with grand plans and vistas of a rich life overseas.

Since then Allah Ditta had grown surly with me and avoided eye contact.

*

Summer was here again with all its battering force, and cockroaches were flourishing in my house.

At first I ignored the plague with ascetic calm. I spoke to them in the soothing tones of St Francis of Assisi as they scuttled past and wagged their antennae at me with squidgy torpitude. But then, as they multiplied and ignored my sermons about their need to live a discreet life, I came to regard them as an extension of my household's mutinous subterfuge. In frenzies of violence I battered them with rolled-up copies of *The Week* or, better still, pristine copies of the weightier *Economist*. Splatting them and smiting them with hatred, their corpses were left strewn about for their stretcher-bearers to carry off at night to bury, or more likely, cannibalise. Battle only made them stronger.

But the gods were kind. A jolly bearded man on a bicycle arrived at the gate. His bike was stacked with cylinders, sieves, rods and clubs; its handlebars were decked out with plastic flowers; and notices on its front, sides and back declared 'Master Sprayman. Cockroaches and all kinds of insect spray complete with destruction guarantee.' I engaged his services. He exterminated them en masse in their Mordor, which he found in a drain outside the walls of the house.

My obsession with cockroaches brought to mind a Graham Greene line: 'Scruples of cleanliness grew with loneliness like the hairs on a corpse.'

In fitful sleep, I had a recurring dream: a mad old man sits in a large chamber on a throne-like chair, wearing a crisp white *shalwar kameez*, knee-length navy-blue *sherwani* and a Jinnah hat. Brandishing a child's black plastic police truncheon in each hand, he is trying to whack large, buzzing flies. I am planning a journey to some frontier place. Pakistani companions think it is a meaningless chore, I that it is adventurous. I have a picture of a map-like landscape, more a feeling of it in my head:

it is all frontiers, borders and hinterland, but there is more stretching unfathomably beyond and around it. There really is no frontier. It hangs in folds, like a coat on a peg, or that Dervish's cloak, in which you could rummage but never find whatever it is you were searching for. That dream morphed into another one where I sit in a military base overlooking the source of the Indus, a glistening cataract of copper sulphate blue crystals, and there on a table are my lost notebooks, and then suddenly all is dwarfed by a giant supermarket, and army officers say that the 'Greenwich river' also rises here. I have come full circle. I would wake with a dread feeling that the whole journey had been a waste, that my search for origins and exoticisms had been futile.

*

But all was not bad. A positive force had arrived in the shape of a large, refractory mongrel mastiff called Fred, whom I had inherited from English friends when they left Pakistan. He had eaten several of my books, most savagely George MacDonald Fraser's *Quartered Safe Out Here*; but, during our walks together, he kept away haranguing *mullahs*. Basil claimed that several locals wanted to buy or steal him as he had the makings of an excellent bear-baiter. I suspected, unfairly as it turned out, that Basil was priming me for his 'theft'.

In the evenings, after work, I drove to a lake to walk Fred, who had met his match there in the form of a pack of wild dogs. At sundown we would watch large colonies of bats take off in a swarm and head off to feed in the folds of the bruised-purple silhouette of the mountains, a happy reminder that beyond Islamabad lay another world.

One day in July, the monsoon rains broke, puckering the earth, and a group of bare-chested young men closed the city's main road by dancing in the middle of it next to their cars, a snub to the stifling rigidity of the covert military regime and the capital's alien orderliness. Women's wet clothing clung to their bodies, and the staid city momentarily had a clammy, jungle sensuality.

*

One morning, a week or so after the rains broke, I squeezed my feet, now swollen from the effects of kidney failure and looking as if they had been severed from an elephant and marinated in the Indus for a week, into a pair of *chappal* (Pathan sandals).

I set off on what was to be my last foray, to the shrine at Buner on the edge of Swat, the resting place of Pir Baba, a saint madly popular among the Pathans. It was not the best moment to visit because Taliban militants had briefly overrun it the previous month and still controlled several neighbouring villages.

In recent weeks, Swat, like other parts of the country, had been shorn of its diversity. I'd met Sikhs from the hills near the shrine, driven out by militants, taking refuge in the fabulous *gurdwara* at Hasan Abdal, and Hindus, also now refugees, whose mountain shrine until recently had been where they and Muslims and Sikhs had congregated together to worship.

After leaving Islamabad by road, we cut through the district of Swabi and entered Swat's periphery at Buner, passing a destroyed police post on the edge of fields of cabbage-like tobacco plants and stacks of straw.

My companion was Muzammil, a photographer who had rediscovered a love for Allah in mid-life, and a Pathan driver who knew the backroads here. Muzammil was determined to treat all people equally in a country where equality was as jovial a notion as revenue collection or free and fair elections.

He intoned *bismillah, inshallah* and great sighs of *Allah Akbar* with monotonous regularity. The journey offered him a good opportunity to catch up on missed prayers and so he constantly, irritatingly, mumbled them under his breath.

Once we were in the hills, the smell of the rotting flesh of a herd of buffalo killed in the recent fighting stayed with us for half a mile. But this soon gave way to the perfume of pine trees and a sonic wall created by clicking cicadas that summoned dreams of holiday indolence and my mother.

As we travelled towards Pir Baba's shrine, I tried to focus on the natural beauty. In fertile fields, beautifully domed, beehive-like stacks of straw stood together like clusters of village huts.

These stacks had long fascinated me. They are made after the wheat harvest by tying together string beds (*charpoy*) in square, hexagonal or octagonal shapes, and filling them up with straw, compressing the straw by jumping on it, then raising the *charpoy* higher, and filling them again, and so on, until finally they are rounded off with a dome. The price of a haystack depends on its size, which is measured in the number of string beds used to make it, starting at four, going up to eight.

'The only framework to hold the straw readily available is the *k't* (Pashto for a *charpoy*), so you build the stack and then take the *k't* back to the *hujra* (male part of the household) for a kip,' a friend, an old Pathan landowners had told me.

In the countryside you were born on a *k't*, you slept on it, you died on it and you were carried on it to your grave.

Farther along the road, solitary low-built, thatched longhouses were dug into the sides of empty hills of cactus and rock. Only sixty miles from Islamabad people were living in primordial poverty.

Soldiers manned lookout posts on the slopes and lower down on the road they had set up checkpoints. We were all jumpy as suicide bombers were on the prowl for targets. We had to get out of the car and walk one hundred yards to checkpoints with our *shalwars* raised to show we had no explosives strapped to our chests.

We were concerned that we didn't have the right paperwork (we had none) and that we would be turned back. And there was always the fear that the soldiers could panic or turn out to be militants in military uniform.

The day was fuzzy with nerves, fear warping time into unaccustomed units, some short, some long, at times pushing reality to a palatable remove, at others giving a second unbearable length and clarity.

At one checkpoint an impatient NCO complained to Muzammil: 'Don't you have a Pakistani you could bring instead?' The complications of a *gora* wandering about the area were evident. After a close inspection of my French Club membership card, which he mistook for official ID, we were waved through.

These valleys were thick with Gandharan Buddhist ruins. We passed the remains of friezes and monasteries and in one or two places bricks from crumbling *stupas* had cascaded from the hills. In this region, Greco-Buddhism flourished and Buddha appeared for the first time in statue form with flowing drapery, top-knot and halo. For hundreds of years, since Mahmud of Ghazni razed Peshawar in the 11th century, Muslim iconoclasts had destroyed Buddhist carvings, statues and buildings and once again they were setting about them with boneheaded determination, destroying the ruins of a world that now was of no importance.

Muzammil was serene, and as we drove towards the Buner shrine he spoke, with I fancied a hint of longing, of heady days in Peshawar, of drinking beer and living at one of the city's famous old hotels. Our conversation jumped about and we discussed doing an article together on aphrodisiacs, and this in turn led to us talking of the sexual tension of the hot season.

'Sometimes this tension is very dangerous,' he said, staring ahead. 'So it is better to fake orgasm through hand practice.'

We finally arrived at the shrine of Pir Baba to find that its mosque had become a Frontier Corps post, with olive military *shalwars* hung over balconies and a heavy machine gun clamped on to the roof next to the mosque's dome. Big fat black rabbits, kept for the soldiers' cooking pot, hopped about in the shade; a colossus of a wild tomcat with protuberant balls studied them from under a vehicle, its eyes slits of idle hatred.

Locals showed a touching concern by insisting that I quickly leave. Militants were still lurking in the town. A couple of days before, the decapitated body of a retired soldier had been dumped on the main road.

We entered the shrine, which was fronted with a chevron of yellow-and-black tiles, its dome thick with green paint. Inside, the four corners of the tomb were marked off with miniature minarets. A profusion of synthetic flowers with vibrant yellow, magenta, crimson and orange bi-pigmentation petals adorned the tomb like cocktail sticks.

The saint's history is obscure. Miangul Aurangzeb, the would-be ruler of Swat, whose family had once ruled Buner, claimed that the holy man was a stooge sent by the Mughals to pacify the tribesmen. But now Pir Baba is revered as a cave-dwelling philanthropist and mystic who had set up a leper colony in these hills.

The slight, white-bearded, gap-toothed guardian of the shrine told us he had been eating when the militants arrived. One of them had said to him: 'We have come to correct things.' Another had taken out a dagger, put it to his throat, and threatened to kill him if he didn't leave.

His large spectacles rested on gaunt cheekbones; he wore a white prayer cap, and two or three fists of beard, twisted like a billy goat's, hung from his chin. 'The militants told me not to live on alms and threw me out,' he whispered, still stammering with shock. 'They said they wanted to destroy the shrine'. But his piety and poverty had forced him to return when they left.

The thugs had broken open the donation box, destroyed some of the surrounding food stalls and stripped many of the decorative religious motifs from its walls.

They had driven out the area's Sikhs and Hindus, who till recently had united with Muslims in gatherings, which included women of all those faiths, to worship here through the night in bewitched vigils of chanting and devotion. In attacking the shrine they had hoped to purge, as they had hoped to do elsewhere, the country of its history, its spirit and to impose their deadening will on it.

They had been driven back this time. But I wondered if they had not succeeded, through fear, of robbing it of some of its unconscious self, and whether places such as this would soon be hollow husks 'where late the sweet birds sang'.

I noticed then that the militants had smashed some twenty to thirty of the shrine's clocks hanging on its walls.

Clocks. I had seen them in so many shrines but had failed to ask why they were there. Now that they were smashed I remembered a note from the book written by the saint of Lahore, Data Sahib, that said we must have 'a knowledge of time' as time is the state that limits us.

Suddenly I didn't feel well. I sat down crosslegged, supporting my back against a wall, and took some deep breaths. The stalking shadow of illness had caught up with me. I tried to expunge what felt like a whirring, nervous tension and shortness of breath. A flickering darkness came over me, with shadows and shades crossing the lids of my closed eyes. I felt without strength or purpose, leaving the solid world, dissolving and fading. I was no longer sure of my aim. What was I doing here? What was I looking for? How far was I trying to get? A chasm opened beneath my existence.

Voices, like tapping on a pane of glass, made me open my eyes. Then, as I sat there, trying to calm my breathing, heart rate and nerves, some plainclothes security men made themselves known, bringing a warning of violence, which then seemed to be falling over all the country, snuffing out hope and cloaking everything in darkness. 'You must leave the town,' one of them was saying to me, politely, with understanding, gently as if he knew I was ill. 'The Taliban are looking for a bargaining chip. It's a difficult time to visit the shrine.'

On the way back, passing through the shot-up landscape, we overtook a ruffle-haired boy riding an emaciated horned buffalo towards a crossroads known as 'the place of tired people'.

EXIT

Last Amble

A MONTH LATER, things hadn't improved. My kidney function had plummeted; cuts on my feet had become inflamed with cellulitis (although I didn't know that then) so I was finding it painful to walk; gastritis ruled my digestive tract; there was a trace of TB on my lung; and I was falling asleep everywhere. 'You are a boat adrift,' said a friend. 'Your sails, masts, oars and rowlocks have gone. Go home for a few months, patch yourself up.'

I dallied for a week or so, struggling to admit to myself that my travels were over. I knew what lay ahead: I would have to, as *mureeds* (saints' disciples) say to explain their devotion, surrender myself 'like a corpse in the hands of a washer man', to submit myself to the skills of nurses and doctors, and a life of chlorined hospital corridors, the nocturnal shouts and screams on the ward, beeping machines, the swearing and dying, with my freedom to roam ended, more isolation and the loneliness of disease.

Illness brought back memories of my first encounter with it, one of those moments that teaches us the bleak truth that there are no certainties, no unqualified right to life: everything is a bonus.

But things were not too bad: a few weeks before a photographer friend had had a leg blown off in Afghanistan. My entire journey here had been a long lesson in other people's suffering, and I knew I was among the privileged, the fortunate few who could take a flight back to a comparatively stable, prosperous and peaceful land.

I knew, living with this illness, dependent on pills and medical practice, that I was from another world, and that I was not strong enough to live in Pakistan. Allah Ditta had once gone to buy a packet of immuno-suppressive pills for me and the chemist, presuming he was too poor to buy an entire packet, had given him one pill. A local newspaper photograph had shown a row of brick-kiln workers, usually trapped in the job as bonded-labourers, with identical scars: they had all sold their kidneys to rich clients in an attempt to pay off debts. Here, if I hadn't enjoyed the advantages conferred by my background, I would likely have died like a dog, as did so many.

*

Sadly, Allah Ditta and I had parted ways.

Months ago I had argued with his new mentor Mahbub Ali over money, and he seemed to have turned Allah Ditta against me in revenge. Basil, who had long wanted his ouster and resented my affection for him, contributed to his departure too. He reported his rival to me for stealing alcohol and money. At first Allah Ditta denied it, and then after painful headmaster-like questioning, he 'confessed'. It was a hollow victory. After the humiliation of the confession, he no longer wished to work for me.

To complete the gloomy picture, my neighbour, the Professor, was gravely ill, having had a stroke severe enough to render him bed-ridden and which, not long after I left the country, led to his death. Torture for a man of dictionaries, he now found it difficult to find the phrase, the words, that brought order to chaos and made him smile.

*

At last, following friends' advice, and heeding that of the consultant, I set off for Lahore, after which I would leave the country.

On the road from Islamabad, I stopped off to pay my respects at the tomb of Nawabzada General Sher Ali Khan Pataudi, a family friend. Known affectionately as 'the General', he was an unusual man: polo player, philosopher, writer, soldier, diplomat and devout teetotal Muslim. His elder brother, who had inherited the mantle of Nawab, chose to remain in India, while he 'opted for Pakistan' in 1947 and was, he said, therefore 'a Pakistani by choice and not by Radcliffe award', referring to the British civil servant who hastily drew up the border dividing the newly created Pakistan from India on the orders of the Viceroy, Lord Mountbatten.

I came to the perimeter wall of the isolated graveyard, where sitting crosslegged and leaning against the walls, a hawker puffed on his *hookah*.

The General had said he discovered his final place of rest in a dream. A figure in armour had appeared to him and complained of being disturbed, demanding that, as a fellow soldier, he should do something about it. The General's enquiries had led him to this place, to an unmarked grave on the Potohar plain, where villagers believed the remains of Shahibuddin Ghauri, a 12th-century Afghan warrior, lay.

Among the General's writings, there is a passage where he describes Ghauri as the early Muslim conqueror who laid the foundation of 'permanent Muslim rule' in India. According to legend Ghauri dreamed that one of the greatest of all South Asia's Sufi saints, Mueen-ud din Chisti (1141–1230), who was then alive, had appeared before him and exhorted him to leave Afghanistan to conquer India, saying: 'Get up, the land of India is yearning to kiss your feet, and the throne and crown are awaiting you there'. Ghauri was assassinated in 1206 near Jhelum, and his body was taken back to his homeland. The General had laughed at the incongruity in the story, that there was a tomb here but no body.

'It being a long journey, they may have buried his innards here and taken the rest of him back to Afghanistan,' he had explained.

He had fenced off Ghauri's untended grave, bought a piece of land next to it, and declared that when the time came he would also like to be buried here.

On reaching the General's tomb, a simple rectangular sarcophagus on a low platform headed by a tombstone, uncertain as ever of how an infidel should behave, I bowed my head and said a little agnostic prayer for his soul.

I remembered him fondly. He was often dressed in crisp white pantaloons that wrinkled tightly around his lower leg like drain-pipe trousers and ballooned at the knee, and an immaculate white cotton tunic. A village boy massaged his legs every night and told him entrancing folk and fairy tales peopled with djinns.

One of Pakistan's founding generation, he was concerned about his country's faltering quest for an identity: during his lifetime the ideal of a Muslim homeland had been sullied. He deplored that increasingly 'low-calibre scoundrels' and ill-educated clergy who knew nothing of Islam, were running the country. 'These bloody fools have just come down from the trees,' he would say, jabbing a raised forefinger into the air. 'We claim in Pakistan to be Islamic? Are we? Islam forbids church and priesthood. Nothing thrives more than these today.'

I saw that nearby, something of this rascally tenor had now overrun Ghauri's tomb. The General had merely tidied it and erected a simple plaque, but A. Q. Khan, a renegade scientist who was under house arrest for being a little too free with his nuclear favours on the international arms market, had stamped his mark on Ghauri's tale. Khan had spent millions of rupees on the tomb, and emphasising his own heroic status, had erected a twenty-feet-high facsimile of a nuclear-capable 'Ghauri' missile next to it. It was a rather absurd totem pole, a red-tipped phallus; a monument to an identity crisis.

Like Pakistan itself, the General was full of contradiction. He revered Ghauri as a symbol of Muslim dominion over Hindus, but he abhorred chauvinists who took warriors from India's complex past and recast them as Hindu or Muslim heroes, when Muslim had fought against Muslim, often alongside Hindu allies, and Hindu against Hindu, alongside Muslim allies. Such lies had led to the Indo-Pakistani border becoming a mirror in which the two countries saw their shared history in separate, bitterly contorted forms. On one side, Indian Hindu fundamentalist nationalists believe the Gita was created by Sanskrit-speaking gods, and writers such as V. S. Naipaul espouse the theory that India's 'purity' was wounded by Muslim invaders; on the other, Pakistani Muslim fundamentalist nationalists repress facts about their mixed racial and religious origins to create a myth about Muslim purity.

The sun lowered, but not the heat, and splintered behind a row of *chinar* trees. I thought of how, in the dusk of his life, the General had described a visit across the border to his old homeland, India, where he had dozed off at a Muslim saint's shrine, a place where traditionally people of different religions had gathered and mixed. He felt at peace, he said, because at that place there was 'no class, no creed, no sense of another country. Here everyone was first and last a human being'. It was an echo of an old, universal ideal, one that had now become almost heretical in the country he had adopted and in which he died.

*

The next day I left for the airport from the Begum's house.

'I'll be back in a month or two,' I told her.

'*Inshallah*,' she replied. 'We must still find you a bride. Not only one who would put up with an impoverished *gora*, but also a sick one.'

As I walked out of the house I bowed my head under a leather-bound Koran that she held up. This was a country that still felt the importance and sorrow of partings. I felt a terrible tightening in my throat as I said farewell. The Begum shed a tear and hurriedly told the driver to go.

On the Mall Road, heading away from the city, everything was again as clear as I had first seen it. Impressions long forced into obscurity by familiarity broke rank and reminded me of the thrill of arrival: the old practices and customs through which one could touch hands across the centuries with the court of Akbar; bottles of warm 7Up, the dissonant calls to prayer.

I thought of Allah Ditta. My conscience had been made lighter by a rapprochement with him before I had left Islamabad: we had exchanged gifts, embraced and let bygones be bygones. He was happy to have returned to driving minibuses in Rawalpindi.

More memories jostled at the exit: fist fights among Pakistani friends who wanted to be the one to pay a restaurant bill; teapots that poured without a splutter into porcelain cups; the view of Lahore from a minaret above Emperor Jehangir's tomb; chance encounters and spontaneous departures; hitching lifts on the back of motorcycles. Then there was the policeman on the long train journey who took off his trousers every time he smoked a joint; and on that much earlier train journey, the poor family who had fed me, and when I was cold put me under a blanket with one of their children tucked under my arm. Street cricket games, the drama of daily life and its intrigues, all flickered before my mind's eye.

Now, smells of sewage, exhaust fumes and perfumed petals fused with the kick of a pinch of snuff in my nostrils. Dust robbed the resinous light of its clarity and coated the scene in a haze. Men walked hand in hand on a torn-up pavement. Plastic bags and rubbish clung like sleeping fruit bats to trees and electricity wires. Knackered old men goaded knackered old donkeys. Schoolgirls in pristine blue uniforms and sprightly pigtails climbed into buses. Other children, caked in black, worked on the streets as mechanics' grease monkeys, and office boys carried trays of teapots and cups among the crowd. A family of five rode a single moped, children clustered on it like bees on a flower.

No longer part of that bustle, saddened that soon I would be lost to it, I wondered if it feels a little like this at the end.

But there would be consolations: to dismount from the merry-go-round of life, to step back and take stock and return to my family, to be cosseted and cajoled in the bantering folds of Ireland.

There, a few years after these travels ended, my elder brother, Chev, would donate one of his kidneys to me, enabling me to have a second transplant, and to return to the shore of forgetting, of fat days and of freedoms.

Acknowledgements

This book took criminally long to write and many people suffered in its making. All those in Pakistan, particularly the Begum and her family, who bore the burden of hosting and ferrying about a *farang*, have my everlasting thanks. I hope you see in these pages my affection for you and your country. Thanks also to my former bosses at the *Daily Telegraph* and the *Economist*, who gave me the freedom to roam, and my Pakistani and Afghan colleagues – some of whom later paid for their work with their lives – who often guided me through dangerous areas.

Gauvin Bailey, Carl W. Ernst, Salman Rashid, Susan Stronge, Frances Pritchett, Francis Robinson, John Mock and Kimberley O'Neil, Alexander Evans, the late Adam Nayyar, experts all, gave me valuable guidance, which I may or not have taken.

Several friends read early drafts and endured much, none more so than Catherine Ann Heaney and Charles Cumming. Other victims include: Alice Albinia, Sarah Gabriel, Alan Philps, Sam Loewenberg, Chris Morgan-Jones, David Sharrock, Robbyn Swann and Tony Summers. I'm grateful to Angharad Kowal, whose encouragement propelled me to complete a first draft, and Marc Lavine of Agence France-Presse, who gave me leeway to get it finished.

Even though hellishly busy, James Astill executed a massively generous, detailed and astute eleventh-hour rescue operation that may have just saved this book's skin; and Joshua Ireland used his wizardry as an editor to try to make it all of a piece. Simply, this book would not exist without the hard work and benevolence of Barnaby Rogerson and Rose Baring of Eland. Their passion for travel and books, and their warmth and unstuffiness made the enterprise a joy. My travels, indeed much of my life, would not have been possible were it not for the staff at the Adelaide and Meath Hospital and Beaumont Hospital in Dublin who have kept me on my feet and toes for nearly twenty years. Among others, I owe thanks to George Mellotte, Maura Looney, Helen McGovern, Donna Johnson and David Hickey.

Praise is due to my old neighbour and steadfast friend, John Ind, who during my periods of illness buoyed me with insults and flights of poetry, and Brian Kelliher and Liz Daly, who tried to make sure I didn't lose the run of myself.

My family also put its shoulder to the book-wheel: brother Gus steered me away from some embarrassing follies; sister Gez urged me on, despite fearing for my sanity; Marina brightened our lives; and all my nieces provided great joy. My beloved and much-tested father, aided by generous and punctilious Juliet, stayed the course right from the book's earliest, tattiest stages and midwifed it through till the end.

I owe an unrepayable debt to Laura, who knocked this book and me into shape, and made us both her own, giving the text a rigorous shake-up and urging me on whenever my spirits flagged. On a trip back to Pakistan in 2016, intrepid and boundlessly curious, she reminded me why I loved the country. It's unfair that I should then have persuaded her to marry me. I can only offer her my dog-eared self.

The last of my thanks goes to: Chev, frequent companion on these sallies, who is missing a vital organ on my account, and without whom this book, and I, would have sunk long ago; Granny (Pam Stephenson, 16.12.1923–15.6.2017), the sine qua non of it all, who saw me through the lowest ebb of sickness; and my mother, who, although now dead for over a decade, is with me always.

Ireland, Budapest and Hong Kong
May, 2017

Index